PITT SERIES IN POLICY AND INSTITUTIONAL STUDIES

The Competitive City

THE
POLITICAL
ECONOMY
OF SUBURBIA

MARK SCHNEIDER

UNIVERSITY OF PITTSBURGH PRESS

To Elizabeth, Johanna, and Susan

Published by the University of Pittsburgh Press, Pittsburgh, Pa., 15260
Copyright © 1989, University of Pittsburgh Press
All rights reserved
Baker & Taylor International, London
Manufactured in the United States of America
Paperback reprint 1991

Library of Congress Cataloging-in-Publication Data

Schneider, Mark.
    The competitive city: the political economy of suburbia / Mark Schneider.
      p.   cm.—(Pittsburgh series in policy and institutional studies)
    Bibliography: p. 231
    Includes index.
    ISBN 0-8229-3610-0—ISBN 0-8229-5452-4 (pbk.)
    1. Metropolitan finance—United States.   2. Metropolitan government—
United States.   3. Municipal services—United States.   4. Cities and towns—
United States—Growth.   I. Title.   II. Series.
HJ9145.S36   1989
363'.0973—dc19   89-30015
                                                      CIP

CONTENTS

TABLES

PREFACE

This book represents one stage of my long-term commitment to the study of local government. My work has been concerned with the two horns of what Arthur Okun called the "big trade-off" between equality and efficiency. For several years, my research (especially with John Logan) explored the inequalities embedded in the development patterns of metropolitan regions. This work investigated the costs that emerged from the differences and inequalities between cities and suburbs and between suburbs themselves in the demographic patterns, the distribution of fiscal resources, and the quality of local services characteristic of development in metropolitan regions.

As that work evolved, I became increasing interested in the efficiency side of metropolitan service delivery. My interest in this issue traces directly to exposure to the work of Elinor Ostrom. A central research theme in Ostrom's work emphasizes the benefits of "polycentricity." Thus while my earlier work stressed the costs of development in fragmented metropolitan regions, I began increasingly to wonder about the benefits of such development.

My interest in the benefits flowing from the structural arrangements of polycentric metropolitan regions was furthered by the growing literature exploring bureaucratic behavior, especially that literature concerned with the ability of bureaucrats as monopolists to control public resources to maximize their own interests at the expense of the society they are supposed to serve. The work of William Niskanen was important, as was the exciting work of analysts such as Terry Moe, Gary Miller, and Jonathan Bendor.

Drawing on these intellectual themes, this book explores the concept of a local market for public goods in which the polycentric structure of governmental arrangements can increase consumer choice and the level of competition bureaucrats face. The book is concerned with identifying the empirical effects of consumer choice and competition on the ability of bureaucrats to exact "rents" from the communities they serve. Thus, it is concerned with efficiency and responsiveness and leaves aside the equality issues which my earlier work investigated.

The second theme in this book is the limited ability of suburban municipalities to control the resources they desire and to achieve the patterns of growth they want. Paul Peterson's concept of "city limits" is central to my work in this vein, although I believe the limits I identify are much broader and more encompassing than those Peterson had in mind.

While I have incurred many broad intellectual debts which are obvious in this book, I have incurred more specific debts which are less obvious, but are as real. I want to thank Bryan Jones for his criticisms and comments at several important junctures. Other thanks are owed to John Scholz, Paul Teske, and

Charles Cameron, for their suggestions. I of course retain full responsibility for any errors of commission or omission in the subsequent analysis.

I have had help from many other people. Several of my students helped in both the intellectual and practical work upon which this book rests. Among them are Byung-Moon Ji (especially for his contribution to the study of the flypaper effect); Fabio Fernandez (for his help in studying the changing suburban economy); Joseph Lenart (for the study of the public sector work force); and Tom Phelan (for help at several places). Both Irene Horn and Anne Giles provided secretarial and moral support.

My wife, Susan Roth, and my daughters, Johanna and Elizabeth, deserve extensive praise for putting up with the abnormal demands on time and emotional resources which writing a book entails.

Finally this book could not have been written without the help of research grants from the National Institute of Child Health and Human Development and the National Science Foundation.

Part I

SIMPLIFYING COMPLEXITY:
MARKETS, MODELS, AND
LOCAL POLITICS

In the United States, local politics are complex, involving large numbers of people and institutions with different goals and varying resources to achieve these goals. The issues of local politics can range from defining what is a stray animal (and then choosing someone to catch it) to allowing the construction of certain types of housing (and deciding where to put them) to the location of facilities (such as garbage dumps and sewer plants) that nobody wants in his back yard. Local decisions, such as these, are driven by local needs and local politics. They are also affected by the multitiered federal system and by the openness of communities to macroeconomic and broad social changes.

Given its complexity, by necessity, any social scientific analysis of local politics must be selective. The full panoply of actors, strategies, institutions, and interactions cannot be described and explained. Instead, every analysis must focus on a set of key terms which underlies what the author considers to be the most important aspects of reality. In the next two chapters I identify the aspects of local politics I consider to be critical. I describe how competition among municipal governments in metropolitan regions creates a marketplace for the public goods and services local governments provide.

In this marketplace, I describe residents and businesses as the "buyers" of the local public goods and services which are provided by municipal governments. In turn, the municipal "sell" decision is dominated by bureaucrats and by politicians. I then explore the role of competition internal to each community as the key actors interact over the allocation of local budgets and other public goods. Just as a city competes with other cities, actors within cities compete with each other.

In describing this internal competition, I define the goals, strategies, and resources that the four key sets of actors (residents, businesses, bureaucrats, and politicians) bring to the local market for public goods.

The chapters in part 1 present the overarching theoretical constructs which inform the empirical analyses in parts 2 and 3. Chapter 1 describes the basic operation of the local market for public goods, comparing it to the much more widely analyzed market for private goods. Chapter 2 describes in detail the key sets of actors in this market and identifies the points of consensus and cleavage between them in the local market for public goods.

1

THE LOCAL MARKET FOR
PUBLIC GOODS

Local governments in the United States are responsible for delivering a wide range of services to their residents: they build streets and then clean and maintain them; they organize police and fire protection; they build and maintain sewer and water systems; they pick up garbage; they provide parks and other recreational facilities—the list goes on. Local governments also raise much of the money to pay for these services. In some places, the local tax bill is a substantial cost to residents. But not every municipal government provides every service and there is wide variation in the taxes municipalities impose to pay for the services they deliver.

In this book, I examine the diversity in the goods and services that local governments, specifically suburban municipal governments, provide. I argue that the diversity in the goods and services offered by local governments and in the local costs of such services creates a local "market" for public goods.

I begin by discussing the much better known characteristics of the market for private goods and by identifying important differences between the private market and the operation of the local market for public goods. While real world market configurations range from perfect competition to monopoly, the model of perfect competition is the analytic baseline to which almost all markets are compared.

The core characteristics of the competitive market for private goods are well known: the idealized model of pure competition in the private market requires a variety of goods and a multiplicity of buyers and sellers. Within their budget constraints, buyers are free to purchase those goods that most satisfy their preferences and needs. Given multiple buyers and sellers, and given freedom of choice, the competitive market place is efficient, an outcome which is normatively desirable. However, efficiency in the private market is conditioned by, among other things, the number of firms, the degree of differentiation between products produced by these firms, and the ease of entry of new firms into the market.

In the model of the competitive market for private goods, the major behavioral assumption for the firm is profit maximization. However, since each firm is so small in comparison to an entire industry, the ability of a producer to maximize profits by inflating the market price for his goods and services is limited. Rather, any single producer must take the market price as given—no firm can affect the price of goods through artificial manipulation. Furthermore, in the perfectly competitive market, a firm faces an extremely sensitive demand for its product; given the assumption of product homogeneity, any unilateral increase in a single firm's price will leave it with virtually no customers. Thus, consumer sovereignty characterizes the market—it is the preferences of the consumer not the wishes of the producer that matters.

The efficient operation of the market is also based on easy entry and exit of providers (see especially Baumol 1982). If supernormal profits ("economic rents") are being made by sellers already in the market, other firms will enter the market until a normal rate of profit is reestablished. Finally, given an ideal market, firms must produce efficiently to survive. Thus, the outputs of firms in competitive markets are produced at the lowest possible cost to society; the market enforces efficiency. This efficient use of societal resources endows the model with normative superiority: since efficiency is highly valued, the market's claim to efficiency endows it with a compelling logic as a social system for the allocation of goods and services. This in turn makes the market an appealing model against which to compare the public sector (which, in general, does not share the market's claim to efficiency).

While the above is an oversimplified depiction of the assumptions of the competitive private marketplace, the key mechanisms required for its operation are evident. However, do these concepts translate into a local market for *public* goods? Who are the buyers and sellers in the local market for public goods? Is there competition in this public market? Does competition increase efficiency and responsiveness in the provision of public goods as it does in the provision of private ones?

THE LOCAL MARKET FOR PUBLIC GOODS: AN OVERVIEW

At this point, I take a "first cut" at describing the characteristics of the local market for public goods. The following sections identify the general setting of the market, the participants in the market, the products that are exchanged, and the institutional and structural constraints that make the local market for public goods different from the idealized version of the competitive private market.

The Setting: Metropolitan Regions

In this book, I argue that a local market for public goods is definable by the interaction of *suburban* governments operating within any given metropolitan region. While I focus almost entirely on how suburban *municipal* governments, and the actors within them, cooperate and compete in the allocation of local resources, budgets and services, the local market for public goods is in reality multitiered: agencies from all levels of government provide goods and services to metropolitan residents. Furthermore, in the ever-changing American system of intergovernmental relations, the responsibilities of agencies at any particular level of government vary over time.

In the multitiered federal system, national and state governments affect the "market" behavior of local governments. For example, higher level governments make money available to local governments in the form of grants. Such grants, by subsidizing the costs of some services but not others, affect local government decisions about which services to offer. Moreover, higher level governments often directly tell local governments what they can and cannot do with their budgets and their policies.

Thus, intergovernmental influences are important in determining how local governments deliver products in the market for public goods. In the analysis in this book, higher level governmental actors are treated as exogenous factors—they define external constraints on the behavior of local governments. While clearly local governments seek to influence the policies undertaken by their states and by the federal government, for analytic purposes, I set the policies of higher level governments as a given, not controlled directly by the actions of local governments. In chapter 10, some aspects of this assumption are more closely examined.

Because the geographic size of the market can be set at different points, there are difficult analytic questions in determining the boundaries of the local market for public goods. Given the high mobility of individuals and capital in the United States, every local government may ultimately be related to every other local government, creating a national market for local public goods. That such a national market exists is evident in the fight for economic development evident between local governments in metropolitan regions of the North and the more recently emergent ones of the South and Southwest. Despite evidence of such a national market, I focus on the interactions between local governments within the *same* region, treating intermetropolitan factors as an external constraint on the operation of local governments within any given metropolitan market.

The Participants in the Local Market for Public Goods

As in any market there are buyers and sellers. The "buyers" in the local market for public goods are the people who choose to reside in the communities of a metropolitan area and the businesses that locate in these communities. These buyers choose to locate in specific communities and then pay for their choice by the taxes they pay to the local government.

Residents and firms have a variety of needs, preferences, and "tastes" for public goods. Some prefer parks to streets, others police services to libraries. Whatever their preferences, residents and firms, similar to buyers in any market, face budget constraints. As rational consumers, buyers want to purchase the products offered in the local market for public goods at the lowest costs. Indeed, this diversity in the preferences of buyers, combined with their desire to satisfy their preferences at minimum cost, are preconditions for the operation of the local market for public goods.

The "sellers" in this model of the public market are local governments. Within each local government, politicians and bureaucrats are the decision makers with primary responsibility for assembling the particular package of goods and services offered by each municipality. Municipalities present a "bundle" (or product mix) of goods and services to buyers, among which firms and residents choose. Municipalities charge for the goods and services they deliver primarily by levying taxes against the consumers of their product (local residents and businesses). As a whole, local governments seek to provide services to mobile "buyers," while keeping local taxes low. This can be accomplished through a variety of strategies. But I will argue that at the core of all these strategies is the desire to increase the local tax base—the wealth against which local property taxes are levied.

Given variation in buyer tastes and given variation in municipal service bundles and tax costs, the local market for public goods operates via two basic mechanisms. Following Hirschman (1970), consumers can use "voice" to affect market choices. For example, they can become involved in political campaigns, they can contact their local elected representatives, or they can use the other prerogatives of citizens in a democratic society to influence the bundles of goods and services made available to them. The efficacy of voice in the system of metropolitan governance has been a major topic of research, especially in those studies comparing the responsiveness of small suburban governments to the responsiveness of the larger central city government found in metropolitan areas (see, for example, Ostrom 1972; or, more recently, Sharp 1984).

While "voice" is clearly important, in many analyses of the local market for public goods the "exit" option is more theoretically central. Following Charles Tiebout, research has extensively explored the creation of the local market for public goods which emerges from the actions of "citizen/consumers" (firms and residents), as they "shop around" between different local governments to find the service/tax bundle that most closely matches their preferences (Tiebout 1956). In the Tiebout tradition, it is the mobility of consumers—their ability and willingness to exit from a community with an unsatisfactory service bundle to locate in a more satisfactory community—which drives the local market for public goods.

My analysis draws on both lines of research. I explore the Tiebout model in more detail in this chapter. In the next chapter, I explore more fully the political incentives and strategies of the most important sets of actors in the local market for public goods and analyze how their political demands and actions are ultimately constrained by the impact of mobility (exit).

The Products Offered and Their Pricing

The products offered for "sale" in the local market for public goods consist of the services local governments provide: streets and roads, parks, libraries, police, and sewers are examples. It should be clear that local governments can act as "assemblers" or "providers" and not only as direct producers of the services they offer. The products can actually be produced by a wide variety of sources besides the municipality itself. For example, a municipality can contract for the delivery of a service produced by another entity such as a private firm or another government. As such, a municipality organizes and supervises the delivery of goods to its residents, but the actual production may be the work of others. Such arrangements actually increase the freedom of governments to assemble efficient service/tax bundles by choosing low-cost producers.[1]

In the local market for public goods, the way in which sellers raise revenues is more complex than in the private marketplace. In the public market, municipalities charge for their bundles of goods and services basically in three ways. The public-sector mechanism most similar to the exchange mechanism used in the private market occurs when governments levy charges or fees directly on consumers of locally provided goods or services. For example, a municipality may levy a daily admission charge on users of a local pool or beach. The appeal of this funding mechanism rests in the benefit principle—only those choosing to partake and benefit from a particular service pay for it. However, direct user charges for services represent only a small source of revenues for local governments.

Local governments can also "charge" other levels of government for the services they deliver. Federal and state governments often provide substantial subsidies to underwrite local government expenses. While intergovernmental aid is explored in detail later in this book, it is important to note here that there is substantial variation in how intergovernmental aid is delivered to local governments. Most notably, in the last three decades there have been wide swings in the level of aid made available to local governments and in the extent to which local governments are restricted in their use of these monies.

Finally, and most important, local governments charge for their products by levying taxes. The most important tax, by far, is the local property tax. The property tax is a proportional tax levied against the owners of local property regardless of the consumption pattern of the individual homeowner—for example, childless couples will pay local property taxes supporting playgrounds even if they do not use them.

Tax rates vary across neighboring local governments, as does the value of the local property against which the tax is levied. Variation in both the local tax rates and the local tax base presents theoretical and practical problems for the analysis of the local market: variation in the local tax base affects the relationship between the costs of local public goods and the quality of services they support. Thus, the pricing mechanism of the local market is affected by the distribution of property values and, somewhat more indirectly, by the level of local income.

Sources of Competition

Central to the operation of any market is competition between alternate suppliers of goods and services. What are the sources of competition facing municipal government agencies operating in the local market for public goods?

Local government agencies supplying goods and services can be in competition with myriad other suppliers, the most common of which are special district governments, county government agencies, and private suppliers. But central to my analysis, municipal governments are also in competition with one another as they try to attract desirable residents and firms by marketing attractive goods and services at a reasonable tax bill. While I return in detail to intercity competion, I first briefly identify several other competitors.

Special Districts   Special districts are the most numerous form of local government in the United States and they deliver a wide range of services to metropolitan residents. It has been frequently argued that the myriad special districts in metropolitan areas, each concerned with only a limited number of services, fragment authority and lead to unresponsiveness in the provision of local services. In terms of intellectual history, special districts were criticized as inefficient, unresponsive, and undemocratic because they fragmented the overall structure of metropolitan government. However, DiLorenzo (1981a) argues that because special districts increase competitiveness in the local market for public goods, they can actually increase efficiency in providing municipal services.

County Agencies   Competition between local government and county agencies as service providers also takes place. In many metropolitan regions, county governments have assumed considerable responsibility as direct service providers, sometimes complementing but often competing with municipalities.

The Lakewood Plan, in which local governments themselves "shop around" among alternate suppliers of public services, is the archtypical example of intergovernmental competitiveness in a county area, with a subsequent increase in the efficiency of local service provision (Miller 1981). But even in regions where a formal Lakewood Plan is not in effect, county governments have greatly expanded their role as direct service suppliers and often compete directly for service contracts with local municipal agencies (Schneider 1980a; ACIR 1972). Deacon (1979) provides empirical evidence that such competition can reduce local service costs by increasing efficiency.

Competition from the Private Sector   The appeal of private-sector firms as competitors to government providers of local services has increased recently. The core assumption in the drive to "privatize" local services is that the competitive environment in which private-sector providers operate will force public providers to deliver services in a more technically efficient manner than would a public bureaucracy (see Savas 1982; Rich 1981; Percy 1984).

As sources of competition, special districts, county agencies, and private firms can all increase the efficiency and responsiveness in the provision of public services. However, competition between municipal governments has been the dominant issue of studies of the local market for public goods since the seminal work of Charles Tiebout. Intercity competition is central to my analysis.

THE TIEBOUT MODEL AND COMPETITION AMONG MUNICIPAL GOVERNMENTS

Tiebout sought to define a local market for public goods based on the interaction of diverse municipal governments; and he sought to show how competition in this market could increase the efficient provision of local public goods.

Tiebout started with several simplifying assumptions. In his model, metropolitan space was presented as an undifferentiated plane across which residents were assumed to have virtually unlimited mobility. Residents were further assumed to have varying "tastes" for public goods: some prefer libraries to parks, other parks to libraries; some residents prefer to devote more of their resources to public provision of goods, while others prefer fewer public goods and more private goods.

Combining variation in preferences with high mobility, Tiebout argued that the existence of numerous local governments could simulate an efficient local market for public goods in which metropolitan residents "shop around" to locate in a community where the service/tax bundle offered by the local government most closely approximated individual preferences. While this public market did not generate all the efficiency gains of the private market, Tiebout demonstrated the importance of "exit" as consumers expressed their preferences through location decisions across multiple local governments providing diverse product mixes.

The Tiebout market increases efficiency in two ways. First, given increased choice between various communities, citizen/consumers in a metropolitan region can maximize the match between their preferences and the actual goods and services provided by their municipality. In a metropolitan region characterized by a single tax level and a single set of municipal services, citizen/consumer preferences can not be as well satisfied as in a market created by multiple municipalities offering diverse bundles. In a region with only one government, the individual who prefers parks to libraries must consume the same service mix as the individual who prefers libraries to parks. In contrast, Tiebout argued that the existence of multiple local governments, providing differentiated bundles, allows citizen/consumers to "vote with their feet," moving across communities to locate in the specific community whose service/tax bundle most closely resembles their preferences. In the Tiebout world, citizen/consumers can purchase their preferred mix of services and pay the corresponding tax bill.[2]

In this differentiated market for public goods, the welfare loss to individuals of forced consumption of unwanted goods and services is minimized. But not only does the polycentric Tiebout model increase the match of preferences, competition between municipalities also encourages the efficient provision of public goods and services.

This aspect of efficiency has been extensively explored in the long standing debate between metropolitan "reformers," who argued for consolidation of local governments to achieve economies of scale and coordination of services, and "polycentrists," who stressed the efficiency gains possible through the quasi market created by fragmented systems of local government. This debate has been resolved in favor of polycentrists, in part because the savings promised by consolidation were not evident in the metropolitan areas that changed their structure of government in the reform era of the 1950s and 1960s (see Schneider 1980a, chap. 6, for a review of these issues). Both Sjoquist (1982) and Schneider (1986b) empirically demonstrate a negative relationship between fragmentation and the level of expenditures for several types of local services. Parks and Ostrom (1981) present a similar finding in which the multiplicity of police departments in metropolitan regions increases efficiency as well as the responsiveness of police services to citizen demands (also see DiLorenzo 1983).

From a Tiebout market perspective, such empirical findings are not at all surprising: in a fragmented metropolitan system of government, competition operates as it does in any market, increasing the incentives for efficient provision of services and for increased responsiveness to consumer demand.

Tiebout's model is built on the concept of citizen/consumer sovereignty and is driven by their mobility. But it has little to say about the independent role of local government agencies as sellers in the market. Local government policies are "more or less set" (Tiebout 1956: 418). This perspective follows directly from the extension of models of pure competition in the private market to Tiebout's concern for a "pure" theory of public goods.

In a pure competitive market, while sellers have interests (such as profit maximization) and develop marketing and production strategies to achieve their goals, their success is constrained by the freedom of buyers to choose between highly similar products offered by a large number of sellers. By extension, in Tiebout's formulation of the competitive public market, municipal governments were relatively passive: as a consequence of the sensitivity of consumer/citizen demand for public goods and the substitutability of alternate locations, competition in the local public market limited the freedom of municipalities as sellers of public goods.

However, there are identifiable structural characteristics of the local market for public goods which distinguish it from the private market: shopping between local governments is not quite the same as choosing between the A&P and Shoprite. As a consequence, the independent role of producers is enhanced.

The Local Market for Public Goods as a Constrained Market

Important structural characteristics limit the operation of the local market for public goods. Perhaps the single most important is that local governments are spatial monopolists. Municipalities "own" a piece of metropolitan space and consumers can purchase the bundle of goods and services offered by a local government only by locating within its boundaries. Consequently, the decision to buy a local service bundle occurs through the locational decisions of residents and firms: the local market for public goods operates as residents and firms shop around.

There are costs associated with shopping in the private market—the drive to the local Shoprite may be longer than the drive to the A&P. But shopping costs in the local market for public goods are much higher: because of the spatial distribution of services, a decision to "buy" a new product mix involves exchanging physical assets such as houses or factories. In the private market, buyers make thousands of highly separable decisions involving the bundles of goods they want. Given spatial monopoly, buyers in the local public market face a much more limited choice among the already assembled packages offered by municipalities.

As noted earlier, the assumption of competition between producers is in part dependent on easy entry of new producers into the market (Baumol 1982). In the local market for public goods, however, competition between sellers is more limited than in the private market and the market is highly regulated. State rules and regulations limit the ability of local governments to offer products and constrain the way in which the costs of local governments are met. But of equal importance, entry into this market is limited by state and local laws. Rather than being free and open, the public market is limited by government regulations in a manner that consistently restrains competition.

The openness of local governments operating in a system of intergovernmental relations adds complexity to local decisions setting the bundle of goods and services they offer. Intergovernmental grants are exogenous, but greatly influence local decisions. These grants can reduce the costs of services subsidized by higher level governments in relationship to unsubsidized services. Such subsidies change the benefit/cost considerations of local residents and can thus distort local preferences. Intergovernmental mandates (Lovell et al. 1979; ACIR 1984) and historical patterns of service responsibility (Liebert 1976) further constrict the freedom of local governments to fashion service bundles to offer in the local market for public goods.

The "pure" version of the private market also makes no allowance for the fact that producers are not unitary actors, but are often large-scale, complex organizations. In reality, the complexity of decision making within organizations greatly affects the goods offered by a producer. This holds true for municipalities as producers in the public marketplace as well as for firms as sellers in the private marketplace.

Within municipal governments, as in any large-scale organization, differences between the preferences and goals of subunits and the associated bureaucratic politics make the setting of policy and service goals difficult (the classic works here are Cyert and March 1963; and, in the public sector, Allison 1971). In municipalities, the interests of politicians and bureaucrats can vary. And different bureaucratic agencies can hold divergent interests in service levels and in the allocation of local monies. Given the weakness of competition in the local market for public goods, and the corresponding weakness of constraints on the freedom of producers, the strategic interests of bureaucrats become important in the public market. Local decisions are further complicated by the nature of municipal governments in a democratic society. Municipalities are political systems in which problems of aggregation and representation must be factored into the process by which local bundles of goods and services are set. The interests of politicians may be particularly affected by the structure of local electoral systems and by variation in how different electoral systems translate local voice into policy demands. In short, the "slipperiness" of local systems of political representation can affect the process by which the local bundles are determined.

Finally, the operation of the local market is structured by a question fundamental to the very goods around which it is built:

Are Local Goods Really Public Goods?

The 1982 Census of Governments identifies over 150 specific services provided by municipal governments in the United States. Typical services include highway maintenance, street repair, street lights, parks, police, fire protection, and sanitation. Less typical municipal services include hospitals, health services, and welfare. To what degree are these really *public* goods?

Because public goods present difficult problems for private markets, they often *require* governmental intervention to ensure their delivery. As is well known, the market problems generated by public goods hinge on two characteristics: externalities and nonexcludability. Externalities are generated when a transaction between individuals imposes costs or benefits on others not directly involved in the exchange. Because some of these costs or benefits escape the parties directly involved in the transaction, externalities can produce a failure in the market and may require collective action to insure that an optimal level of a good or service is provided.

Education is often cited as an example of a local service with public good characteristics requiring governmental intervention. Society as a whole benefits from a highly educated work force. But given local funding of education and given the high mobility of Americans, an individual will likely make economic contributions to a community other than the one which paid for his or her education. One local government pays, but another local government reaps the benefits of the higher productivity resulting from this human capital investment.

Relying simply on the private benefits accruing to an individual investing in education or allowing local governments to consider only their own benefit/cost considerations could produce a suboptimal level of education. Consequently, government subsidies are necessary to reduce the local costs of education and to insure societally optimal levels of provision.

Nonexcludability refers to the fact that individuals cannot be easily prevented from using true public goods. Given the difficulty of exclusion, public goods generate the problem of the "free rider," individuals who use a public good but avoid paying for it. One of the major functions of government is to provide the coercive structure to limit free rides and force individuals to pay their fair share.

However, the "publicness" of the services provided by local governments is widely debated. Perhaps the most direct evidence to show the "privateness" of urban services is that almost every service offered by local governments as a public good is also offered by private firms. For example, for every municipality that collects garbage as a municipal service, many other municipalities rely on private carters. For every community that runs its own swimming pool or golf courses, many others rely on private firms to provide recreational opportunities. Even residential fire protection can be provided by private firms on a contractual basis without extensive municipal intervention. In more analytic terms, Bergstrom and Goodman (1973), among others, have shown that the goods provided by local governments resemble private goods in that they are "congestible."

Since the late 1970s, the concern for private provision of urban services has become a strong ideological and practical force in the analysis of the local market for public goods. At the core of the debate is the central belief that most services provided by local governments can be offered by private firms because there is nothing inherently "public" about them.

Absent the rationale that local services are truly public goods requiring government provision, we are faced with the question of explaining municipal choices in constructing the package of goods and services they offer. While there are institutional limits on the freedom of local government to choose among services, right now I want to emphasize the freedom they have to structure their public service packages. If local services are not truly public goods, local governments are not compelled to offer most services. Instead, within limits, they can design packages of services to satisfy the demands of their present residents and they can construct bundles of public goods to achieve local policy goals.

Given the imperfectness of competition and given the nature of the goods and services which local governments offer, the local market for "public goods" is a market in which local governments have freedom to design service packages: budgeting for public services can be regarded as a strategy chosen by municipalities working in a particular local market. The strategic importance of local budgets and services has been widely recognized and is the core of one of the most important works on local politics: Paul Peterson's *City Limits* (1981).

Peterson's Model of Strategic Budgeting

Peterson specifically links municipal budgeting to strategies of local growth. Peterson's argument hinges on the concept of a benefit/cost ratio relating the benefits of local services (benefits) to the local tax bill (costs). By explicitly including service cost considerations into locational decisions, Peterson extends Tiebout's model of the market and focuses attention on the strategic implications of local budgeting.

Cost considerations are major factors in locational choices because local governments vary not only in the kinds of services they provide but also in the tax levels they impose to support their services. Because of reliance on property taxes, and because of variation in local property tax bases across municipalities, communities with similar packages of goods do not necessarily levy equal taxes. While the question of unequal tax base is investigated in more detail later, at this stage let us take as given that the existing local market for public goods is characterized by variation in the benefit/cost (service/tax) ratio offered by local governments.

Given such variation, Peterson's specific argument is driven by the benefit/cost ratio experienced by above-average-income residents and by the businesses which strengthen the local tax base and reduce the taxes levied on present property owners. High-income residents and business firms are important to communities because they affect the size of the local property tax base, which in turn leads to improved local services, lower local tax rates, or, in the neatest fiscal trick of local government, both.

In Peterson's model, local governments which consistently offer poor benefit/cost ratios to above-average-income actors will witness their out-migration and will be unable to attract desirable new residents. This erodes the local tax base, which in turn leads to higher taxes in relation to service levels. Thus, a cumulative pattern of escalating taxes and deteriorating services ensues. According to Peterson, local budgetary politics are driven by the need of municipalities to avoid these negative consequences.

Peterson divides municipal expenditures into three categories: developmental, allocational, and redistributive. The classification of specific municipal expenditures into these categories is determined by the effect any particular service has on the benefit/cost ratio of an above-average-income resident of a community. Thus, Peterson links budgetary politics and the politics of growth.

Specifically, developmental policies provide the infrastructure necessary to support further growth, particularly economic development. While the exact identification of "developmental" policies varies across the many studies following Peterson, expenditures on streets and highways, transportation facilities, and utilities are the most commonly used examples of developmental policies. Because these municipal investments reduce the costs of doing business in a specific location, they improve the benefit/cost ratio experienced by mobile and desirable actors and promote further growth in local wealth.

At the other extreme are expenditures for redistributive functions, such as social welfare, housing, health and hospitals, which provide benefits primarily to lower income individuals. Since they pay lower taxes than those with higher incomes, and since they benefit disproportionately from these services, the potential redistributive impact of such services is clear. According to Peterson, local governments which engage extensively in redistributive activities will present an unattractive benefit/cost ratio to desirable, mobile, fiscal resources. Consequently, such a community will experience declining fiscal wealth with strong negative implications for remaining residents.

Finally, in Peterson's analysis, allocational policies are the "housekeeping" functions of government—such as general administration— that all local governments undertake simply to keep going day-to-day. They are, according to Peterson, neutral with regard to benefit/cost considerations.

With this background, it is now possible to present a second more developed "cut" at the local market for public goods, integrating the work of Peterson and Tiebout into a more extended presentation of its operation.

THE MODEL OF THE MARKET

1. The local market for public goods is "polycentric": in most metropolitan regions, there are multiple municipal governments with responsibilities for delivering a variety of goods.

2. The polycentric market for local public goods is characterized by a Tiebout sorting process which matches metropolitan residents and communities: buyers, such as families or firms, compare the product mix offered by different communities and locate in a community whose package most closely matches their preferences.

3. "Sell" decisions are dominated by politicians and bureaucrats, who influence the actual determination of the bundle of goods and services a municipality offers. The interests of politicians and bureaucrats when assembling the local service/tax bundle will vary with conditions in the local market for public goods and with the conditions of the local "political market" in which they operate.

4. Local governments must raise the revenue necessary to support local services. In the present configuration of local government, the property tax is central to the generation of the local revenues. Nation-

wide, the property tax accounts for over 75 percent of local tax collections and about half of total revenues (ACIR 1985: table 39). These local taxes represent direct costs to residents of local communities.

5. Wide differences are found in the levels of services supported by local governments. These differences derive from the distribution of "tastes" or preferences across communities and from variation in the assignment of functional responsibility to different government or nongovernment agencies. Such differences also derive from the unequal capacity of local governments to pay for the services they deliver.

6. Unequal fiscal capacity is largely caused by the unequal distribution of the local tax *base,* which directly affects the relationship between local tax rates and service levels. With a strong property tax base, a community can support a high level of local services without necessarily imposing high property tax rates—a low rate applied to a large base can produce revenues sufficient to support quality services. Alternately, a community with a strong tax base can choose to offer lower service levels, with even lower tax rates. Thus, a strong property tax base allows a community wide latitude in framing attractive service/tax bundles. In communities with a poor tax base, even high rates will not yield high revenues, and they will be forced to offer relatively unattractive service/tax bundles.[3]

7. As a result, widespread inequalities exist in the taxes charged by communities, and these tax costs do not vary directly with the quality of local service: widespread differences in the benefit/cost ratio of local service bundles may exist in the metropolitan market.

8. Consequently, informing the matching process noted in proposition (2) above is a benefit/cost analysis undertaken by buyers linking local public services to local taxes: when the benefits of location in a specific community exceed the associated costs, buyers (firms or residents) will either move into or remain in a community. In contrast, when the community benefit/cost ratio falls, out-migration of mobile resources will follow (Peterson 1981; Pack and Pack 1978; Bradford and Kelejian 1973; Schneider and Logan 1982a).

9. From a *community's* standpoint, not all resources are equally desirable. Desirable resources are those that contribute more to the local tax base than they cost in services—these resources will improve the community's benefit/cost ratio. However, desirable resources are potentially more mobile than less fiscally productive ones, that is, given the high costs of moving, wealthy families or profitable firms are most likely to be "footloose." This means that local governments will compete for

desirable units and offer inducements for relocation or for retention in the community.

10. Therefore, in the competitive market, in order to attract desirable resources, local governments enact policies they think increase their local benefit/cost ratio. For example, they will offer locational inducements for firms, they will engage in fiscal zoning, or they will incorporate to protect a local tax base. In their budgets, municipalities will favor what Peterson (1981) calls "developmental" expenditures and what others have called "economic overhead" or "social capital expenditures" (Hansen 1965, 1977; Holland 1975; O'Connor 1973).

Consequently, it is in the shared interests of members of municipalities to maximize their tax base. For residents and local business firms, a stronger tax base means a better benefit/cost ratio between services and associated tax bills. For elected officials, a stronger tax base allows them to take credit for more and better services at any given tax rate. For local bureaucrats, a stronger tax base allows larger budgets or the accumulation of perks with potentially less resistance to the associated tax costs. In short, powerful interests in the city combine in the pursuit of local property wealth—the city becomes a "growth machine" (Molotch 1976; also Stone 1980).

The risks to communities that do not undertake such investments are potentially severe: fiscally productive resources will leave and the community can fail to attract new ones. The resulting stagnation or decline in local property wealth can force remaining residents and firms to pay even higher taxes, further increasing local costs in relation to local benefits. This will make a community even less attractive in future competition for mobile resources—a cumulative process of decline is possible with increasingly adverse consequences for those who remain (Schneider and Logan 1982a; Logan 1978).

CONCLUSION

There are sources of both conflict and consensus among the actors in the local market for public goods. As in any market setting, the interests of the buyers and the sellers diverge at key points. In part 2 of this book, I look at a particular set of conflicts pitting the interests of bureaucrats against those of other actors in the community. I explore this conflict as it manifests itself in the setting of local budgets (chapters 3 and 4), in the labor policies adopted in the local public-sector (chapter 5), and in the allocation of intergovernmental aid (chapter 6).

But my model also points to a core of consensus in the dynamics of this market: tax base maximization lies at the direct intersection of the interests of the diverse sets of individual actors within any local municipality. As illustrated in greater detail in the next chapter, it allows both buyers and sellers to pursue their own particular interests, without necessarily detracting from the interests of others in the community. In part 3, the analytic emphasis is on exploring the ability of communities to maximize the local service/tax ratio. The analysis thus shifts from conflict and disagreement to the pursuit of a goal shared by all major actors in the local market for public goods.

2

ACTORS, INTERESTS, AND CONSTRAINTS

Chapter 1 described the local market for public goods. In this market, firms and residents are the buyers of the bundles of goods and services offered by municipal governments, which are the sellers. The "sell" decisions of municipal governments are dominated by the interests and actions of bureaucrats and politicians, which are both driven and constrained by the mobility of resources. However, the original Tiebout model paid scant attention to the independent interests of providers: in a purely competitive market, their interests are fully constrained by consumer (or, in the Tiebout model, citizen/consumer) sovereignty. In a democratic society, the market force of citizen/consumer sovereignty is reinforced by norms of government responsiveness to the interests and demands of its citizens and by the various electoral processes that enforce these norms.

In the local market for public goods, however, the forces which transform local governmental service decisions into a set of responses directly mirroring the interests of local consumers are weak relative to those in the private market. Both economic and democratic political theory emphasize the need for competition to enforce consumer sovereignty. Yet the local market for public goods may be more similar to a regulated oligopolistic market than it is to a purely competitive one. In an oligopolistic market, producers have considerably greater freedom in their actions than do producers in a competitive market. Given his concern for a "pure theory" of public goods, Tiebout was able to concentrate on citizen/consumer sovereignty, but a more developed model must take into account the motivations, interests, and strategies of the bureaucrats and politicians who dominate local decisions.

The local market for public goods is also driven by a political economy linking the structure of local government to decisions about service and tax bundles. The desire to maximize the local tax base is a key ingredient of this political economy. Emphasizing this link, Peterson integrated the voice and the exit dimensions of the local market for public goods. His extension of the Tiebout model is based on explicit ties between the mobility which is central to the Tiebout model and the different worlds of political demand resulting from the need to maximize the tax base.

This chapter explores more fully the incentives and interests of the actors in the local market, showing how their goals and strategies are rooted in the characteristics of the market described in chapter 1. I discuss in more detail the interests of the four sets of actors (residents, business firms, bureaucrats, and politicians) whose actions drive the local market, assessing the degree to which their interests are homogeneous and identifying the source of conflict between them. Some cleavages are internal to any given set of actors: for example, the interests of residents will differ depending on income and housing tenure. Other conflicts occur between sets of actors: residents and firms may disagree over the desirability of future economic growth or over the optimal level of funding for any particular service.

Despite multiple lines of cleavage and conflict among actors in the market, I show that there is at least one interest upon which consensus is more easily achieved—the desire to increase the fiscal wealth of the community. This shared interest derives from the structural arrangements of the local market for public goods in which the relationship between service levels and tax rates is directly tied to the strength of the local tax base.

The last section of this chapter demonstrates that the market is open to exogenous influences. As a result, the ability of the actors in the local market to achieve their policy goals may be limited. The ultimate irony of the local market for public goods is that the most consensual goal held by the main actors in the market may be beyond the reach of the strategies and tools they have at their command.

THE ACTORS: THEIR INTERESTS AND THEIR STRATEGIES

Residents

Individual residents of municipalities have different needs and tastes for public services. These differences emerge from a variety of complex factors, including demographic conditions (such as age, race, or income) and ideological preferences for more or less government. There are significant political problems in aggregating the diverse needs of a population into a single community preference order, adding complexity to the operation of the local market.

Satisfaction of aggregate residential demand for public services is ultimately limited by the municipality's income. While the national government can run on debt financing, local governments cannot. Municipalities must balance their books every year, and most face strict debt limits imposed by state governments. Cities that violate these practices, such as New York City in the early 1970s, are eventually called to account for their sins.

The basic goal of residents is to increase the flow of dollars into the local government's coffers to support higher services while not increasing the local taxes they pay. In this way both private *and* public consumption can increase. But how can this fiscal legerdemain be accomplished?

Strategies There are several strategies which can ease the municipal budget constraint without increasing the direct taxation of residents. Some strategies shift the local tax burden to other actors either inside or outside the community, while other strategies reduce the cost of government. Here, I briefly identify four specific strategies with varying appeal to residents: increasing intergovernmental aid; increasing local efficiency in providing services; increasing reliance on user charges; and strengthening the local tax base.

Intergovernmental aid means that higher level governments subsidize local services. This in turn means better services at the same local tax rate or a reduction in local taxes. While intergovernmental aid can be cheap, it is usually not free. For example, many grants require the local government to find matching money. Grants may also force local governments to deliver services they would prefer not to deliver or to deliver them in a way contrary to local preferences. Thus, intergovernmental conditions of aid and other types of mandates may be costly to local government and alter local policies in ways not desired by local residents.

Intergovernmental aid, especially from the federal government, has been an erratic source of income. These fluctuations in the flow of aid increase uncertainty in local budgeting processes and can leave localities holding the bill for services they purchased on the assumption of continued aid. For example, Stein (1984) shows that after refusing to increase personnel costs that were subsidized by the flow of federal money during the 1960s, local governments in the early and mid-1970s finally expanded their work force, in effect betting their budgets on the continued flow of federal monies. Unfortunately, by 1978 the Carter administration began cutting federal intergovernmental aid, a process accelerated by the Reagan administration. Local governments were left with higher personnel costs than they would have had otherwise— relatively permanent costs that had to be met with local resources.

Thus, while intergovernmental aid can be appealing, there are risks involved which may lead to disagreement over the optimal level of aid a community should pursue. Furthermore, at any given level of aid, conflict can emerge between residents and other actors in the community over the use of such aid. This is particularly evident in the allocation of unrestricted funds, as in the federal General Revenue Sharing program (discussed in detail in chapter 6). Residents will rationally prefer to divide intergovernmental monies between tax reduction (to increase their consumption of private goods) and additional public goods in a manner similar to the way in which they allocate their own incomes. Bureaucrats, however, will prefer to use intergovernmental aid to increase the size of government rather than return it to residents as tax relief. This·conflict has been investigated in the literature as the colorfully named "flypaper effect"—intergovernmental money sticks where it hits (see, for example, Courant et al. 1979a; Schneider and Ji 1987).

Increasing local government efficiency, which allows more services to be delivered per tax dollar, is a second strategy for easing budget constraints. However, drives to increase local government efficiency have encountered difficulties, chiefly because we cannot monitor and improve something we cannot measure—and measuring local government performance has proved elusive. Measuring the inputs is not particularly difficult—labor constitutes the bulk of most municipal service costs and can be relatively easily assessed; but without assessing output, efficiency measures cannot be readily constructed. While some urban analysts are seeking more rigorous measures of government output (see Hatry 1977), others have proposed "privatization" of municipal services. Through privatization, local governments rely on private firms to produce and/or deliver public services. According to its proponents, privatization increases efficiency by expanding the range of potential suppliers of municipal services. Competition among them, including private firms accustomed to the rigors of the private marketplace, supposedly leads to greater efficiency in the provision of local public goods. Privatization has been a popular concept since the mid-1970s and was a key component of the urban policies proposed during the Reagan administration (Savas 1987; DeHoog 1984).

To the extent that privatization increases efficiency, it should appeal to residents. Private-sector firms will support privatization if it increases their opportunities to do business with government, but bureaucrats will not necessarily share their enthusiasm. To the extent that better efficiency measures increase the information available about the operation and costs of government programs, bureaucrats lose one of their major sources of power—the control over information. Bureaucrats will also oppose privatization if it reduces the size their agencies.

The response of politicians to calls for privatization can vary widely. Some may try to build a political constituency by endorsing the efficiency of the private marketplace and engaging in "bureaucrat bashing," a style characteristic of the "new fiscal populists" identified by Terry Clark and Lorna Ferguson (1983). But more traditional politicians may be less enthusiastic, since private-sector firms intent on profit maximization may resist political demands to deliver services in a manner for which a politician can claim credit.

Fees and user charges represent yet another strategy by which more services can be provided without increasing taxes. User charges are levied directly on consumers and shift the cost burden of a service to its direct beneficiaries. This in turn eases pressure on the general residential population, many of whom might not use the service.

Despite its justification in the benefit principle, user charges have not been as widely adopted as one might expect. Critics argue that they discriminate against low-income residents, forcing people who cannot afford a publicly provided good or service to forego it; although this is how the private market works, critics argue that governmental services in a democratic society should be available regardless of the ability to pay. Furthermore, the complexity of pricing local public goods and services reduces the appeal of user charges. While economists have invented ingenious techniques for determining market prices for many local public goods and services, determining and implementing user charges remains a difficult task for most local governments.

Intergovernmental aid, privatization and user charges, are all part of the new grab bag of local fiscal management. But there are limits to the success local governments have had in adopting these strategies. Some relate to technical problems, but much of the slow response stems from the political problems of each strategy—some powerful set of actors in the local community can be expected to oppose each of these avenues.

In contrast, the desire to increase the local tax base is more consensual. Because communities with a strong tax base have a greater capacity to deliver services at moderate tax rates, this is the strategy perhaps most frequently and ardently pursued by residents, and, indeed other actors in a community. Tax base maximization can be accomplished in several ways, but the most common are to control the entry of new residents and to promote local economic development.

Present residents of a community want newcomers to be richer than they themselves are. They will favor exclusionary zoning and other local policies to help ensure new entrants are of higher income, primarily by increasing the price of housing. Forcing new residents to buy housing with a price tag above the existing median generates a fiscal dividend to the present residents: since a household's property tax bill is a direct function of the value of its house, new residents buying an expensive house contribute more money to the local treasury. To use Buchanan's terminology, the "membership dues" of a new resident who has purchased a house with an above average price tag are higher than the median dues. This transfers wealth to existing members of the "club" and shifts local costs from present residents to new ones (Buchanan 1981).

While this strategy is clearly appealing, it is limited by the number of wealthy families in a region and by their willingness to buy expensive housing in any given community. Only attractive communities, located with access to some geographical amenity or with other appealing characteristics, can successfully pursue this strategy. Residents may turn instead to economic development as a means by which to diversify and strengthen the local tax base. To the extent that business growth produces a net fiscal plus, economic development reduces the "membership dues" of residents: the costs of local public goods and services are shifted from residential housing to business firms. Indeed, this strategy has become extremely attractive to local governments in recent years, and may actually be the dominant approach to tax base enhancement (see, for example, Beaumont and Hovey 1985; Blair et al. 1984). However, it too has limits.

For example, residents live in a community for a variety of reasons, some of which might be adversely affected by economic growth. They may prefer the local quality of life or desire a particular ambiance that makes economic development unpalatable. If it affects the qualities for which they chose that community, residents will oppose development that would otherwise be fiscally productive. This conflict can place a coalition of residents in opposition to the "growth machine"—the usually dominant coalition of actors in communities who pursue economic growth (Molotch 1976; Sanders and Stone 1987; Swanstrom 1985; Logan and Molotch 1987).

Internal Splits Among Residents   If residents can generally agree on the need to improve the fiscal base of the community, increasing the level of services in relation to tax costs, there will nonetheless be disagreements over desirable service and tax levels. There are at least three lines of cleavage differentiating the way in which residents evaluate the relative value of local services and the relative pain of local taxes. These lines of cleavage distinguish the interests of homeowners and renters; of income groups; and of racial groups.

Homeowners more directly face the costs of local taxes than do renters. For the typical homeowner, the local property tax bill is concrete, and increases in property taxes are direct and palpable. In contrast, the property tax costs of local services are more diffuse for the renter. The local tax bill is certainly reflected in rents; but since local property taxes usually are not separately enumerated on rental contracts, their impact can be hidden. Furthermore, because most contract rents are for a set period of time, the impact of property tax increases is not as directly experienced by renters as by homeowners. If the demand for public goods is similar to the demand for private goods, then higher prices decrease demand. Thus, if the renter's "fiscal illusion" dilutes information about the true tax costs of public services, renters will demand more services than will homeowners.

Residential interests are also affected by the distribution of income in a community. In order to extract a fiscal dividend, present residents of a community will try to limit entry to individuals with incomes higher than theirs. However, the payment of fiscal dividends is not limited to *new* upper income residents. Because municipal services can transfer income from higher income to lower income individuals, fiscal dividends can emerge in the relationship between above- and below-average residents already in a community.

The potential for income transfer through municipal services results from two factors. First, once a service is provided the exclusion of community residents may be legally impossible, for example, a municipal park or beach will be open to all residents (Jones et al. 1980). Second, higher income individuals with expensive houses pay more taxes than individuals with less expensive ones. Yet, because of the openness of local public services, wealthier residents do not necessarily get more services in return for their higher tax payments. This can produce a net fiscal dividend to lower income residents: higher income residents pay higher taxes but do not consume more services; lower income residents pay lower taxes and get the same services.

The redistribution inherent in this arrangement can result in conflicts over service levels between income groups within communities: in communities heterogeneous with respect to income, lower income residents may prefer more services, perhaps even at higher tax rates, than will upper income residents, who rationally prefer less government to limit the payment of a fiscal dividend to the less wealthy. Their most common strategy is to limit the ability of lower income residents to enter the community. Homogeneous high income communities face less potential redistribution than do heterogeneous communities. Consequently, exclusionary zoning is a rational strategy which is widely pursued. But despite such efforts, many if not most suburbs house a diverse population (Schneider and Logan 1982a). Given such income diversity, the potential for class based conflict over service levels exists. Thus the extent of income homogeneity in a community may affect the interests of residents in service provision (Schneider 1987).

Racial differences provide another line of cleavage among residents. Most suburbs are overwhelmingly white, and blacks historically have been confined to a small number of black suburbs. However, increasing numbers of blacks and other racial minorities are now finding suburban residences. While not conclusive, there is evidence that suburban blacks prefer higher levels of public services than whites (Clark and Ferguson 1983; Schneider and Logan 1982b), perhaps because they have, on the average, lower incomes and may need more public goods and services. But different preferences might also result from the fact that blacks are more recent migrants into suburbia and may have developed a taste for the higher levels of services provided by central cities.

Firms

Beginning in the 1960s, business firms became increasingly important actors in the local market for public goods, especially as the perceived contribution of business to the fiscal well-being of local communities increased.

Early forms of business growth in suburbs produced a negative image of the relationship between economic growth and desirable community development. Suburbs with concentrations of business and industry were central cities writ small, marked by low incomes, high concentrations of racial minorities, and an older housing stock. But the transformation of the U.S. economy from heavy manufacturing to high tech and services, especially coupled with rapid economic growth outside of the central cities, changed the nature and appeal of economic development. New development was of high quality, clean, offered convenient employment for local residents, and eased pressure on residential property taxes. Consequently, suburbs began to engage actively in the effort to attract firms.

The Interests of Firms   While a large, diverse, and often contentious literature has examined the role of firms in local politics, I assume that firms are overwhelmingly interested in reducing their costs and thereby increasing their profits. This motivation drives businesses to participate in local politics and enter cooperative agreements with other actors in local communities: if local governments want economic development to diversify the local tax base and create jobs for local residents, and are willing to pay for such growth, a congruence of interests of firms and other local actors can emerge.

But some researchers have questioned the degree to which local economic development produces actual fiscal benefits for municipalities. The costs of the inducements offered by a municipality, such as tax abatements or subsidies to improve local infrastructure, reduce the flow of fiscal benefits it receives. In the extreme, economic development subsidized by local governments may lead to net losses (see especially Rubin and Rubin 1987; also Logan and Molotch 1987; Swanstrom 1985; Friedland 1983; Stone and Sanders 1987).

Other research shows that the possible success of local government policies to attract firms is constrained by a very basic economic fact. The costs constituting the bulk of business expenses are not really under the control of local governments: firms usually choose locations which maximize access to raw materials and markets or which minimize labor costs. Despite such problems, most local governments, in fact, still actively support economic development and negotiate fervently with firms.

Several lines of research have explored the nature of the negotiations between firms and other local actors. Some analysts, especially those working from a neo-Marxist perspective, argue that local policies favoring development result when business interests coerce city decision makers (for example, Fainstein et al. 1984). This power of firms results from a fundamental asymmetry in business-municipal negotiations: a business knows its "bottom line," the terms and conditions it really requires to locate in a specific place. Municipalities lack this information. As a result of this "corporate information surplus," local governments in competition with other municipalities to attract a firm can be manipulated into offering more subsidies than the firm actually requires (Jones et al. 1986).

Other research stresses the importance of bureaucratic power in the "market for jobs." There is now a well-developed stockpile of tools for economic development, and a large number of government professionals to use them. This has eased transaction costs between cities and business and has created a powerful bureaucratic structure with the specific mission of encouraging economic development (Blair et al. 1984). These bureaucrats may pursue deals to justify their jobs and their salaries, without judging the more general societal payoffs of their actions.

Differences Among Firms   The ability of firms to locate according to fiscal criteria varies across the sector of the economy in which they operate. Most studies of the locational decisions of firms are based on manufacturing firms, especially large ones (Humberger 1983). However, retail, wholesale, and manufacturing firms respond to different characteristics of local communities (Schneider 1985).

Consider, for example, the locational needs of manufacturing firms. Since manufactured goods are often sold in large markets with many alternate suppliers, price differentials are important and the firms must be sensitive to differences in local costs. Therefore, they seek lower taxes. In contrast, retailers compete in much smaller and limited markets. The most important characteristics of location may not be tax costs, but proximity to a quality market defined by large numbers of individuals with high income (Schneider 1986a). Thus a local economic development strategy designed to appeal to manufacturing firms (through tax abatements or the support of infrastructure) might have no effect on retail development. Indeed, if the development of an infrastructure to support manufacturing lessens a community's appeal to higher income groups, manufacturing interests and retail interests can be in direct conflict.

Bureaucrats

Considerable work in the past few years has identified the interests of bureaucrats and the degree to which these interests match those of their "sponsors" and the external constituencies bureaucrats are supposed to serve. Building on the arguments developed by Anthony Downs, Gordon Tullock, James Buchanan, and others, the work of William Niskanen (1971, 1975) has informed a large body of subsequent research with the assumption that bureaucrats seek to increase their control of public resources, often independent of societal needs.

In Niskanen's view, bureaucrats seek to maximize agency budgets, since budgetary expansion allows them to achieve a variety of goals.

Niskanen argues that "a bureaucrat can increase his salary, perquisites, etc., *only* by increasing his budget or by demonstrating that he can manage another bureaucracy with a larger budget. Budget maximization, thus, probably explains most of the use of managerial discretion in a bureaucracy" (1974: 44). Niskanen's argument has led to a large body of research, which has raised at least two questions that deserve comment.

First, one may question why *overall* budgetary expansion should be the ultimate goal of bureaucrats. In fact, at the national level, many agencies with large budgets are not noted for the power of their bureaucrats (Meier 1986). Such agencies process entitlement claims and have little or no administrative discretion over the flow of their budgets. Thus it is arguable that what bureaucrats seek to maximize is not the total agency budget but rather the slack in the budget or the degree of discretion in spending (Niskanen 1975; Moe 1984: 763). However, because the measurement of these terms is difficult (Dunleavey 1985), empirical research has tended to focus on total budgets.

Researchers have also sought to identify a wider range of bureaucratic objectives than stipulated by Niskanen. Consequently, his emphasis has been broadened by expanding the number of terms in the bureaucratic utility function (for example, Mique and Belanger 1974; Stockfish 1976; Langbein 1980) and by identifying conditions under which bureaucrats might *not* seek to maximize control over local resources (Mique and Belanger 1974; Breton and Wintrobe 1982). Similarly, Ostrom (1981) and Parks and Ostrom (1981) have sought to develop a bureaucratic utility function including terms measuring the rewards bureaucrats receive from satisfying the demands of their community. Theoretically, terms measuring "responsiveness" can be added to the more "selfish" goals of bureaucrats at the core of models based on Niskanen.

Research identifying a more inclusive bureaucratic utility function and identifying the mechanisms by which bureaucrats achieve these goals is a major task in the present analysis of public organizations (see, for example, Moe 1984; Miller and Moe 1983; Bendor 1987). This work, while developing rapidly, is plagued by numerous theoretical and empirical problems. As a result, the most developed research still centers on the ability of bureaucrats to control more budgetary resources than are "objectively" required by their communities. These larger than necessary budgets are used to indicate bureaucratic success in achieving their diverse (and at present not fully specified) goals. I accept the core assumption that bureaucrats indeed seek to increase their budgets.

Strategies Theoretically, the ability of bureaucrats to control public resources and to augment "real" community demand stems from their monopoly of information about the true costs of services, and relatedly, their ability to determine the public policy agenda. This control of information is based on bureaucratic claims to expertise (Bendor et al. 1987).

The implications of bureaucratic control of information was recognized by Niskanen. Indeed, emphasizing the asymmetry in information possessed by bureaucrats and their "sponsors," Niskanen transformed his basic model, in which bureaucrats and sponsors negotiated more or less on an equal basis, into one in which bureaucrats had virtually all the power. In this new version, politicians were relatively passive and powerless in the face of bureaucratic control. Given this imbalance, Niskanen and others have argued that a "monopolistic" bureaucratic agency operating in a noncompetitive environment may consume anywhere from two to four times the level of resources as an agency operating in a competitive environment (see Niskanen 1971, 1975; Conybeare 1984; also Stockfish 1976; Mackay and Weaver 1978; McGuire et al. 1979; Romer and Rosenthal 1982).

Others have rejected the extreme bureaucratic monopoly model and argued instead that the outcome of bureaucratic strategies depends on the *relative* strength of bureaucrats: that is, bureaucratic demands must be analyzed in a framework which defines the strength of bureaucrats in relation to their sponsors (see, especially, Miller and Moe 1983; Moe 1984; Eavey and Miller 1984; Bendor et al. 1987).

Most later research seeks to identify the conditions under which politicians can counter bureaucratic demands; and constraints on the power of bureaucrats have become theoretically central. Most important is the belief that *competition* can limit the size of government caused by excessive bureaucratic demands and can increase pressure on bureaucrats to be responsive to public demands (Breton and Wintrobe 1984; Niskanen 1975; Ostrom 1981; Miller and Moe 1983; Conybeare 1984). Competition is central because it increases the level of information in the environment about the true costs of services and about alternate modes of service delivery. Thus, competition decreases the basic source of bureaucratic power—the monopoly of information.

Conflicts As long as bureaucrats want larger budgets, conflict may be inevitable. Most important, bureaucrats in any given local government represent different agencies, and their perspectives and interests will be shaped by their experiences in and loyalty to their own agency. Conflict can emerge as they compete with one another within the limited budget of the community to enlarge their own agency's budget.

Bureaucrats may also disagree about how to spend their budgets. Consider, for example, the merits of capital goods versus current expenditures. Some analysts argue that bureaucrats seek to maximize current labor expenditures as an input into the production process, with the result that the labor/capital ratio may be higher in bureaucratic environments than in competitive ones (see Staaf 1977; Courant et al. 1979b; Spizman 1980; for a contrary view, see DeAllesi 1969). This may result because, as Noll and Fiorina (1978) argue, bureaucrats want to enhance the patronage value of public-sector jobs. Moreover, bureaucratic salaries are often a direct function of the number of workers supervised. But if this is true, bureaucrats may seek to maximize the size of their work force, and not the size of their overall budget as predicted by Niskanen (also see Downs 1967; Staaf 1977).

A large work force may also be desired by bureaucrats since government workers can be a political base supporting bureaucratic demands for resources and directly fueling further budgetary growth (Burkhead and Grosskopf 1980; Kau and Rubin 1981; Frey and Pommerehne 1982; Bennett and Orzechowski 1983; Cummings and Ruther 1980). However, there are limits on the size of the public work force and its salaries—a trade-off between wages and workers may ultimately have to be made (see chapter 5).

Politicians

Politicians constitute the last set of actors in my model of local decision processes. Following the work of Downs, Fenno, Fiorina, and others, I stipulate that the overriding goal of politicians is reelection. There are psychic and often monetary rewards for winning reelection and policy goals can be accomplished only by remaining in office.

Obviously, to remain in office politicians must continue to attract enough votes to win election. Local politicians increase the likelihood of winning election by providing quality services to their constituents. But the benefits of this strategy are realized only if local taxes are kept low. Thus, politicians benefit from improving their community's tax base, since this allows more demands to be satisfied within a given tax rate.

The interests of politicians in improving their community's benefit/ cost ratio may align them with business firms: to the extent that economic development improves the local tax base, it can help incumbents win reelection. As I noted earlier, some analysts argue that politicians are too pro-business, granting concessions in excess of returns to the local electorate. This "critical" perspective raises an important question: how long and how far can a local politician deviate from the interests and demands of local residents? The answer may largely determine the degree of freedom politicians have in formulating local policies.

There are compelling theoretical reasons to believe that the freedom of local politicians as policy entrepreneurs is limited. Competitive elections push candidates toward the ideological center of their community: those who stake out positions too far from the center will lose to a more centrist candidate. This concept underlies the logic of the median voter model, which emphasizes the interests of the median voter as a constraint on the independent behavior of politicians (see Inman 1978). Politicians act as conduits for the interests of their voting constituents and cannot consistently take positions which violate these interests. From this perspective, politicians reflect the interests of the community and do not have an independent influence on policy. This theory may help explain why studies of urban policy processes have shown that local politicians have only a limited impact on policy (Pressman and Wildavsky 1973; Morgan and Pelissero 1981; Morgan and Brudney 1985).

Constraints on the Strategies of Politicians   Several factors may affect the goals and strategies of local politicians and how they respond to local demands for services; their freedom to stake out independent positions (rather than simply reflect the demands of other local actors) may depend on local political conditions. In the classic work of V. O. Key (1949), competitive, partisan, political groups seek to win elections by gaining the votes of low-income voters through the expansion of public expenditures that benefit such groups; party competition leads to larger budgets, especially for social services. Despite the compelling logic of Key's hypothesis, empirical work has not consistently identified any effects of partisan conflict. Some studies find a positive (but usually weak) relationship between competition and government expenditures, while others find no association at all (see, for example, Cameron 1978; Lowery and Berry 1983; Gray 1976; Winters 1976; Jones 1974; Flanigan and Zingale 1980).

Inconsistent results may stem in part from the lack of specification of the prerequisite conditions linking partisan conflict to policy outputs. The effect of party politics on the size of government logically depends on the shape of preferences in a community, which in turn depends on the demographic characteristics of the population. Key's hypothesis assumes a sufficient number of low income individuals in an electorate who prefer higher public expenditures. It further assumes that such individuals exercise a critical role in the electoral process (see Jennings 1977 for an exploration of these assumptions). Other studies examining the link between the shape of the income distribution of communities and their expenditure patterns have found patterns not predicted by Key.

Peltzman (1980), for example, argues that the size of the *middle class,* not the lower class, determines the size of government. As the middle class grows, it constitutes an organized and articulate group with an interest in expanding the size of government transfer payments it receives (also see Stigler 1970). However, Peltzman did not examine explicitly the interaction effects of party politics and income distribution.

While this research into the effects of party politics on service demand has produced a set of relatively weak findings, investigation of the role of strong urban political parties in mediating bureaucratic demands has led to more consistent results.

Research on urban service delivery systems has often concluded that the level and distribution of local services are largely determined by "bureaucratic decision rules"—local political parties do not significantly affect service patterns (for example, Lineberry 1977; Mladenka 1978). In such work, politicians are assumed to be either neutral to demand or helpless in the face of bureaucratic power. While the lack of political impact is the most common finding of recent service delivery research, Jones (1981), in his study of Chicago, a city with a strong political organization, shows that entrenched political parties do play an important intermediary role in bureaucratic decisions, increasing demands on the local bureaucracy and influencing the services delivered by the local government.

This highlights an unresolved but basic theoretical problem in the investigation of the relationship among political parties, bureaucrats, and local services. In Jones's argument the *lack* of political party conflict characteristic of political machines *increases* the size of local government. Key, and others following in his tradition, postulate the opposite: the stimulative effect of competition.

Research on the effects of party control on the size of local government is almost as confused as the research on party conflict. However, there is somewhat more consistent empirical evidence that Democratic party control is associated with larger government (Winters 1976; for a comparative perspective on liberal versus conservative parties see Cameron 1978). At present, we can probably accept as a working hypothesis that Democrats are less likely to oppose bureaucratic demands for services and hence Democratic control of local governments would lead to larger local governments. However, because many municipal governments, especially suburbs, are nonpartisan, the importance of this hypothesis for research in the local market for public goods is vitiated.

The prevalence of nonpartisanship in local elections results from the periodic waves of political reform that have swept local governments since the early 1900s. According to Hofstadter (1955), Americans have an almost uncontrollable need to tinker with the structure of local governments under the rubric of reform. Given this tinkering and the variety of political forms it has produced, the effects of reform on local politics have attracted considerable research attention. But research on the effects of reform on local government expenditures and services has reached contradictory results.

Three dimensions of reform have most often been identified as potentially affecting public policy outputs: partisan versus nonpartisan elections; ward-based versus at-large elections; and city manager versus mayoral administrative leadership. Lineberry and Fowler (1967) argued that reformism affected policy outputs by isolating bureaucratic decisions from the "divisive" demands of the electorate. Furthermore, in reformed cities, bureaucrats are supposedly more responsive to the demands of the middle class for less spending and lower taxes (also see Banfield and Wilson 1963), an assumption which runs contrary to Peltzman's empirical finding that the size of the middle class is most strongly associated with size of government.

Research following Lineberry and Fowler has failed to find a consistent effect of reform on local policies. For example, in an empirical investigation of the effects of reformism on tax and expenditure patterns over time, Morgan and Pelissero (1981) conclude reform had little long-range effect on local fiscal decisions, did not limit city spending, and did not change the incentives of politicians to oppose underlying expansion of local government.

THE EXTERNAL LIMITS ON SUBURBAN STRATEGIES

The model of the local policy process developed in this book revolves around four sets of actors: residents, firms, bureaucrats, and politicians. These local actors share a common goal: they want maximum services in relation to tax costs. In the context of suburban politics, a major avenue for accomplishing this goal is maximization of the tax base. Many of the most noted characteristics of suburban politics, especially fiscal zoning, the politics of incorporation, and local budgetary politics, flow from this union of the incentives of these major actors.

There are limits, however, to how far any local community can maximize its tax base. Some limits result from internal conflicts over the extent and distribution of the benefits of economic growth (see especially Logan and Molotch 1987). But there are also strong external constraints: the potential success of the strategies for tax base maximization is limited. In the next few pages I identify three type of external constraints that limit the strategic success of the municipal governments in pursuit of tax base. These limits emerge from strong demographic/ ecological factors shaping growth, from the changing economy, and from the multitiered system of federalism. In section 3 of this book, I examine empirically how these factors affect the accumulation of the local tax base.

Ecological Limits

Since the 1920s, an "ecological" perspective on urban growth has affected our understanding of metropolitan development. It holds that the distribution of income groups across metropolitan communities is the outcome of the "organic" processes driving metropolitan development, especially the process of differentiation natural to the development of any ecological system (Hawley and Rock 1975; Burgess 1927). From this perspective, the development of local communities and their level of wealth are constrained by their physical location in metropolitan regions, their age, and other ecological attributes.

The classic ecological model predicts a continuous cycle of growth and decline as higher income residents move to newer communities, abandoning the deteriorating housing of older ones. Ecological forces produce a "life cycle" of community development, in which older communities lose social status to the newer communities growing on the metropolitan periphery. The ability of local communities to resist this life cycle can be expected to be as successful as individuals seeking to arrest their own life cycle by finding a fountain of youth.

Recent theoretical investigations have modified the classical assumptions of urban ecology to develop a "persistence model" of social status in the distribution of wealth across urban areas. It shares a core theoretical perspective with the ecological approach in that both attempt to model the locational choices of households within the constraints of transportation technology and economic development. But in the persistence model, there is high stability in wealth—a community will retain its status whether high or low. Rather than a life cycle, re-

searchers such as Farley (1964) and Guest (1978) have shown remark-
able stability in the social status of suburban communities over periods
as long as fifty years.

While research by Collver and Semyonov (1979) and Logan and
Schneider (1981) demonstrated more complexity to the patterns of the
distribution of wealth than the ecological models predict, stability over
time in the location of wealth across communities is the overwhelming
finding documented in most research. Such stability limits the ability of
local governments to attract the wealthy families they want to contribute to tax base maximization.

The Transformation of the Economy

The growing literature on the transformation of the national and the
international economy identifies further limits on the success of local
policies in maximizing the local tax base. At least since the 1920s, innovations in manufacturing and transportation technologies (electrifica-
tion, the introduction of trucks) allowed business firms to move out of
central cities to suburbs. New forms of decentralization became even
more evident in the United States after the 1950s. There was a pronounced shift of economic activity from the northern "snowbelt"
regions to the South and West. Paralleling this regional change was a
growth of manufacturing activity outside metropolitan regions entirely—
manufacturing firms found sites in nonmetropolitan areas cheaper.
Because the interstate highway system virtually links the entire country,
such location did not hinder the transport of goods to the large markets
of metropolitan regions.

More recently, to minimize labor costs and often to avoid environmental regulations, manufacturers have moved to off-shore locations.
In turn, there has been a shift in the American economy from manufacturing toward services. The implications of this transformation for local
governments have been much debated. And whether or not local governments can at all control this transformation has been subject to even
more debate.

For example, according to Noyelle and Stanback (1983), the rate and
composition of economic growth in any metropolitan region as a whole
is strongly affected by where it fits in the *international* economy (also see
Rodriquez and Feagin 1986). It is difficult, perhaps even impossible, for
a metropolitan region to alter its fate in this complex system. The worldwide economic system is driven by changes in technology and the
demands for goods and services, all of which affect the rate of economic
growth of regions and local communities, and none of which is ame-

nable to local control. While local governments seek to increase their own rate of growth, and control its composition, ultimately exogenous economic forces limit what any individual community can do.

Intergovernmental Limits

Local governments also face intergovernmental rules and regulations restricting both the flow of money into the community and its freedom to design the service/tax product mix it wants to offer in the local market for public goods.

Local governments want intergovernmental aid to reduce the costs of local services, but their interests are not always congruent with higher level governments. The payment of monies has been volatile, and local governments have been at the mercy of policy changes at the higher level. Furthermore, local governments desire to use their budgets to fashion service/tax bundles attractive to higher income families or to businesses. However, local governments often face severe intergovernmental restrictions on the freedom they have to design policy tools.

During the 1970s, the system of intergovernmental relations took a new direction as higher levels of government began to rely more on the regulation of the behavior of local governments, regulations not tied directly to specific subsidies. New intergovernmental mandates are often more coercive than the rules and regulations of intergovernmental grant programs. Furthermore, higher levels of government do not necessarily provide the money to offset the administrative and policy costs associated with mandates (Lovell et al. 1979; ACIR 1984).

Municipal freedom in the design of marketing strategies is also restricted by patterns of functional responsibility. Liebert (1976) conducted the first extensive study of the distribution of major governmental functions performed by city governments. He identified an ordered historical process in which cohorts of cities (those reaching a threshold of 10,000 population at about the same time) share patterns of functional responsibility. In his analysis, the oldest cities in the United States had more inclusive sets of functions than newer ones. Given historical growth patterns, in which many more cities in the Northeast and Great Lakes regions reached this critical size earlier than cities in the South and Southwest, the process has clear regional implications: cities in the North do more than cities in other parts of the country. While such practices can be changed legislatively, the forces of historical practices and expectations constrain the operations of the local market for public goods and the role of municipal providers in that market.

CONCLUSION

The local market for public goods is driven by the structure of local government and the preferences of actors as conditioned by this structure. Local actors will prefer different service/tax bundles. But the extent of disagreement and its impact on the actual policies enacted by local governments are affected by the degree of competition in the local market and will be constrained by the structural characteristics of the market. For example, bureaucrats want to maximize their budgets. But their ability to do so will be constrained by the degree of competition between alternate service providers found in the local market for public goods. Part 2 of this book examines these conflicts in more detail.

Similarly, many of the shared interests and policy goals of local actors are a direct function of the desire for increased tax base. This consensual goal is, in turn, a direct result of the way in which service and tax levels are determined in the presently configured local market for public goods. Basically, a community's service/tax ratio is driven by its tax base, and maximizing this service/tax ratio can increase the well-being of local actors.

Thus, strong incentives to pursue growth of the local fiscal base cut across the major actors in suburban communities. While a strong service/tax ratio has immediate pay-offs, there are also long-run, cumulative benefits to a strong service/tax ratio. These incentives derive ultimately from the "exit" option—given an unattractive service/tax ratio, all actors in a community suffer if desirable fiscal resources either avoid or leave a community. In contrast, a strong service/tax ratio can attract desirable growth. Despite recently noted problems in the growth machine, incentives to pursue growth in the local tax base remain strong.

Ultimately driven by this exit option, local actors will use their political resources, their "voice," to compel local governments to undertake policies in pursuit of higher service/tax ratios. But there are severe limits on the ability of local governments to fashion policies which successfully achieve this goal. In part 3 of this book, I look at the impact of strategic budgeting on the attraction of rich people, business firms, tax base, and intergovernmental aid. The core question motivating the analysis in part 3 is simply stated: Can local governments actually achieve the outcome most desired by the actors who make local policy decisions?

Part II

DISAGREEMENT OVER THE ALLOCATION OF LOCAL RESOURCES

Four sets of actors in suburbia are central to the operation of the local market for public goods. In this section I examine the conflict between local bureaucrats and other actors over the allocation of local resources. Each chapter analyzes conflict over a particular local resource. Chapter 3 analyzes the size of total municipal budgets while chapter 4 analyzes local budgets in the budgetary categories suggested by Peterson (developmental, redistributive, and allocational). Chapter 5 examines the size and cost of the local public work force. Finally, chapter 6 examines the conflict between bureaucrats and residents over the allocation of intergovernmental aid.

The analysis in each chapter unfolds in a parallel fashion. First, I briefly review the distribution of benefits and costs of the specific resource across the sets of suburban actors—actors may view each particular local resource somewhat differently. I particularly emphasize the interests of bureaucrats.

I then present a multivariate empirical analysis of the distribution of the resource, integrating factors measuring local demand, exogenous constraints, and competition in the local market for public goods. The question underlying the analysis is simply stated: how does the structure of the local market for public goods affect the ability of bureaucrats to control local resources and to extract "economic rents" from their community?

3

SUBURBAN EXPENDITURE PATTERNS

Of the multiple lines of conflict dividing the actors in my model of local politics, I focus on those which hinge on the demands of bureaucrats for more resources. The bureaucratic quest for resources is thus the mainspring for the subsequent analysis of the local resource allocation process. Using the perspective developed in chapter 2, I postulate that a fundamental conflict emerges as bureaucrats use their control over information to manipulate the design of policy and to control consideration of policy alternatives. Control of information allows bureaucrats to demand local budgets larger than the level desired by other actors in their community (Bendor et al. 1987; Moe 1984; Mitnick 1986).

To recapitulate briefly, bureaucrats demand large budgets because they have few incentives to minimize societal inputs into their bureau's production process. According to Niskanen, bureaucratic salaries, promotions, and other perks are contingent upon their success in achieving larger budgets. In a similar vein, Moe (1984) argues that bureaucratic "slack" may be the closest analogy to the "residual" which private sector managers seek. Given the structure of public bureaucracies, budget maximizing behavior emerges because slack is produced only to the extent that an agency's budget exceeds the true costs of production (also Niskanen 1975).

Because a successful Niskanen-like bureaucrat will exact more money from the community than objectively required by others, the level of government expenditures for the provision of public goods and services in relationship to demand is central to this argument.[1] While bureaucrats prosper from their budget maximizing behavior, bureaucratic "profits" or "rents" come at the expense of other members of the local community: since the successful exercise of bureaucratic power shifts resources away from goods preferred by others, monopolistic bureaucratic outputs are, by definition, not optimal.[2]

It also follows that the ability of local bureaucrats to exact larger budgets from their communities will be inversely related to the degree of competition in the local market for public goods.[3] To see this, imagine a metropolitan "market" in which there is only a single community. Citizens and politicians, who have their own preferences for local expenditures, will find it difficult to gather information about alternate service delivery modes and input costs. In this restricted environment, bureaucratic control over information is maximized and the ability of other local actors to gather information about the true costs of services and alternate policy choices is low. Citizens and politicians will find it difficult to monitor and control bureaucratic budget proposals and agency performance. At the other extreme, in a market with perfect information, the power of bureaucrats is reduced, because its source has been eroded. Of course, perfect information never exists. But the local costs of gathering information can vary widely and these costs can be radically lower in a municipality surrounded by many other suburbs with different input/output mixes.

Competition between municipalities can also increase pressure for efficiency and responsiveness. Politicians and citizens must retain fiscally desirable resources; if these resources leave a community, politicians can face reduced chances for reelection and residents will face higher taxes. Where there is choice across neighboring communities with alternative service/tax mixes, the pressure on citizens and bureaucratic sponsors to control costs and to increase the efficiency of government production will therefore be higher. While bureaucrats share the need to retain desirable fiscal resources, their benefit/cost calculations differ from other actors in the community. Bureaucrats will favor larger budgets because the benefits of higher expenditures are concentrated and directly experienced by them. Given such incentives, it is irrational to forego concentrated benefits for the more diffuse benefit of general economic growth (Olson 1982; also see Wilson 1980).

In the next four chapters, I investigate empirically the extent to which competition and consumer choice in the local market for public goods affects the size and growth of suburban government. To the extent that competition actually limits local public expenditures in relation to local demand, the assumption that the monopoly power of bureaucrats allows them to maximize their budgets, by shifting resources from private pocketbooks to public ones, is supported.

I begin by presenting descriptive data on the services delivered by the suburban municipalities in this sample. I first report the total number of services for which different suburbs are responsible. Following Liebert's work (1976), many studies have documented the importance of functional responsibility in determining the size of local budgets. I then present data on the total expenditures of local governments over time and across regions.

Once these broad trends are described, I develop a demand model for suburban municipal expenditures. I extend this simple model to include measures of competition in the local market for public goods. If the local market for public goods operates in a manner similar to the market for private goods, competition will *limit* local government expenditures. This reduction is achieved by encouraging the efficient provision of goods and services and by limiting rent seeking by local bureaucrats.

The empirical investigation begins with a pooled cross-sectional analysis. I then turn to an investigation of *change* in the size of suburban budgets.[4] For the analysis of change, I follow the same steps as in the cross-sectional analysis. I develop a demand model explaining changes in local expenditures and then investigate the effects of market competition on change. Again, to the extent competition restrains growth in local expenditures, I take this as evidence that competition limits the exactive capabilities of bureaucrats.

SUBURBAN SERVICE DELIVERY

Patterns of Functional Responsibility

The number of services which a municipality delivers drives its expenditures: municipalities which do more, spend more. In the parts of the United States settled earlier, local governments traditionally have more responsibility than in newer parts of the country, but as time passed, the expected role of local government narrowed. The distribution of functional responsibility is thus intimately tied to the historical timing of settlement (Liebert 1976).

In this section, I briefly review levels of total service responsibility across 31 service areas listed in the Census of Government Finance. I use a simple index of functional responsibility in which a municipality is assigned a value of "1" for each service for which it expended any monies for current operations. The total functional responsibility index is the sum of these values, with a range of 0 to 31.[5]

Suburban municipalities provide far fewer than the entire range of services enumerated by the Census of Governments. Table 1 reports the average total functional responsibility score for suburbs by geographical region in 1972, 1977, and 1982. Across regions, suburbs in New England

TABLE 1

INDEX OF TOTAL FUNCTIONAL RESPONSIBILITY

	1972	*1977*	*1982*	*Number of Cases*
New England	13.3	15.6	16.7	21
Mid-Atlantic	9.3	10.3	11.1	368
East North Central	8.2	10.2	10.3	451
West North Central	7.8	9.5	9.8	160
South Atlantic	8.0	9.6	9.7	112
East South Central	7.5	9.2	9.9	29
West South Central	8.1	9.3	9.9	101
Mountain	8.2	10.8	11.9	34
Pacific	8.1	10.2	10.9	176
All suburbs	8.4	10.1	10.5	1452

NOTE: The functional responsibility index is the total number of services on which a suburb expends any money whatsoever for current operations. It is computed over the 31 major functional areas reported in the Census of Government Finance. See Appendices for a discussion of the distribution of cases across regions and SMSAs and the number of cases included in analyses.

provide by far the most services, a result directly paralleling Liebert's analysis of larger cities. However, in other regions, average differences in total suburban functional responsibility are not as dramatic as documented by Liebert. While the direction of differences is similar—suburbs in the South and both the East and West South Central regions provide fewer services than do suburbs in the Mid-Atlantic or East North Central regions—the magnitude of the differences are small. Furthermore, levels of functional responsibility in the Mountain SMSAs are relatively high, despite the "newness" of this region.

Patterns of Suburban Total Expenditures

Table 2 reports total suburban expenditures in 1972, 1977, and 1982, in constant 1967 dollars, adjusted by changes in the consumer price index (CPI). Substantial changes in the real expenditures of suburban governments are evident. Nationwide, suburban municipal expenditures per capita rose by an average 16 percent between 1972 and 1977, but then fell sharply in the following five years. Consequently, real public expenditures on the total package of goods and services delivered by suburbs were actually lower in 1982 ($110) than in 1972 ($117).

TABLE 2
TOTAL EXPENDITURES PER CAPITA, IN CONSTANT DOLLARS

	1972	1977	1982
New England	$343	$442	$349
Mid-Atlantic	107	118	100
East North Central	120	135	109
West North Central	122	121	101
South Atlantic	109	145	98
East South Central	117	156	80
West South Central	90	112	98
Mountain	88	119	102
Pacific	121	148	134
All suburbs	117	134	110

NOTE: Expenditures have been adjusted by changes in the consumer price index, with 1967 as the base year.

Regional differences abound. For example, among this small set of New England communities, expenditures were by far the highest in the nation. This should not be surprising: municipalities in New England have the greatest functional responsibility and usually do not have viable county governments with which to share the delivery of urban services.

Suburbs in the Pacific SMSAs also spend more than the nationwide average, although much less than New England suburbs. Between 1972 and 1977, expenditures in suburbs in the South Atlantic and East South Central regions shot up rapidly: in real terms, expenditures increased by about one-third among the suburbs in the SMSAs in the South Atlantic and the East South Central SMSAs. But these increases were not sustained. Suburbs in the Mid-Atlantic and the North Central SMSAs shared a similar, but much less pronounced, pattern of increase between 1972 and 1977, followed by decline in the last half of the decade.

These geographic and temporal patterns of change suggest the openness of local budget decisions to outside forces: a changing economy and changing expectations about the value of local goods and services produced large changes in suburban budgets across the country. Within the boundaries of these overall secular shifts, individual budgetary decisions are made by each suburban municipality. Thus my empirical models of the causes of variation in total expenditure look at local budget decisions as a function of both exogenous and endogenous factors.

THE "OBJECTIVE" DEMAND FOR LOCAL SERVICES: EXOGENOUS FACTORS

Among the exogenous influences which help determine local budgetary decisions, variation in the rate of growth in local economies is clearly important. In particular, in the 1970s economic growth was faster in some regions than in others. Furthermore, local governments faced runaway inflation during the 1970s and had to struggle just to keep up with escalating costs. On the whole, local governments failed in this effort and real total expenditures in 1982 were lower than in 1977 or 1972.

Another exogenous force potentially affecting local budgetary decisions is variation in the availability of intergovernmental grants. Grants affect local budgetary decisions by shifting the local budget line, increasing local income and allowing the purchase of more goods and services at a constant tax rate. But the flow of intergovernmental monies in the 1970s was highly erratic, due to the fiscal and ideological changes in state and federal politics (see chapter 10).

In addition, many local governments faced a harsh evaluation from the "buyers" of their services in the local market, as citizen/consumers began to denigrate the value of the packages of goods and services offered for sale. This was particularly clear in the mid to late 1970s, when the tax-expenditure limitations movement led residents in many communities to view the operations of their local government as wasteful and inefficient (Sears and Citrin 1983).

ENDOGENOUS DEMAND

Given these broad parameters, objective demand for public goods and services within any given community will vary with the needs and preferences of the residents of that community. Variation in demand and tastes can be approximated as a function of measurable demographic characteristics of a community. Among the most important determinants of local demand are the following.

Community Income

We can reasonably expect income to affect preferences for local public goods. However, there is debate about the *direction* of its effect.

Private goods are generally "normal" goods—consumption increases with income. However, some analysts argue that local public goods are "inferior" goods. For example, if a city devotes a large share of its expenditures to welfare services, public health facilities, or certain types of municipal recreational facilities (swimming pools, for example), local demand could actually decrease with income. Higher income individuals and families would either have no use for these services or would prefer more exclusive private facilities. In turn, higher income families would rationally reduce their willingness to pay local taxes. The withdrawal of their support could ultimately force reductions in local services.

Some researchers have documented empirically that the demand for urban public services indeed declines with income (see, for example, Jones et al. 1980; Stein 1986). But these data have been generated from the study of central cities, and there are at least two characteristics of suburban public goods which can cause the relationship between income and demand in suburbia to differ from central city results.

First, the package of goods and services of suburban municipalities varies from central cities in the extent to which redistributive services are offered. Most suburbs devote only a small share of their budgets to typical redistributive services such as health, welfare, and housing. For example, in 1972, the average suburb spent only $2.11 per capita on redistributive services. By 1977 this had increased to about $2.50. Despite radical changes in the demography of suburbia in the 1970s and wide changes in service responsibilities, in 1982 less than $3.50 per capita was spent supporting these services. Moreover, most of these monies went to housing and community development—a program area which often provides low-income housing but which also invests in more general development activities with benefits beyond the lower classes.

Furthermore, many suburbs are relatively homogeneous with respect to income; and virtually all suburbs are more homogeneous than central cities. Homogeneity further reduces possibilities of redistribution. In the extreme case, a homogeneous and affluent suburb can spend all its public revenues on services tailored for the wealthy, such as tennis clubs, golf courses, limited access swimming pools or beaches. Since these services would be tailor-made for the affluent and would be used only by members of the community (who are all affluent) no significant redistribution takes place. Consequently, homogeneous suburbs can purchase more public goods without considering the redistributive implications of budgetary decisions. Since community homogeneity increases with community income, this homogeneity effect might produce higher demand for local services with increases in community income (Schneider 1987).

Given these characteristics of suburban services, the general package of goods and services delivered by suburban governments should be a normal good, that is, demand should increase with income.

Housing Tenure

As I argued in chapter 2, the distribution of local home ownership can also affect the demand for services by changing both the goods and services needed by a community and the perception of costs. Despite consistent efforts to diversify sources of revenue, the primary source of local revenues is still the property tax which homeowners pay on a regular basis. Consequently, homeowners directly experience the costs of local governments and should moderate their demand for public goods as their costs increase.

Renters face a different decision calculus, and they may operate under a "fiscal illusion" in which their calculation of the relative benefits and costs of services are skewed by an underestimation of local costs.

Racial Effects

The racial composition of a suburb can further shift local demand. Blacks generally are of lower income than whites and there is a negative correlation between the concentration of black population and a community's median income. This can affect local demand in contradictory ways. In the first case, given the positive correlation between income and consumption of public goods, and given that blacks, as a whole, have lower incomes than whites, black concentrations might be associated with lower expenditures. But given higher objective need for local services, blacks may demand more municipal services.

Further, blacks are often recent migrants to suburbia from central cities, where services are more abundant. This could produce expectations of higher services compared to white families of similar income. This differential experience with local service levels would couple with a possible preference of blacks for higher local service levels to increase aggregate demand for services in communities to which blacks have access (Clark and Ferguson 1983; Schneider and Logan 1982b).

Population Size and Growth Rate

Among other broadly defined demographic factors affecting local expenditures may be the size of the community itself. Some analysts have argued that important economies of scale exist in the provision of local services, that larger communities require less expenditure per capita than smaller ones (see, for example, Committee for Economic Development 1967). However, others argue that larger communities provide a milieu in which political pressures more than offset any savings from economies of scale in the provision of services. Hirsch (1967), for example, shows that large cities have a larger municipal work force, which in turn increases the political power of municipal workers. These workers then lobby successfully for higher expenditures (also see chapter 5). Furthermore, according to Hirsch, few local government services actually can be organized to achieve economies of scale. Consequently, the political forces for higher wages which accompany large size easily outweigh any savings from production economies.

Population growth may also change the demand for services, by forcing local governments to expend more on the urban infrastructure, such as sewers, a safe water supply, streets and highways.

Demand may also be affected by a community's "ecological position" in its region (Hawley and Rock 1975; Schnore 1961), which is reflected by the distance between a suburb and its central city and by its density.

Economic Composition

The composition of the local economy can also affect community demand. Some suburbs are exclusive residential enclaves which limit commercial development. At the other extreme are communities, such as Industry City, California, where businesses seek to exclude residential development, so as not to dilute the benefits of a strong local tax base with demands for services such as schools or parks.

A large literature, much of it focused on central cities, has investigated the role that business firms play in determining local spending decisions (for example, Fainstein et al. 1984; Friedland 1983). Any local demand model must include measures of the relative size of different sectors in the economy.

Fiscal Factors

The ability of local communities to pay for local services at a reasonable tax cost varies widely and will affect local demand. A stronger tax base redefines the relationship between local taxes and service levels, increasing the policy options available to local communities and allowing communities to offer a better service package at any level of taxation.

The local tax bill can act as a fiscal constraint. In a purely economic model, since taxes represent the amount paid by a household for local services, higher taxes should be translated into lower demand. But some analysts argue taxes represent the extractive capacity of government, rather than a cost mechanism. From this perspective, higher taxes allow local governments to generate even bigger and more expensive government. This was the argument which underlay the general tax limitation movement of the 1970s: by limiting local taxation, the unnecessary size and functions of government will be reduced, without affecting the services truly desired by the local community.

Functional Responsibility

Lying somewhere between endogenous factors and exogenous ones is functional responsibility: the number and range of services local governments deliver. Some governments deliver a wide range of services, while others offer minimal services. This variation affects the size and composition of local budgets (Liebert 1976; Schneider 1980b; Clark and Ferguson 1983).

In the next section I look at total suburban municipal expenditures as a function of these endogenous and exogenous factors. I use these factors to estimate the objective demand for local public goods. I then add indicators of intercommunity competition to this demand model to see how expenditures are affected by competition in the local market for public goods. The ultimate objective is to assess the extent to which marketlike conditions limit local expenditure levels, which are driven by the rent-seeking behavior of bureaucrats.

TOTAL EXPENDITURE PATTERNS: A FIRST CUT

To increase the sample size and to enhance the efficiency of the estimates of structural effects in this demand model, I combined the three years of data into a single pooled cross-sectional analysis. This analytic technique is a powerful statistical tool—but as with any other technique there are associated costs. The major problems result from a complicated error structure, including problems caused by the shared contemporaneous effects of "neighboring" cases. There are a variety of techniques to deal with these problems, of which I use the Least Squares Dummy Variable (LSDV) method suggested by Stimson (1985).

Within the pooled cross-section research design, it is possible to assess the extent to which the coefficients of the independent variables vary from year to year. I initially ran a model in which each variable was allowed to have its own slope in each year. By imposing restrictions across panels and using the Chow test, I found the structural relationships did not vary significantly across time. Therefore only a final model is presented in which the slope of each variable is constant over time. To allow the intercepts to vary, I introduce a time dummy variable. I thus begin by estimating the following demand model of total expenditures:

(1) Total Expenditures$_{i,t}$ = f(SMSA$_i$

+ Demographic Factors$_{i,t}$
+ Economic Composition$_{i,t}$
+ Intergovernmental Factors$_{i,t}$
+ Functional Responsibility$_{i,t}$
+ Fiscal Factors$_{i,t}$
+ Time).

Where:

SMSA = a set of dummy variables representing metropolitan regional location. They control for unmeasured variables, the effects of which are shared by neighboring cases in the sample, and thus correct for problems resulting from the correlated error terms.

Demographic Factors = a vector of demographic characteristics which affect demand: community median income, percent renters, percent black, percent poor in each community as reported in the 1970 and 1980 Census of Population, and adjusted to estimate 1972, 1977, and 1982 values matching the years in which the governmental data were collected.[6] To tap the ecological dimension of demand, a set of four variables was developed, including population size, which can affect local expenditures through its affect on economies or diseconomies of scale; density; percent change in population, which can affect expenditures as the need for an urban infrastructure increases with growth; and distance from the central city, which reflects a community's stage in its life cycle.

Economic Composition = a vector of four variables measuring separately the number of workers in the wholesale, retail, manufacturing, and service sectors in a community relative to community population. These are variants of the traditional Employment/Residents ratio used in ecologically oriented work and measure the relative strength of the economic interests in each sector in a community (see, for example, Schnore 1961).

Intergovernmental Factors = a set of three indictors of potential intergovernmental influences on local decisions. Two of them, total intergovernmental grants per capita from the federal government and total grants per capita from the state government, reflect the fiscal presence of higher level governments in the local revenue picture. To measure the effects of regulatory federalism I rely on Hill et al.'s (1978) work on state mandates. Hill surveyed state governments to determine the number of mandates they imposed on their local governments in several specific functional areas, such as the form of government, annexation, and financial management. I "attached" state scores in each of these areas to each suburban municipality within its jurisdiction—the state mandate "environment" is a cross-level contextual variable which all suburbs in a state share.[7] After experimenting with several combinations of the counts reported by Hill, I found that simply using the total number of mandates was representative of the effects of the other more detailed forms of state regulatory involvement in local decisions.

Functional Responsibility = a single measure of the total number of services a community offers. This measure is created by counting the total number of services for which a suburban government has budgeted current operating expenditures, regardless of the amount.

Fiscal Factors = a vector of two variables reflecting the fiscal capacity of each local government.

The effective median tax bill reflects the cost of local services. This tax bill is computed by multiplying the effective local tax rate by the median home value in a community.[8] True value per capita is measured because of its mediating effect on the tax/service ratio (see chapter 9).[9]

Given inflation, all dollar figures were converted to constant dollars using changes in the consumer price index as the adjustment factor with 1967 as the base year.

Time = a vector of two dummy variables, one recorded 1 for observations in 1977, the other recorded 1 for observations in 1982. These dummy variables help control the effects of exogenous factors affecting local decisions resulting from changes in the macroenvironment which local governments face and the corresponding problems in the error structure resulting from the pooled cross-sectional design.

Results

I created a baseline model of total expenditures as a function of the variables described above. In subsequent analysis I add several variables measuring the extent of competition in the local market for public goods in order to test the effects of the market on expenditure levels. I first regressed total expenditures against the set of SMSA dummy variables. This simple regression model explained 27 percent of the variance in total expenditures (measured by the adjusted R square). While geography clearly matters, so do other characteristics. When I add the remaining variables, the variance explained rises to 61 percent, a substantial increase in explanatory power. (See table 3.)

The overall budgets of suburban governments represent a response to a mixture of both endogenous and exogenous factors, but exoge-

TABLE 3

Total Expenditures as a Function of Local Demand and Exogenous Factors, Controlling for SMSA, Pooled Cross-Sectional Analysis, 1972, 1977, 1982

Variable	B	SE B	Beta	T-Test
DEMOGRAPHIC FACTORS				
Median income	1.71	0.05	.067	3.41
Poor (%)	34.70	22.72	.035	1.52
Rent (%)	35.00	11.42	.056	3.06
Black (%)	40.35	13.10	.044	3.07
Population	0.19	0.06	.051	3.25
Population growth	−0.45	1.62	−.003	−0.28
Distance	0.38	0.18	.031	2.14
Density	−0.02	0.00	−.092	−5.67
ECONOMIC COMPOSITION				
Manufacturing	3.67	6.79	.008	0.54
Services	225.69	25.58	.151	8.82
Retail	51.73	21.33	.035	2.42
Wholesale	111.37	24.08	.082	4.62
INTERGOVERNMENTAL FACTORS				
Federal aid	1.23	0.08	.197	14.88
State aid	1.28	0.04	.387	26.60
Mandates	1.18	0.63	.103	1.86
Functions	8.02	0.61	.217	12.98
FISCAL FACTORS				
True value	2.40	0.32	.152	7.33
Tax bill	0.75	1.06	.011	0.71
TIME				
1977 dummy	−19.86	3.23	−.098	−6.13
1982 dummy	−47.79	3.71	−.228	−12.85
Constant	−99.07	34.19		−2.89
Adjusted R square, SMSA only,	.27			
Adjusted R square, full model,	.61			

NOTES: In this and all similar tables, SMSA location is controlled by a series of dummy variables, the coefficients of which are not reported; all dollar figures are in constant 1967 dollars, deflated by the CPI; population, true value per capita, and median income are measured in thousands; expenditures and intergovernmental grants are computed per capita; and economic composition is the number of workers in a given sector per 1000 residents in a suburb.

Number of cases in pooled sample = 2517.

nous factors seem to be more important. SMSA location effects are clearly important. Time effects are also strong. In 1977 and 1982, real expenditures, *ceteris paribus*, were significantly lower than in 1972. During the 1970s, inflation, tax and expenditure limitations movements, and the general conservative ideology of limited government, all outside the control of local governments, acted to reduce local expenditures.

Consider too the strong effect of intergovernmental aid on local expenditures. State aid has the single largest effect (as measured in standardized regression coefficients) of the variables measured: where states give more money, local governments spend more.[10] Similarly, federal aid also stimulates local expenditures.

Intergovernmental grants are not purely exogenous—that is, local governments have the option of applying or not applying for project grants, and they could have turned down revenue sharing monies (although few did). But throughout the 1970s the amount of money available in the intergovernmental grant system was driven by exogenous forces. Most notably the growing conservative ideology of the Carter and Reagan administrations produced a dramatic reduction in federal intergovernmental aid, and the growing fiscal problems of many states also led them to cut back aid to localities.

Functional responsibility also affects local budgetary outlays. If Liebert is correct, the distribution of functional responsibility is also largely an exogenous factor determined by historical choices, and local governments do not have the ability radically to redefine their responsibilities. Consequently, another major determinant of suburban expenditures is beyond local control.

After taking into effect these exogenous factors, a few local conditions still significantly affect the size of the local budget. Total expenditures are a function of community income. Note that the total package of goods and services delivered by local governments appears to be a normal good. But the effects of the local tax base are even stronger. Fiscal wealth affects the benefit/cost ratio of communities and reduces individual costs. In turn, actors in communities with a strong tax base rationally choose to buy more public goods and services.

As expected, both the concentration of renters and the concentration of blacks increase total expenditures, but the effects are small. Population size also increases expenditures, but if we control for population size, density has the opposite (and stronger) effect. Change in the size of the population does not affect total expenditures.

Among the measures of strength of the sectors of the local economy, note that a larger concentration of each economic sector is associated with larger public expenditures. However, these effects are not very large, and in the case of the manufacturing sector not statistically significant. Of the four sectors, the size of the service sector exerts the strongest effect on local expenditures. In short, larger and more powerful business concentrations do seem to increase the size of the local budget. In the next chapter, the relationship between the size of the local economy and budget allocations across specific categories of expenditures is examined, specifically, does the political strength of business groups actually force local governments to spend more on the services (such as infrastructure) that business needs?

MEASURING MARKET EFFECTS

In the next stage of analysis, the effects of competition on local expenditure decisions are explored. If bureaucrats exact additional local resources by using their monopoly over information and their ability to set policy agendas, it logically follows that bureaucrats operating in an environment with more information will be less successful in exacting rents from their community. But given the complexities and limitations in the local market for public goods, what are the sources of competition?

The Tiebout Model of the Local Market for Public Goods

In Tiebout's model, given a number of different local governments in a metropolitan region, citizens and firms as buyers of local public goods and municipalities as sellers interact to create competitive marketlike conditions. The Tiebout market is driven by the locational decisions of citizen/consumers, who shop between communities and ultimately "vote with their feet."

This "shopping around" is informed by strategic fiscal behavior in which citizen/consumers try to maximize the benefit/cost ratio of location, buying into efficient municipalities which offer the package of services the consumer most prefers at the most reasonable tax level. Inefficient and unresponsive jurisdictions will lose mobile and fiscally desirable citizens to more efficient ones (see especially, Peterson 1981; Epple and Zelenitz 1981; Sjoquist 1982; also Aronson 1974; Pack and Pack 1978; Schneider and Logan 1982a; Sharpe and Newton 1984).

The Tiebout model is ultimately based on the mobility of citizen/consumers and, therefore, is logically contingent upon the presence of alternate municipalities. The importance of this structural condition is at the core of the polycentric version of the local market, where a number of local governments in a metropolitan region is required to simulate marketlike competitive forces (see especially Ostrom et al. 1961; Bish 1971; Ostrom 1972).

I operationalize the concept of alternate providers in two ways. First, I counted the number of incorporated suburbs in each SMSA. This reflects the number of municipal providers in the general market for public goods. This is a contextual variable identical for each suburban municipality in each SMSA. In addition, I computed a community level measure of proximate alternate providers by counting the number of other municipal governments located on the border of each municipality in the sample. A greater number of contiguous providers stimulates more competition for at least two reasons: first, increasing the number of neighboring municipalities theoretically increases the amount of information about alternate patterns of service delivery available in the environment. It will cost an isolated community more to discover the true costs of service delivery and to discover alternate service delivery patterns. In contrast, with greater proximity comes lower information gathering costs, restricting bureaucratic monopoly control of information. Second, moving costs increase with distance. Thus, residents in a local government surrounded by other municipalities will find it easier (cheaper) to leave a community when faced with inefficient or unresponsive services.

Clearly, indicators of the number of alternate providers alone are not enough to describe the structure of the local market. While large numbers of proximate alternate providers may encourage competition in the local market for public goods, this by itself is not a sufficient condition. If a large number of suburbs offer identical service/tax bundles, a robust market for local public goods would not exist. Therefore, the degree to which local governments actually provide a differentiated product mix, offering a range of different services and tax levels from which local residents can choose, must be measured.

Measuring Consumer Choice in the Local Market

I developed two measures of the range of consumer choice in the local market for public goods. One assesses the range of consumer choice in service levels (local benefits). This measure is the standard deviation of total suburban municipal expenditures across all the municipalities in a region.[11] Correspondingly, to assess the degree of variation in the local taxes paid to local government, I first computed the tax bill assessed against the owner of a house with the median value in a community. The extent of variation in taxes is measured by the standard deviation in the municipal tax bill across all suburban municipalities in an SMSA.

Adding these two indicators to the measures of alternate municipal providers yields four empirical indicators of the degree of choice available to consumers in the market for public goods: the total number of municipalities in an SMSA, the number of contiguous municipalities, variation in expenditures, and variation in the local tax bill.

Like the total number of suburbs in an SMSA, the measures of choice in expenditure and tax bill are "contextual" variables measured at the regional level—each municipality in a region has the same score as every other municipality in its region, but municipalities in different regions have different scores. The method thus assumes that individual municipalities in the same region face the same conditions in the local market for public goods, but these market conditions vary from one SMSA to another. In contrast, the number of contiguous suburbs varies across individual communities.

These factors are external to the organization of the local government. McGuire et al. (1979) argue that the structure of the bureaus that politicians face will also affect their ability to control bureaucratic demands. Specifically, they argue that multiple bureaus reporting to the same sponsor and competing for limited resources increases the ability of sponsors to extract more information about the true costs of services from bureaucrats, thereby limiting expansionary bureaucratic demands (also see Miller and Moe 1983; Stockfish 1976).

To assess the degree to which bureaucracies are unified within each individual government, I computed a Herfindahl index based on data from the Census of Government Employment: a score of 1 indicates all government workers work for only one bureau; a value of 0 means all bureaus are of equal size. By extension, McGuire et al. predict a positive coefficient between the Herfindahl index and the size of government: that is, municipalities with more concentrated work forces will have larger governments which grow faster.

To examine how competition affects the total expenditures of local governments I added the competition variables to equation 1. Table 4 reports the results of estimating empirically this expanded equation. Because the effects of individual community variables do not change across the two equations, I discuss only the effects of the market variables on expenditures.

First, the overall number of municipalities in an SMSA drops out of the estimation because of its multicollinearity with the SMSA dummy

TABLE 4
TOTAL EXPENDITURES AS A FUNCTION OF LOCAL DEMAND, EXOGENOUS FACTORS,
AND MARKET COMPETITION, CONTROLLING FOR SMSA, POOLED
CROSS-SECTIONAL ANALYSIS, 1972, 1977, 1982

Variable	B	SE B	Beta	T-Test
DEMOGRAPHIC FACTORS				
Median income	1.73	0.05	.068	3.44
Poor (%)	34.87	22.73	.035	1.53
Rent (%)	32.95	11.45	.053	2.87
Black (%)	38.45	13.15	.042	2.92
Population	0.21	0.06	.060	3.63
Population growth	−0.56	1.62	−.004	−0.35
Distance	0.32	0.18	.026	1.75
Density	−0.02	0.00	−.096	−5.92
ECONOMIC COMPOSITION				
Manufacturing	4.02	6.80	.009	0.59
Services	227.11	25.65	.152	8.85
Retail	45.28	21.85	.030	2.07
Wholesale	111.13	24.02	.081	4.62
INTERGOVERNMENTAL FACTORS				
Federal aid	1.24	0.08	.199	15.02
State aid	1.28	0.04	.387	26.60
Mandates	1.17	0.63	.102	1.84
Functions	7.67	0.63	.208	12.08
FISCAL FACTORS				
True value	2.54	0.32	.160	7.73
Tax bill	2.85	1.21	.044	2.35
TIME				
1977 dummy	−20.87	3.27	−.102	−6.37
1982 dummy	−44.53	3.84	−.212	−11.57
COMPETITION				
Borders	−1.26	0.63	−.030	−2.00
S.D. expenditures	0.01	0.01	.016	1.15
S.D. tax bill	−0.05	0.01	−.100	−3.82
Herfindahl index	−17.77	12.05	−.020	−1.47
Constant	−79.24	34.66		−2.28
Adjusted R square, SMSA only,	.27			
Adjusted R square, full model,	.64			

NOTE: The "Borders" variable is the number of contiguous municipalities;
"S.D." = standard deviation. See text for complete description.

variables.[12] However, the number of bordering communities has a significant negative effect on expenditures: a greater number of proximate providers does restrict successful rent-seeking by bureaucrats.

The effects of the consumer choice variables are more problematic. Variation in taxes affects local governments as expected: more variation across suburban municipal taxes generates competitive pressure to keep expenditures low. Thus, where lower (tax) price providers are available in a local market, pressure is exerted on bureaucrats to lower their demands on communities. But variation among the "products" offered by local governments does not affect demand: more variation in service levels does not restrict bureaucratic behavior.[13]

In the cross-sectional analysis, outcomes congruent with the expected results of competition in the local market are evident, but are not overwhelmingly strong.

COMPETITION AND CHANGE IN THE SIZE OF LOCAL GOVERNMENT

Measuring the rate of change in the size of local government is conceptually distinct from measuring the size of local government at a single point in time. Cross-sectional analysis focuses on a present equilibrium: that is, it measures present "solutions" to the processes driving the market. In contrast, analysis of rates of change focus on perturbations in a system which can cause shifts to a new equilibrium. Despite this conceptual difference, the large literature examining growth in government overlaps the literature examining the size of government in cross-sectional terms (see, for example, Larkey et al. 1981; Lowery and Berry 1983).

In the next section I test empirically the effects of the competition in the local market for public goods on the rate of growth of local government.

Measuring Change

To control for demand and to identify the effects of competition on change in the size of local government I estimate the following model:

$$(2) \quad Y_t = \alpha + \beta Y_{t-1} + \beta X_{t-1} + \beta \text{COMPETITION}_{t-1} + \text{Error.}$$

This is a lagged endogenous variable model in which government expenditure measured at time (t) is a function of its previous value, a set of community characteristics (measured at t-1) used to estimate local demand, plus competition. Following Markus (1980) I interpret this model as an investigation of the causes of change in the dependent variable.[14] Because this is a change model, only two panels can be used (change from 1972 to 1977; change from 1977 to 1982) and information from independent variables measured in the third wave of observations (1982) is lost. To control contemporaneous effects, the SMSA dummy variables are again introduced.

To estimate demand, the same community factors used in the first section of this chapter are used. Once local demand for services is controlled, municipalities located in metropolitan regions with more competition should experience slower growth than municipalities in less competitive regions, that is, competition will restrain the growth of local government.

Results Table 5 reports the results of this analysis. The model explains 56 percent of the variance in expenditures. Not surprisingly, most of the local characteristics which affected local expenditures in the cross-sectional analysis significantly affect the rate of change in local expenditures. More surprising is the fact that the relationship between present expenditures and the lagged measure is weak.

Intergovernmental effects on the growth of local government are clear. State aid stimulates more rapid growth in local budgets; in contrast, federal aid does not. But recall both federal and state aid stimulated cross-sectional expenditures. This difference in cross-sectional and over-time effects of state and federal aid likely results from the stability of state aid and the volatility of federal aid. Local governments are reluctant to rely on federal aid for long range budgetary plans. Instead, communities spend federal aid for capital equipment or other "big-ticket" items which will not disappear when federal aid is cut (hence, a large cross-sectional effect). In contrast, given the greater stability of state aid, communities are apparently more inclined to factor such aid into both their current and long-term budgetary planning (producing both cross-sectional and longitudinal effects).

The cross-sectional and longitudinal effects of income and fiscal factors also differ. Median income had a significant positive effect in the cross-sectional analysis, but its effect on changes in total expenditures is not significant. In contrast, community fiscal wealth clearly allows for the expansion of local government. Also note that similar to the cross-sectional analysis, a higher tax bill is associated with greater increase in the size of local budgets.

Larger concentrations of wholesale, manufacturing, and service industries in a community are significantly associated with more rapid

TABLE 5

CHANGE IN TOTAL EXPENDITURES: TOTAL EXPENDITURES AS A FUNCTION
OF PREVIOUS EXPENDITURES, LOCAL DEMAND, EXOGENOUS FACTORS, AND
COMPETITION, CONTROLLING FOR SMSA, POOLED ANALYSIS, 1972–1977 AND 1977–1982

Variable	B	SE B	Beta	T-Test
LAGGED VALUE				
Expenditures $(t-1)$	0.06	0.01	.118	6.29
DEMOGRAPHIC FACTORS				
Median income	0.04	0.06	.017	0.73
Poor (%)	0.55	0.86	.007	0.64
Rent (%)	57.90	15.13	.088	3.82
Black (%)	67.23	17.55	.068	3.83
Population	0.25	0.00	.062	2.86
Population growth	−3.06	3.61	−.015	−0.84
Distance	−0.16	0.24	−.013	−0.66
Density	−0.02	0.00	−.110	−5.11
ECONOMIC COMPOSITION				
Manufacturing	24.56	8.90	.055	2.75
Services	280.33	43.52	.141	6.44
Retail	35.88	29.59	.022	1.21
Wholesale	141.94	40.15	.082	3.53
INTERGOVERNMENTAL FACTORS				
Federal aid	0.16	0.10	.029	1.66
State aid	0.59	0.06	.181	9.25
Mandates	0.69	0.83	.059	0.83
Functions	6.01	0.90	.151	6.63
FISCAL FACTORS				
True value	3.26	0.47	.196	6.92
Tax bill	6.76	1.88	.104	3.58
TIME				
1972 dummy	49.91	3.79	.254	13.15
COMPETITION				
Borders	−1.28	0.86	−.030	−1.48
S.D. expenditures	−0.05	0.02	−.054	−2.49
S.D. tax bill	−0.03	0.03	−.050	−0.90
Herfindahl index	−58.78	18.08	−.059	−3.25
Constant	−52.13	45.48		1.14
Adjusted R square, lagged value,	.13			
Adjusted R square, + SMSA,	.32			
Adjusted R square, full model,	.56			

NOTE: Number of cases in pooled sample = 1678.

increases in total expenditures. Of the business sectors measured, the service sector has the strongest and most consistent effect on total expenditures.

Let us return to the central theoretical question: does competition between suburbs act as a brake on growth of government? The answer is again mixed. Communities surrounded by a greater number of alternate providers do expand their budgets more slowly, but the effect is small and not significant. Variation in the tax bill also has the predicted sign, but its coefficient just misses being statistically significant at the conventional .05 level, using the appropriate one-tailed t-test.

Consistent with the anticipated results, greater competition in the service offerings of local governments in a region acts as a brake on growth: the coefficient of the lagged value of the standard deviation of expenditures is negative and significant.

Finally, the Herfindahl index is not well behaved. Contrary to the argument of McGuire et al. (1979), a more fragmented bureaucratic structure within a local government does *not* seem to increase the ability of sponsors to control the demands of their bureaucrats. The negative coefficient on the Herfindahl index shows that expenditures increase more slowly in a more concentrated bureaucratic structure (at least as reflected in the relative size of agency work forces). Competition between workers in different bureaus may actually force local governments to expend more money, perhaps because concessions made to a set of workers in one agency must be matched with concessions in all the others.

CONCLUSIONS

It is widely believed that local governments spend more than needed by the society they serve. Alternate theories have been proposed to explain the size and rapid growth of government. In crafting these theories, analysts draw on a wide range of political, economic, and demographic factors (see, for example, the summary by Lowery and Berry 1983). In contrast, there are far fewer theories describing how to limit such growth. The most powerful seek to design service delivery systems which maximize competition between alternate service providers, increasing the information in the service delivery environment to counter the expansionary demands of bureaucrats (see Bennett and Johnson 1980; Wagner and Weber 1975). The importance of this approach is most directly seen in the growing interest by policy analysts in devising service delivery systems, such as the Lakewood Plan, contracting, voucher systems, and "co-production," which build directly on competitive mechanisms.

Accumulating evidence shows these direct changes in service delivery systems can limit government (Savas 1987 is a good summary). The evidence presented in this chapter suggests that "macro-level" competition between different communities can also limit the size and growth of local government. In regions where there is more variation in tax bills across communities, expenditures are lower. This is exactly what would be predicted by a competitive market model, as variation in tax costs pressures sponsors to limit the expansionary demands of bureaucrats and keep expenditures more in line with objective local need. This argument is bolstered by the consistent effects of the "border" variable. Bureaucratic suppliers facing more intense competition from neighboring communities and operating in an environment with more information are less able to expand local agency budgets than are bureaucrats facing less competitive environments. In a more competitive and more information-rich environment, communities can more easily monitor their bureaucrats and test the veracity of bureaucratic claims about the costs of supplying public goods and services.

In the cross-sectional analysis, communities facing a market with greater variation in service expenditures spend neither more nor less, *ceteris paribus,* than communities in environments with less competition. But over time, variation in expenditures does have the expected result, limiting growth in local budgets. Thus, in the long run this form of competition may also produce the expected result: eventually the expenditures in communities operating in competitive environments will grow more slowly than expenditures in other communities.

Finally, the Herfindahl index created to tap the effect of a fragmented bureaucracy does not operate in the predicted direction. The effects predicted by McGuire et al. may be more than offset by dynamic forces in the interplay of the demands of government workers—a factor I consider in chapter 5.

The effects of competition are not as uniform nor as strong as the direct application of a competitive private market model would predict. However, given the complexity of the local market for public goods, given the spatial monopoly held by municipal providers, and given the powerful control over agendas and information which public bureaucrats possess, it is perhaps more surprising that the effects of competition are so consistently found.

Just as competition in the direct provision of services, for example through contracting or through privatization, reduces the costs of local government by restraining the demands of bureaucrats, increased macro-level competition build into the structure of the local market for public goods can also restrict the size and growth of local government.

4

COMPETITION IN THE THREE WORLDS
OF MUNICIPAL EXPENDITURES

Intermunicipal competition has theoretically interesting effects on the total expenditures of local governments. By limiting the monopolistic power of bureaucrats to maximize their budgets, competition restrains the size and growth of local government. However, using total budgets alone to assess the effects of competition on bureaucratic power may mask as much information as it provides. Disaggregating total expenditures into more discrete categories of expenditures allows for a fuller examination of the workings of the local market for public goods.

Local governments invest their budgets in a variety of functional areas. Following Peterson (1981), these can be divided into three categories. Developmental expenditures support the urban infrastructure, have positive effects on the future fiscal development and growth of the community, and are popular in local governments. In contrast, redistributive services transfer resources to lower income individuals, have negative effects on the benefit/cost ratio experienced by above-average income residents of a community, and are thus conflictual and unlikely to be well funded. Finally, there are allocational services, which, theoretically, are neutral with respect to the redistribution of resources, fund the housekeeping functions of local government, and, according to Peterson, are not entangled with the politics of fiscal growth.

Peterson argues that each type of expenditure has a distinct form of politics associated with it, resulting from the impact each has on the local benefit/cost ratio. I explore this idea more fully through the analysis of the local market for public goods. Specifically, if Peterson is correct, in more competitive markets the incentives for local governments to invest in developmental expenditures should be especially strong. Competition to lure attractive, fiscally productive individuals, families, and firms increases the incentives of local governments to invest in the developmental services which will appeal to them. Conversely, competition should lead to lower expenditures on redistributive services. Municipalities facing more competition have less ability to levy higher taxes on wealthier residents to pay for redistributive services. Finally, competition should have little or no effect on allocational expenditures.

In contrast to this idea of differential impacts, the "greedy bureaucrat" model makes no distinction across policy domains. From the budget maximizing perspective, there are no reasons *a priori* to expect bureaucratic demands to vary. Rather, bureaucrats seek to increase their consumption of local resources, and it is competition, not the substantive policy domain of an agency, which limits bureaucratic demands for resources.

To test these two perspectives on the effects of competition on the bureaucratic consumption of local resources, I will examine the effects of competition in each of the three domains of local expenditures. Using the mode of analysis established in the previous chapter, I begin with a brief review of suburban expenditures of the three service areas. A demand model of expenditures in each domain, including indicators of competition, is then estimated and the effects of competition on the level of expenditures in each service area examined.[1] As in the previous chapter, the empirical work is based on data from suburban municipalities observed in 1972, 1977, and 1982, using constant 1967 dollars.

THE SUBURBAN SERVICE DELIVERY ROLE: AN OVERVIEW

Developmental Services

Developmental expenditures are defined as current operating outlays on streets and highways, sewers, sanitation, transit, transportation, and utilities.[2] On the average, about 25 percent of total local budgets is spent on these services. Nationwide, in 1972, suburbs spent an average of $27 per capita on developmental services (measured in constant 1967 dollars), a figure which rose only slightly over the next decade. (See table 6.)

Stability in outlays for developmental services most likely results from the centrality of these services to the role of local government. The most typical service responsibilities of municipal governments include maintaining streets and keeping the urban environment clean. Variation in the need for expenditures on these services across regions and across time appears to be limited.

Stability in developmental services is also evident in levels of func-

TABLE 6
PER CAPITA EXPENDITURES ON DEVELOPMENTAL SERVICES, IN CONSTANT DOLLARS

	1972	1977	1982	(N)
New England	$32	$33	$26	21
Mid-Atlantic	27	27	27	368
East North Central	31	31	34	451
West North Central	21	23	22	160
South Atlantic	28	33	33	112
East South Central	25	24	26	29
West South Central	25	25	31	101
Mountain	24	25	29	34
Pacific	23	26	27	176
All suburbs	27	28	29	1452

TABLE 7
FUNCTIONAL RESPONSIBILITY INDEX, DEVELOPMENTAL SERVICES

	1972	1977	1982
New England	3.8	3.8	3.8
Mid-Atlantic	3.1	2.8	3.0
East North Central	3.4	3.2	3.2
West North Central	2.9	2.7	2.8
South Atlantic	3.3	3.0	3.0
East South Central	2.9	2.8	3.1
West South Central	3.7	3.1	3.4
Mountain	3.8	3.7	3.8
Pacific	3.1	2.9	3.0
All suburbs	3.3	3.0	3.1

tional responsibility. Of the eight developmental services measured, most suburbs offer between three to four such services, a figure which has remained relatively stable from 1972 to 1982. (See table 7.)

Allocational Services

Table 8 reports average per capita expenditures for allocational services, defined as the costs of administration and general management.[3] Nationwide, these services constitute a smaller share of local budgets than do developmental services. Furthermore, there is greater variation over time and across regions. Between 1972 and 1977, average alloca-

TABLE 8
PER CAPITA EXPENDITURES ON ALLOCATIONAL SERVICES, IN CONSTANT DOLLARS

	1972	1977	1982
New England	$28	$58	$53
Mid-Atlantic	15	24	26
East North Central	12	19	23
West North Central	9	16	19
South Atlantic	12	20	21
East South Central	7	13	14
West South Central	8	12	18
Mountain	10	15	19
Pacific	18	25	25
All suburbs	13	21	23

TABLE 9
FUNCTIONAL RESPONSIBILITY INDEX, ALLOCATIONAL SERVICES

	1972	1977	1982
New England	4.0	4.0	4.0
Mid-Atlantic	3.8	3.5	3.3
East North Central	3.7	3.4	3.1
West North Central	3.7	3.4	3.3
South Atlantic	3.6	3.3	3.0
East South Central	3.6	2.8	2.5
West South Central	3.8	2.8	2.6
Mountain	3.6	3.5	3.5
Pacific	3.6	3.6	3.4
All suburbs	3.7	3.4	3.2

tional expenditures increased by over 60 percent nationwide. However, between 1977 and 1982, further growth in such expenditures was slow. Moreover, the number of allocational functions offered by suburbs declined over time. (See table 9.) Suburbs thus engaged in "load shedding": they passed allocational services off to other governments, privatized them, or eliminated them altogether.

Redistributive Services

Similar to allocational expenditures, variation across regions and over time is also evident in the redistributive services (health, hospitals, welfare, and housing/community development) examined here. But they consume only a small share of local budgets in most suburbs. Expenditures are low throughout the period studied, with a slight upward drift. In most suburbs, housing/community development expenditures account for most of this outlay. (See table 10.) The number of redistributive services offered by suburbs is also relatively low (table 11).[4]

Given these broad outlines, I next look at the effects of competition in the market for each type of service. Because each type of expenditure may be determined within a distinct policy arena, characterized by dif-

TABLE 10
PER CAPITA EXPENDITURES ON REDISTRIBUTIVE SERVICES, IN CONSTANT DOLLARS

	1972	*1977*	*1982*
New England	$15.70	$22.39	$28.79
Mid-Atlantic	1.42	1.13	1.75
East North Central	3.25	3.13	3.66
West North Central	0.42	2.23	3.41
South Atlantic	1.35	1.40	3.13
East South Central	0.16	0.99	0.35
West South Central	4.46	5.46	6.24
Mountain	0.47	0.30	1.43
Pacific	0.31	1.21	2.78
All suburbs	2.11	2.49	3.43

TABLE 11
FUNCTIONAL RESPONSIBILITY INDEX, REDISTRIBUTIVE SERVICES

	1972	*1977*	*1982*
New England	2.6	2.9	3.2
Mid-Atlantic	1.1	0.8	1.0
East North Central	0.7	0.6	0.7
West North Central	0.7	0.6	0.6
South Atlantic	0.6	0.3	0.5
East South Central	0.5	0.5	0.4
West South Central	0.6	0.4	0.6
Mountain	0.5	0.5	0.8
Pacific	0.4	0.6	0.9
All suburbs	0.8	0.6	0.8

ferential levels of competition and information, to reflect the range of consumer choice, I use the standard deviation of each specific area of expenditure in the equation measuring local demand for that type of service, rather than using the standard deviation of total expenditures. I thus "partition" one dimension of competition into three submarkets.

THE DEMAND FOR DEVELOPMENTAL EXPENDITURES

Table 12 reports an analysis of developmental expenditures in the pooled cross-section of suburbs. While most of the variables that affected total expenditures also affect developmental expenditures, there are some differences worth noting briefly.

Regional location explains less of the variance in developmental expenditures (17 percent) than in total expenditures (24 percent). This may reflect the shared need for developmental services across suburbs regardless of regional location. Furthermore, recall, *ceteris paribus,* total expenditures declined over time: the coefficients for both time dummies in the demand equation for total expenditures were negative. In contrast, for developmental expenditures there is a significantly *positive* coefficient on the 1982 time variable. Thus, developmental expenditures withstood better the deteriorating fiscal condition of suburban governments than did total expenditures.

Note, too, that the effects of intergovernmental aid are weaker in the developmental expenditure equation than in the equation for total expenditures. While intergovernmental aid may allow a local government to purchase "frills" or items lower in its preference order, core developmental services may be priority goods and services funded by local revenues, regardless of the flow of intergovernmental monies.[5]

Among economic indicators, the local manufacturing ratio has a significant *positive* impact on the level of developmental expenditures (recall it had no effect on total expenditures). Manufacturing interests apparently use their political power to influence those outlays on the infrastructure in which they have the most interest. Paralleling total expenditures, a larger service sector also exerts a significant influence on local developmental expenditures.

Median income appears more strongly related to developmental expenditures than to total expenditures. And a stronger fiscal base, not surprisingly, leads to higher expenditures for these services. Thus, within the total package of goods and services that suburban municipal governments provide, developmental expenditures are clearly normal goods.

TABLE 12

DEVELOPMENTAL EXPENDITURES, AS A FUNCTION OF LOCAL CONDITIONS AND COMPETITION, CONTROLLING FOR SMSA, POOLED CROSS-SECTIONAL ANALYSIS, 1972, 1977, 1982

Variable	B	SE B	Beta	T-Test
DEMOGRAPHIC FACTORS				
Median income	0.04	0.01	.109	4.57
Poor (%)	4.31	4.73	.025	0.91
Rent (%)	9.91	2.38	.093	4.15
Black (%)	0.41	2.74	.002	0.15
Population	−0.08	0.00	−.130	−6.76
Population growth	−0.95	0.33	−.046	−2.81
Distance	−0.05	0.03	−.024	−1.34
Density	−0.00	0.00	−.095	−4.83
ECONOMIC COMPOSITION				
Manufacturing	6.18	1.42	.081	4.35
Service	27.85	5.34	.108	5.20
Retail	2.94	4.55	.011	0.64
Wholesale	−8.65	5.00	−.036	−1.72
INTERGOVERNMENTAL FACTORS				
Federal aid	0.06	0.01	.057	3.59
State aid	0.09	0.01	.164	9.37
Mandates	0.03	0.13	.015	0.23
Developmental functions	7.05	0.30	.400	23.37
FISCAL FACTORS				
True value	0.46	0.06	.170	6.77
Tax bill	0.47	0.25	.043	1.89
TIME				
1977 dummy	0.22	0.66	.006	0.34
1982 dummy	1.42	0.75	.039	1.87
COMPETITION				
Borders	−0.37	0.13	−.052	−2.82
S.D. tax bill	−0.00	0.00	−.047	−1.49
S.D. developmental exp.	0.00	0.00	.042	2.58
Herfindahl index	−15.82	2.53	−.104	−6.25
Constant	2.10	7.17		0.29
Adjusted R square, SMSA only,	.17			
Adjusted R square, full model,	.48			

NOTE: Number of cases in pooled sample = 2517.

But let us turn to our central question: does competition affect developmental expenditures?

Local governments facing more competition from neighboring municipalities spend less on development. Similarly, when there is more variation in the taxes of local governments, expenditures on infrastructure are also lower (although the level of statistical significance is only .06, using the appropriate one-tailed test). These forms of competition limit the growth of government. However, a wider range of service choices across developmental service expenditures is associated with higher expenditures on local infrastructure.

Competition between public-sector workers in a community (as measured by the Herfindahl index) is associated with higher expenditures on developmental services. As with total expenditures, the effect implies that competition between workers, perhaps represented by different unions, may force local governments to provide more perks and higher salaries to their workers, thus forcing up expenditures.

In short, the local market for the developmental goods and services provided by local governments is not a perfect market. While tax competition limits municipal outlays, and while the number of alternate providers in a market also constrains expenditures, some forms of competition actually increase the developmental outlays of local government. Thus, the evidence from this service area provides some evidence to support both Peterson's argument and a greedy bureaucrat perspective.

Change in Development Expenditures

Replicating chapter 3, change in current operating outlays for developmental expenditures is examined. Table 13 reports a lagged endogenous variable model in which current developmental expenditures are a function of developmental expenditures five years earlier, plus the lagged values of the characteristics reflecting local demand.

Similar to the weak lagged effects in total expenditures, the effect of past developmental expenditures on present ones is weak. Also similar to the pattern for total expenditures, regional patterns of change are evident. But individual community characteristics still increase the variance explained to 47 percent. Among individual community characteristics, the size of the service sector emerges as a clear predictor of growth in developmental expenditures. A larger manufacturing sector is also associated with more rapid growth of developmental expenditures over time.

Intergovernmental influences play a major role in changes in developmental expenditures: higher levels of federal and especially state aid lead to a more rapid increase in developmental expenditures. The

TABLE 13

Change in Developmental Expenditures, as a Function of Local Demand, Other Local Conditions, and Competition, Controlling for SMSA, Pooled Analysis, 1972–1977 and 1977–1982

Variable	B	SE B	Beta	T-Test
LAGGED VALUE				
Developmental exp. $_{(t-1)}$	0.00	0.00	.010	0.57
DEMOGRAPHIC FACTORS				
Median income	0.01	0.01	.029	1.17
Poor (%)	0.01	0.95	.008	0.01
Rent (%)	8.01	2.95	.068	2.71
Black (%)	4.00	3.43	−.022	−1.16
Population	−0.00	0.00	−.129	−5.61
Population growth	−3.27	0.70	−.095	−4.63
Distance	0.00	0.04	.003	0.17
Density	−0.00	0.00	−.106	−4.52
ECONOMIC COMPOSITION				
Manufacturing	2.93	1.74	.036	1.68
Service	48.37	8.50	.136	5.69
Retail	0.12	5.78	.000	0.02
Wholesale	−12.79	7.86	−.041	−1.62
INTERGOVERNMENTAL FACTORS				
Federal aid	0.08	0.01	.078	4.11
State aid	0.16	0.01	.279	13.39
Mandates	0.04	0.16	.022	0.28
Developmental functions	5.22	0.38	.281	13.74
FISCAL FACTORS				
True value	0.62	0.09	.211	6.82
Tax bill	0.77	0.36	.066	2.10
TIME				
1972 dummy	1.94	0.71	.055	2.70
COMPETITION				
Borders	−0.30	0.16	−.040	−1.83
No. of cities	−0.07	0.05	−.207	−1.49
S.D. tax bill	−0.00	0.00	−.025	−0.40
S.D. developmental exp.	0.00	0.00	.014	0.64
Herfindahl index	−27.11	3.58	−.152	−7.55
Constant	26.13	12.59		2.07
Adjusted R square, lagged value,	.10			
Adjusted R square, + SMSA,	.17			
Adjusted R square, full model,	.47			

NOTE: Number of cases in pooled sample = 1678.

assignment of functional responsibility also pushes up expenditures. A stronger tax base is associated with a more rapid increase in developmental expenditures, and communities with higher tax bills expand their developmental expenditures faster than do communities with lower taxes.

But how do competitive market forces affect growth in these service expenditures? Among these market measures, there is a limiting effect of the number of bordering communities on the rate at which expenditures grow (see Sjoquist 1982, and Schneider 1986c). However, neither the service nor tax choice variables are associated with change in expenditures. Finally, as in the cross-sectional analysis, competition among public workers increases local developmental expenditures over time.

ALLOCATIONAL EXPENDITURES

According to Peterson, allocational expenditures fund the day-to-day "housekeeping" operations of local government and are not central to competitive local growth strategies. Table 14 reports an analysis of allocational expenditures in the pooled cross section of suburbs.

Regional patterns are important in the distribution of allocational expenditures: over 20 percent of variation in allocational expenditures is explained by SMSA location. Time effects are also evident: by 1982, constant allocational expenditures were significantly higher than 1972 levels.

Intergovernmental aid, from both the federal and state governments, has a positive effect on allocational expenditures. While it is not technically correct to compare coefficients across equations, note that intergovernmental aid stimulates allocational expenditures less strongly than they stimulated total expenditures, but more strongly than they affected developmental ones. This suggests that allocational expenditures, like developmental ones, are more likely to be supported by local resources, while intergovernmental aid allows local governments to purchase additional items lower on their preference order.

The size of the local service sector has a significant positive effect on allocational expenditures similar to its effect on both total and developmental expenditures. To the extent the service sector expands in the future, as it inevitably will, upward pressure on suburban expenditures may follow. In comparison, while manufacturing had a positive impact on developmental outlays, it has no effect on allocational expenditures. To the extent that the manufacturing sector exerts influence on local

TABLE 14

ALLOCATIONAL EXPENDITURES AS A FUNCTION OF LOCAL CONDITIONS AND COMPETITION,
CONTROLLING FOR SMSA, POOLED CROSS-SECTIONAL ANALYSIS, 1972, 1977, 1982

Variable	B	SE B	Beta	T-Test
DEMOGRAPHIC FACTORS				
Median income	0.03	0.01	.070	3.03
Rent (%)	10.19	2.47	.089	4.12
Poor (%)	13.41	4.92	.074	2.72
Black (%)	15.09	2.85	.089	5.29
Population	0.00	0.0	.005	0.26
Population growth	0.00	0.35	.000	0.02
Distance	− 0.13	0.04	− .061	− 3.46
Density	− 0.00	0.00	− .086	− 4.54
ECONOMIC COMPOSITION				
Manufacturing	0.23	1.47	.002	0.15
Service	31.93	5.54	.115	5.75
Retail	5.95	4.72	.021	1.26
Wholesale	16.47	5.19	.065	3.17
INTERGOVERNMENTAL FACTORS				
Federal aid	0.15	0.01	.131	8.43
State aid	0.12	0.01	.199	11.76
Mandates	0.12	0.13	.056	0.87
Allocational functions	0.39	0.36	.020	1.07
FISCAL FACTORS				
True value	0.61	0.07	.209	8.60
Tax bill	1.55	0.26	.132	5.93
TIME				
1977 dummy	− 1.00	0.89	− .026	− 1.11
1982 dummy	4.49	0.84	.116	5.31
COMPETITION				
Borders	− 0.56	0.13	− .074	− 4.13
S.D. allocational exp.	0.70	0.08	.251	8.67
S.D. tax bill	− 0.01	0.00	− .173	− 5.70
Herfindahl index	− 11.03	2.54	− .067	− 4.33
Constant	− 8.45	7.43		− 1.13
Adjusted R square, SMSA only,	.21			
Adjusted R square, full model,	.51			

NOTE: Number of cases in pooled sample = 2517.

budgets, it influences the size of the infrastructure expenditures most important to the profitability of its activities.

As with the other forms of expenditures examined, the local tax bill is positively associated with allocational expenditures: higher taxes support bigger government. And allocational expenditures are higher in communities with a stronger tax base.

Market conditions affect allocational expenditures in a manner similar to their effect in other expenditure domains examined so far; but the coefficients are actually *larger* than in previous equations. Thus, as predicted by a market perspective, greater variation in the local tax bill produces lower allocational expenditures, and competition with bordering communities exerts significant negative pressure on allocational expenditures. However, again contrary to the market model, the effects of consumer choice in allocational expenditure packages produces higher allocational expenditures. These results directly contradict Peterson's implication that competition will not affect levels of local allocational expenditures.

Change in Allocational Expenditures

Table 15 reports the analysis of change in allocational expenditures over time. Compared to the other change models previously investigated, a much higher level of stability in allocational expenditures over time is evident: over 38 percent of the variance in present expenditures is explained by expenditures five years earlier. Regional patterns explain an additional 5 percent in the variance. When I add the remaining local lagged variables of our model, the explained variance increases to 54 percent.

Of local factors, intergovernmental factors play only a small role in changes in allocational expenditures. Federal aid has no impact, and the effect of state aid is much smaller than its effect on total expenditure or developmental expenditures. Of the four economic sectors, only the size of the service sector has a significant effect, increasing growth in allocational expenditures.

Similar to previous results, the number of bordering communities reduces the rate of growth on allocational expenditures, and the Herfindahl index of worker concentration is associated with slower growth. And there is significant negative impact of consumer choice across service expenditures on the rate of growth of allocational expenditures. The impact of the choice variables and the border variable is consistent with a Niskanen perspective: competition reduces the growth of government.

TABLE 15
CHANGE IN ALLOCATIONAL EXPENDITURES, AS A FUNCTION OF LOCAL DEMAND,
OTHER LOCAL CONDITIONS, AND COMPETITION, CONTROLLING FOR SMSA,
POOLED ANALYSIS, 1972–1977 AND 1977–1982

Variable	B	SE B	Beta	T-Test
LAGGED VALUE				
Allocational exp. $_{(t-1)}$	0.38	0.02	.331	14.18
DEMOGRAPHIC FACTORS				
Median income	0.00	0.01	.006	0.26
Poor (%)	0.02	0.84	.002	0.03
Black (%)	19.36	3.52	.101	5.49
Rent (%)	9.19	3.02	.072	3.04
Population	0.00	0.00	.008	0.38
Population growth	−0.57	0.71	−.015	−0.79
Distance	−0.13	0.04	−.055	−2.73
Density	−0.00	0.00	−.077	−3.47
ECONOMIC COMPOSITION				
Manufacturing	1.94	1.77	.022	1.09
Service	53.82	8.66	.139	6.21
Retail	3.16	5.89	.010	0.53
Wholesale	13.07	8.00	.039	1.63
INTERGOVERNMENTAL FACTORS				
Federal aid	0.02	0.02	.022	1.22
State aid	0.05	0.01	.082	4.04
Mandates	0.07	0.16	.035	0.48
Allocational functions	1.26	0.59	.038	2.12
FISCAL FACTORS				
True value	0.41	0.09	.127	4.30
Tax bill	1.43	0.37	.114	3.77
TIME				
1972 dummy	−2.84	1.08	−.074	−2.61
COMPETITION				
Borders	−0.72	0.17	−.088	−4.23
No. of cities	−0.06	0.05	−.157	−1.17
S.D. tax bill	−0.01	0.00	−.114	−1.95
S.D. allocational exp.	−0.59	0.11	−.205	−5.39
Herfindahl index	−7.65	3.60	−.039	−2.12
Constant	18.24	13.05		1.39
Adjusted R square, lagged value,	.38			
Adjusted R square, + SMSA,	.43			
Adjusted R square, full model,	.54			

NOTE: Number of cases in pooled sample = 1678.

REDISTRIBUTIVE EXPENDITURES

With the exception of suburbs in New England and several widely scattered SMSAs, most suburban municipalities do not spend significant sums of money on redistributive services. Suburban municipalities do not have a mandate from their state governments to provide these services and suburbs have strong incentives to avoid them. To the extent that a single local government makes what Mayor Beame of New York City termed an "error of the heart" and dilutes its benefit/cost ratio by offering redistributive services, undesirable consequences follow. Consequently, local governments try to invest as little as possible in such services. In the Peterson model, investments in these services should decrease as competition increases.

In the pooled cross-sectional analysis of redistributive expenditures, the single most surprising finding is the low predictive power of the demand model. In the other domains of local expenditures, the demand model was relatively robust. But the same model explains less than 15 percent of the variance in redistributive expenditures. (See table 16.) Given this low explanatory power, it is not surprising that very few terms have significant effects on local redistributive expenditures.

Of these few indicators, the strongest is the functional index of redistributive services: suburbs that deliver more social services spend more on them. Larger suburbs also spend more than smaller ones. Somewhat surprisingly, intergovernmental transfer payments do not increase local expenditures on these services. And neither do indicators of potential need in a community drive expenditures: the percent of the local population that is in rental housing or the percent that is black is not associated with redistributive services. Furthermore, community income levels are not related to the support of redistributive services.

Among market effects, communities in proximity to more bordering communities spend less for redistributive functions. This is congruent with the Peterson model, but it is also consistent with a Niskanen-like market approach. The direction of the effects of the consumer choice variables is similar to other equations: more tax competition reduces redistributive expenditures, more service competition increases expenditures, but neither coefficient reaches levels of statistical significance. Finally note the relatively large coefficient on the Herfindahl index. In this policy arena, a more concentrated work force is associated with higher expenditures.

TABLE 16

REDISTRIBUTIVE EXPENDITURES AS A FUNCTION OF LOCAL CONDITIONS AND COMPETITION,
CONTROLLING FOR SMSA, POOLED CROSS-SECTIONAL ANALYSIS, 1972, 1977, 1982

Variable	B	SE B	Beta	T-Test
DEMOGRAPHIC FACTORS				
Median income	0.00	0.00	.003	0.10
Poor (%)	13.90	6.30	.080	2.20
Rent (%)	3.21	3.17	.029	1.01
Black (%)	2.93	3.65	.018	0.80
Population	0.01	0.00	.157	6.34
Population growth	−0.33	0.45	−.015	−0.74
Distance	0.09	0.05	.045	1.91
Density	0.00	0.00	.033	1.31
ECONOMIC COMPOSITION				
Manufacturing	1.81	1.88	.023	0.95
Service	4.27	7.13	.016	0.60
Retail	−2.54	6.07	−.009	−0.41
Wholesale	3.78	6.67	.015	0.56
INTERGOVERNMENTAL FACTORS				
Federal aid	0.03	0.02	.034	1.63
State aid	0.00	0.01	.010	0.47
Mandates	−0.11	0.17	−.057	−0.65
Redistributive functions	0.96	0.53	.038	1.81
FISCAL FACTORS				
True value	−0.00	0.09	.000	−0.02
Tax bill	0.27	0.33	.024	0.82
TIME				
1977 dummy	−0.33	0.88	−.009	−0.37
1982 dummy	0.64	1.06	.017	0.60
COMPETITION				
Borders	−0.39	0.17	−.054	−2.24
S.D. tax bill	−0.00	0.00	−.001	−0.03
S.D. redistributive exp.	0.13	0.07	.112	1.77
Herfindahl index	30.77	3.31	.197	9.28
Constant	−9.84	9.84		−0.99
Adjusted R square, SMSA only,	.06			
Adjusted R square, full model,	.14			

NOTE: Number of cases in pooled sample = 2517.

Change in Redistributive Expenditures

Paralleling the generally poor explanatory power of the cross-sectional demand model, local conditions do not strongly affect change in redistributive expenditures. The single most important factor, indeed virtually the only factor, affecting the present level of redistributive expenditures is previous expenditures on such services. Simply regressing redistributive expenditures at time t on these expenditures at time t-1 explains 68 percent of the variance. Indeed, neither regional location nor local factors increase the amount of variance explained by this single variable model. Given this, virtually no community level variable has a statistically significant relationship with change in redistributive services. (See table 17.)

Of the competition indicators, the number of bordering communities has no effect. Consistent with both Peterson and Niskanen, indicators of consumer choice in the tax bill and in the service expenditures both reduce the rate of growth in expenditures, although the coefficient on the tax bill is not significant. Finally, the Herfindahl index has a weak, but significant, positive effect: a more concentrated work force is associated with a slightly more rapid increase in redistributive expenditures.

TABLE 17

CHANGE IN REDISTRIBUTIVE EXPENDITURES, AS A FUNCTION OF LOCAL DEMAND, OTHER LOCAL CONDITIONS, AND COMPETITION, CONTROLLING FOR SMSA, POOLED ANALYSIS, 1972–1977 AND 1977–1982

Variable	B	SE B	Beta	T-Test
LAGGED VALUE				
Redistributive exp. $_{(t-1)}$	0.93	0.01	.802	54.79
DEMOGRAPHIC FACTORS				
Median income	0.00	0.00	− .013	− 0.69
Poor (%)	0.00	0.05	.002	0.11
Rent (%)	0.58	2.30	.005	0.25
Black (%)	− 8.04	2.69	− .045	− 2.98
Population	0.00	0.00	.039	2.17
Population growth	− 0.28	0.54	− .008	− 0.51
Distance	0.03	0.03	.015	0.91
Density	0.08	0.08	.017	0.95
ECONOMIC COMPOSITION				
Manufacturing	− 0.88	1.35	− .011	− 0.65
Retail	− 2.15	4.50	− .007	− 0.47
Service	− 1.63	6.62	− .004	− 0.24
Wholesale	0.48	6.12	.001	0.07

Continued on next page

TABLE 17—*Continued*

Variable	B	SE B	Beta	T-Test
INTERGOVERNMENTAL FACTORS				
Federal aid	0.01	0.01	.015	1.07
State aid	0.00	0.00	.008	0.52
Mandates	−0.03	0.12	−.018	−0.31
Redistributive functions	0.08	0.35	.004	0.24
FISCAL FACTORS				
True value	0.03	0.07	.010	0.43
Tax bill	0.19	0.28	.017	0.69
TIME				
1972 dummy	−1.07	0.55	−.030	−1.92
COMPETITION				
Borders	0.03	0.13	.004	0.24
No. of cities	−0.02	0.04	−.065	−0.60
S.D. tax bill	−0.00	0.00	−.032	−0.67
S.D. redistributive exp.	−0.17	0.06	−.131	−2.76
Herfindahl index	7.44	2.74	.041	2.70
Constant	5.87	9.79		0.60
Adjusted R square, lagged variable,	.68			
Adjusted R square, + SMSA,	.68			
Adjusted R square, full model,	.68			

NOTE: Number of cases in pooled sample = 1678.

CONCLUSIONS

Peterson identifies three worlds of local budgeting: distributive, allocational, and redistributive. These policy domains, according to Peterson, are each characterized by distinct political conflicts and outcomes generated by the differential impact each type of expenditure has on the benefit/cost ratio a municipality offers in the local market for public goods. According to Peterson, there are thus clear links between intercommunity competition, the local benefit/cost ratio, and the politics of local budgeting.

I used this argument to predict the effects of competition in each of the three policy domains: competition in the local market for public goods should increase developmental expenditures, decrease redistributive expenditures, and be unrelated to allocational ones. The empirical results are mixed, but taken as a whole tend to disconfirm key parts of Peterson's argument, while confirming a more generally restrictive role of competition in the local marketplace.

Most anomalous to Peterson's theory is the impact of competition on allocational expenditures: local allocational expenditure decisions are clearly affected by competition in the local market for public goods. The results show a greater similarity between the effects of competition on local expenditures for allocational and for distributive services than Peterson predicts. In the suburban environment, allocational expenditures, which support and maintain the infrastructure purchased by developmental expenditures, seem to be allocated in response to competitive conditions in a manner similar to the way in which local developmental expenditures are set.

The results do confirm that redistributive expenditures are a distinct policy domain. These expenditures consume only a small share of most suburban municipal budgets and in general do not seem to be determined by local community characteristics. Instead, past practices alone almost completely determine local involvement in redistributive expenditures.

The effects of specific competition measures in each of the policy domains are often not confirmatory of Peterson. Most notably, competition as measured by the number of nearby local competitors and by variation in the taxes paid for local services consistently restrains expenditures in virtually all policy domains. The direction of these effects is more consistent with a market model in which competition limits the rent-seeking behavior of greedy bureaucrats and limits the bureaucratic consumption of resources. Competition has broader effects than Peterson predicts, and the direction of those effects tends toward restraining expenditures, even developmental ones, rather than stimulating them.

5

SUBURBAN PUBLIC EMPLOYMENT:
THE SIZE AND WAGES OF THE
LOCAL PUBLIC WORK FORCE

In this chapter, I shift from the analysis of expenditures to an investigation of the labor inputs required to provide local public goods and services. This subject is important because local public goods and services are labor intensive and the bulk of local expenditures are labor related. Whatever increases either the number of workers in a community or the wages they are paid also increases local budgets.

In this chapter, I also expand the term *bureaucrats.* Following common usage, in previous chapters, the term encompassed public-sector managers who manipulated information to maximize their agency budgets. But in addition to managers, public-sector workers in bureaucratic agencies are also actors in the process which determines budgets and service levels.

While workers will usually support the budget maximizing goals of managers, workers and managers may disagree about the allocation of the monies their agencies receive. Workers will almost always demand higher wages, and they will often demand the expansion of the work force. Managers may support these goals because higher labor costs translate immediately into a larger agency budget and a larger work force. This growth creates demand for more managers. But to the extent that increased labor costs are tied to specific nondiscretionary categories of expenditures, managerial powers and budgetary slack may actually be reduced, perhaps causing the interests of managers and workers ultimately to diverge. Despite this possible conflict, I assume both workers and managers agree on the desirability of increasing workers' wages and expanding the size of the work force. My analytic goal is to determine if the structure of the local market for public goods restrains these demands.

As in previous chapters, I begin with the basic assumption that a (if not *the*) primary role of local governments operating in a polycentric system of metropolitan governance is to satisfy the interests and demands of their residents by providing service/tax "bundles" responsive to residential tastes. However, the local response to residential demand is structured by the conditions of the local market for public goods. As I have shown, among the most important constraints facing local governments are the variation in fiscal capacity, which affects their ability to deliver public services at any given tax level, and the multitiered structure of federalism, in which both the fiscal and regulatory actions of higher level governments affect local policy decisions.

Local decision making is also open to macroeconomic and societal trends which affect the general demand for local government services. In general terms, there was extensive growth in the size and cost of the local public work force between the early 1950s and the mid 1970s, a secular trend in which virtually all local governments across the United States participated. The recession of 1975 derailed this growth (ACIR 1981). At about the same time, movements to limit taxes and expenditures caused a widespread recalculation of demand and pressured local governments to reduce the cost of their work force (see, for example, Pascal et al. 1979; Clark and Ferguson 1983; Sears and Citrin 1983). While pressures were most intense in those local governments facing budgetary shortfalls or grappling with laws limiting local budgets, more generalized effects rippled across the nation.

THE DEMAND FOR THE LOCAL WORK FORCE

To extend the model of the local market for public goods to the specific analysis of the size and wages of the local public work force, I make the following five assumptions.

1. There is an endogenous demand for local public-sector workers within the individual community, generated by the interplay of residents, firms, politicians, and public "bureaucrats" (here including the interests of managers and workers).

2. The response to such demand is conditioned by (at least) two sets of exogenous factors: the intergovernmental setting in which local governments operate, and general macroeconomic and societal trends.

3. The demand for the local work force decomposes into two different but possibly related decisions: one sets the number of workers employed and the other the level of wages paid. Given budgetary constraints, governments may hire fewer workers at higher wages, or more workers at lower ones (Courant et al. 1979b).

4. The ability of local government to meet demand is constrained by variation in local fiscal capacity.

5. The ability of local workers to increase labor related costs is limited by the degree of competition in the local market for public goods. Communities facing more competition have greater incentives to control labor costs—if they don't they lose mobile resources to other communities. Competition also limits the ability of workers and their bureaucratic managers to exact economic rents through the monopoly control of information.

Endogenous Demand

While the interests of the key sets of actors in local labor policies run parallel to their goals in the politics of expenditure, it is useful briefly to restate them.

Local political decision makers (such as a city council) set the size of the public work force and determine wage rates in response to the demands for services from local residents. However, they must cope with demands from other local actors, in this case the most important being public-sector workers, who can present intense demands for higher wages and for the expansion of the public work force. Further, political decision makers may have their own interests, such as using local policies to maximize their chances of reelection or, relatedly, to minimize conflict with municipal unions, which may shift the policy response to local demands.

The Demands of Residents   As in previous chapters, aggregate residential demand for local workers is identified as a function of the distribution of identifiable demographic characteristics in the local population affecting the preference for services, the ability to pay for them, and how the costs of such services are perceived.

As we have seen, the goods and services delivered by local public-sector workers are "normal goods": demand increases with income. Moreover, given the generally nonprogressive nature of local taxes, the bill for local public goods becomes less onerous with higher income, further increasing the demand for services and the workers who provide them.

The distribution of housing tenure in a community also affects demand because renters may need more of some services (such as parks and recreation, or sewers and sanitation) than do homeowners. But renters can also experience a "fiscal illusion" in which they underestimate the true costs of local services and consequently demand more services than do homeowners.

The Interests of Firms   Business firms will be interested in constraining local government costs. Given the labor intensity of local public services, this can be directly accomplished by holding down local labor costs. However, localities with larger economic sectors may present more complex environments requiring greater monitoring and servicing by local government. For example, communities with a large economic base may require more government workers to maintain the larger infrastructure that business activities require. Thus the effect of business development on the size of the local work force may be indeterminant.

Similarly, the effect of business interests on wage rates is hard to predict in advance. Holding down public-sector wages may appeal to business interests for two reasons. First, lower wages directly reduce the costs of local government and hence local tax costs. Second, to the extent that local government offers attractive wages, it can become another competitor for labor, forcing local firms to offer higher wages. On the other hand, a large local economic base may offer alternate job opportunities for public-sector workers, and local governments may be compelled to offer higher wages to retain their own workers.

The Demands of Public-sector Workers   Political decision makers face strong demands from the existing public work force. These demands may be particularly intense when workers are organized into unions (Spizman 1980). Probably the single most important demand from the public-sector is higher wages, since the benefits of higher wages accrue directly to the recipient workers, while the costs are diffused throughout the community.

As a secondary goal, workers may also prefer a larger work force, in part because it can help them achieve their primary goal of higher wages. A larger work force enhances the bargaining power of workers and subsequent political pressure for higher wages. Furthermore, in the public-sector, wages often increase with the number of people whom a worker supervises, and a larger work force produces more supervisors. However, when faced with a choice between higher wages for already employed workers and expanding the work force at potentially lower wages, members of a public work force, especially if unionized, will likely pursue higher wages.

Higher demand may also result from a concentration of public-sector workers in a community. According to the "factor supplier hypothesis," public-sector workers will demand larger local budgets than will residents who work in the private sector. Courant et al. (1979b) show that if public-sector workers constitute even a small share of a local population, their concerted interest can produce high wages for local public-sector workers, the cost of which is passed along to the general population of the community (also see Tullock 1974; DiLorenzo 1981b; Frey and Pommerehne 1982).

The Demands of Politicians   Identifying the interests of residents and workers is a relatively straightforward exercise; however, the interests of politicians represent a more difficult problem. Politicians can be viewed as entrepreneurs with their own goals, especially winning reelection. As entrepreneurs they should use their strategic position in local government to manipulate policy in pursuit of their goals. And their freedom and success as entrepreneurs should be directly related to the structural conditions of the political marketplace within which they operate.

This concept of politicians as policy entrepreneurs facing structural constraints is the often unarticulated underpinning of the large body of research investigating the effects of political and governmental reform in cities on local policies. Unfortunately, this research tradition has not produced solid empirical evidence that these political conditions strongly affect the role politicians play in setting local policy.

Combine weak empirical results with a plethora of conflicting theories about local politicians as policy entrepreneurs, then add the lack of a rigorously defined demand function for politicians—given this recipe, it is perhaps not surprising that existing research has not documented a strong independent role for politicians in setting local policies. Instead, as Pressman and Wildavsky (1973) argue, local politicians may be mediators and conduits of the demands presented by other actors (also see Morgan and Pelissero 1981).

Exogenous Demands

The satisfaction of endogenous demands does not take place in a vacuum. To the contrary, the boundaries of local governments are highly permeable.

The size of the local work force is affected by the availability of intergovernmental grants and the extent of intergovernmental regulation. State and federal governments make grants available to local governments, easing local budget constraints and allowing local governments to hire more workers (Stein 1984) and to purchase more services (Gramlich 1977; Inman 1979). More recently, faced with their own budgetary problems, higher levels of government have turned to mandates which force local governments to undertake policies without necessarily paying the costs for changes in local policy.

As seen in previous chapters, local government policies are also affected by changes in the economy and society at large, defining the broad parameters within which local governments operate. Such macro-factors affect the demand for services, as well as the willingness and ability of a community to support its local work force.

Constraints on Local Decisions

Municipalities must satisfy the demand for workers and determine local wages within at least three types of constraints: budget constraints imposed by local fiscal capacity; constraints on objective demand conditioned by the size of the community; and constraints generated by competition in the local market for public goods.

Given the decentralized system of finance built on the property tax, local fiscal capacity is a function of the personal wealth of the local population and the strength of the property tax base. Debt levels may also constrain local government budgets (Ehrenberg 1973a).

Objective demand for the public-sector work force may also be conditioned by the size of the community itself. Some studies argue that economies of scale in the provision of local public goods should require a smaller per capita work force in larger cities (for example, Committee for Economic Development 1967). Others strongly disagree, arguing that larger cities are more likely to experience *diseconomies* of scale and employ an even larger work force. Most germane is Hirsch's (1967) argument that larger cities provide a milieu in which government workers have greater opportunities for organizing and lobbying successfully for a larger per capita work force and higher wages.

But more central to my analysis, the structure of the local market for public goods should affect the number and wage rates of local public-sector workers. Competition should limit the ability of workers and their managers to exact economic rents from their community and should limit the willingness of politicians to accede to excessive demands from local employees.

METHOD

Data on public-sector employment levels and wage rates were gathered from the 1972, 1977, and 1982 Census of Government Employment. The independent variables are from matching years, creating a three wave panel design.[1] Following the methods used in previous chapters, I sought to increase the efficiency of my estimates of the structural effects of the independent variables on measures of local work force by pooling cross sections, using the Least Squares Dummy Variable (LSDV) method (Stimson 1985). Adopting this approach, the following model was estimated:

(3) Work Force$_{i,t}$ = f(Demand$_{i,t}$

+ Constraints$_{i,t}$

+ Intergovernmental Factors$_{i,t}$

+ Economic Composition$_{i,t}$

+ Public Work Force Factors$_{i,t}$

+ Political Factors$_i$

+ Competition$_{i,t}$

+ Time + SMSA$_i$).

Where:

Work Force = the size and wages of the local public work force for each suburban municipality i measured at t = 1972, 1977, and 1982, analyzed in two separate equations.

The size of the public-sector work force is measured by the number of full-time equivalent (FTE) workers per 1000 residents. The FTE measure includes full-time workers plus an adjustment for the size of the part-time work force. According to Stein (1984), no information is lost by combining these two categories of public-sector workers into a single measure.

Following Ehrenberg (1973b), the compensation level is measured by the ratio of the average monthly pay of local public-sector workers to the average monthly pay of workers in the local manufacturing sector. This ratio establishes the private-sector wage as the baseline labor cost in the local area. The ratio also adjusts for differences in wage rates caused by inflation and for regional variation in the cost of living.[2]

Demand = a vector of three community characteristics. Median income is classified as a demand variable, although it is also related to local fiscal capacity. The percent of rental households is measured, since renters demand more workers than would homeowners. A new variable specific to this particular analysis is added: the percent of the local population working in the public sector is measured, since government workers living in a community may demand a larger work force and higher wages.[3]

Constraints = a set of variables affecting local demand and the ability to meet it. Included are three measures of local fiscal capacity: true value per capita and the local tax bill, which were used in previous chapters.

Debt per capita is added to the model. Debt may be a particularly salient fiscal constraint on local government decisions determining the size of the local public work force, since it was the accumulating fiscal strain experienced by many cities reflected in increasing debt that ultimately led to reductions in the local work force and in compensation levels after 1975.

Additional variables reflecting local conditions include the population of community i at $t = 1972$, 1977, and 1982, estimated from the 1970 and 1980 Census of Population. The ecological indicators, distance and density, are included as control variables.

Intergovernmental Factors = a vector of six indicators of intergovernmental influences on local decisions.

Intergovernmental transfer payments received by the local government are measured by categorical aid per capita from the state and federal government and by general revenue sharing type grants per capita from the two higher level governments.[4] While categorical aid may be more stimulative of local expenditures than less restricted general aid (Gramlich 1977; Inman 1979), all four types of aid ease local income constraints, potentially increasing the demand for workers.

Mandates can also affect local policy decisions. As in previous chapters, I rely on research by Hill et al. (1978) and use the total number of mandates to assess variation in state regulatory effects on local decisions.[5] Functional responsibility also affects local policies. To measure its potential effects on local labor practices, I constructed a measure of functional responsibility counting the total number of services for which each suburban municipality had *any* fiscal outlays on current operations.

Economic Composition = a vector of indicators of the relative size of each of the four sectors (retail, wholesale, service, manufacturing) of the local economy.

Public Work Force Factors = a set of indicators which varies slightly across the two equations.

Unions represent a potentially powerful force affecting the demand for services, and the percent of the local public work force that is unionized is measured. Second, since there may be a trade-off between wages and the size of the work force, the pay ratio is included in the equation estimating the size of the work force, and the size of the work force is included in the equation estimating the pay ratio.[6]

When estimating the pay ratio equation, the percent of the local work force in police work is included. Empirically, police are the highest paid local public workers. Local governments with greater functional responsibility for police services will therefore experience an upward bias in the pay ratio equation. Including the percent of the work force in police limits this bias.

Political Factors = four indicators of reform and competition are introduced to assess the effects of political interests and entrepreneurship.

Two indicators of structural reform are used. First, a dummy variable was created, coded 0 for a city manager or commission (reformed) government and 1 for a mayor. Similarly, a partisan dummy variable was coded 0 if the city used non-partisan elections and 1 for partisan elections.[7]

The association of efficiency and reform might produce a leaner local work force. It is difficult to predict the effects of reform on wage rates. On one hand, politicians in reformed cities may prefer to save money by paying lower wages; on the other, the concern for efficiency may produce higher wages to attract higher quality workers.

Party competition can also affect the interests of politicians. While party competition is usually measured by the closeness of parties in elections, this type of measure could not be used here for two reasons: first, most suburban elections are nonpartisan; second, it was virtually impossible to reconstruct the detailed electoral statistics from past local elections necessary to compute such a measure.

But, ultimately, if political competition affects policies it is because in more competitive situations, politicians fear loss of their jobs and use government policies to increase the likelihood of remaining in office. Given this underlying logic, it is possible to construct an alternate measure of the likelihood that chief political and/or administrative officers in a community will lose their jobs. Specifically, I measure turnover in the chief executive offices by the number of changes in the office of mayor and city managers between 1972 and 1982 in appropriate cities, as an indicator of "competition."[8]

These political data are available only by surveying local sources and were difficult to assemble. As a result, the data were obtained for only about half the suburbs used above. Therefore, in the empirical analysis which follows two sets of results are reported. The first is based on the larger sample of suburban municipalities used in chapters 3 and 4. I then reestimate the model in the sample of 531 suburbs for which all variables, including the political ones, could be gathered. This second model assesses the degree to which political factors affect local labor practices.

Competition = the five competition variables used in previous chapters: the degree of consumer choice in expenditures and in taxes; the number of other communities on any given suburban municipality's borders; the number of municipalities in a region as a whole; and the Herfindahl index of community bureaucratic concentration.

Time = a vector of two dummies: the first recorded 1 for observations in 1977 and the other for observations in 1982.

After 1975, the general conditions facing the local public work force deteriorated and the two dummy variables summarize unmeasured exogenous factors affecting demand.

SMSA = a vector of thirty-eight dummy variables representing the SMSA in which community *i* is located. These dummy variables help control the contemporaneous effects that emerge because "neighboring" cases usually share the effects of unmeasured variables. (As in other analyses, the coefficients of these variables are not reported.)

After appropriate tests, I pooled the data and found the structural relationships in the model did not vary significantly across time. Therefore only a final model is presented in which the slope of each variable is constant over time, while intercepts are allowed to vary.[9]

RESULTS

Table 18 reports general nationwide and regional trends in the size of the suburban municipal work force. Table 19, below, reports comparable data for the pay ratio. Nationwide, suburban municipalities supported more workers in 1977 than they did in 1972 and 1982, but the size of the municipal work force may have peaked in 1975 for suburbs as it did for central cities. Because these data are reported only every five years, the exact turnaround year cannot be pinpointed. Across regions, not surprisingly, New England suburbs support the largest work force. While in most other regions, county governments employ some of the workers necessary to deliver local services, in New England, municipalities absorb more responsibility. Outside New England, local governments in the South Atlantic and South Central regions support the largest local work force, a fact which has been previously noted but never satisfactorily explained (see Bahl 1984). Overall, suburbs "track" together: in every region they employed more workers in 1977 than 1972 and fewer in 1982. This general trend in part indicates the overall importance of macroeconomic factors cutting across local governments.

Table 19 reports the public/private-sector pay ratio across regions at the three points in time. On average, local public workers are paid less than 90 percent of private-sector manufacturing wages. The lowest

TABLE 18

Size of Suburban Public Work Force (FTE per 1000 Population) by Census Regions

	1972	1977	1982
New England	26.90	29.52	25.42
Mid-Atlantic	6.40	6.97	6.60
East North Central	6.24	7.27	7.00
West North Central	5.04	6.26	6.24
South Atlantic	8.39	10.25	9.17
East South Central	9.73	10.12	8.66
West South Central	7.41	9.15	9.33
Mountain	5.84	6.98	6.94
Pacific	6.24	7.13	6.53
All suburbs	8.65	9.84	9.08

Sources: Number of public-sector workers: Census of Governments, Employment, 1972, 1977, 1982, File A. Population: Estimates of 1972, 1977, 1982 population derived from Census of Population, 1970, 1980.

Note: number of suburbs = 1081.

TABLE 19

Ratio of Suburban Public-Sector to Private-Sector Wages, by Census Regions

	1972	1977	1982
New England	0.96	0.88	0.88
Mid-Atlantic	0.91	0.85	0.85
East North Central	0.87	0.83	0.85
West North Central	0.80	0.78	0.82
South Atlantic	0.87	0.87	0.89
East South Central	0.73	0.69	0.77
West South Central	0.68	0.69	0.76
Mountain	0.87	0.91	0.95
Pacific	1.06	1.05	1.10
All suburbs	0.88	0.85	0.88

Source: Public-sector wages: Census of Governments, Employment, 1972, 1977, 1982, File A. Private-sector wages: Census of Manufacturing, 1972, 1977, 1982.

Note: number of suburbs = 1081.

wages occurred in the South Central suburbs, which may partially explain their larger work force. Pay ratios across regions tracked together: there was an overall decline between 1972 and 1977 in seven of the nine regions. Between 1977 and 1982 gains are evident in eight of the nine regions. In the remaining region (the Mid-Atlantic) wage ratios remained constant.

Within these overall regional and secular trends, local governments determine their public-sector work force. I turn first to an analysis of the relative size of the local public-sector work force.

Multivariate Analyses: The Size of Work Force

At the individual community level, the relative size of the local work force increases both with higher median income and higher true value per capita. (See table 20.) The number of workers also increases as intergovernmental monies ease local budget constraints. Comparing standardized regression coefficients, note that state categorical aid is more strongly related to the size of the work force than is any type of federal aid. Local governments are apparently more willing to make a commitment to personnel based on relatively permanent state monies than they are to using federal monies, which have fluctuated widely in the recent past (Stein 1984). Furthermore, note the strong effects of functional responsibility—where local governments are assigned or assume more responsibility for service delivery, the size of their work force increases.

There is a small positive relationship between population size and the number of workers per capita. A more robust relationship, and one fully consistent with the concept of fiscal illusion, exists between the concentration of renters in the local population and the size of the local work force. While unionization is associated with a larger work force, there is no support for the "factor supplier" hypothesis: a greater concentration of government workers living in a community is not associated with more public workers in that community.

The effect of the pay ratio on the size of the local work force is negligible, and the presumed trade-off between the size of the work force and their wage rates is not evident in this sample. Time had a strong independent effect on size: between 1972 and 1982 it decreased significantly.

The size of a community's economic base generally exerts an upward pressure on the size of its public-sector work force. Thus, despite business interests in containing local government costs, a more developed local economic base probably requires more servicing from local government.

Market effects are small but consistent and interesting. The number of bordering suburban municipalities exerts a significant negative effect on the size of the work force (using a one-tailed t-test), as does both the

TABLE 20

GOVERNMENT WORKERS (FTE PER CAPITA) AS A FUNCTION OF LOCAL COMMUNITY FACTORS, MARKET FACTORS, AND EXOGENOUS CONDITIONS, CONTROLLING FOR SMSA, POOLED CROSS-SECTIONAL ANALYSIS, 1972, 1977, 1982

Variable	B	SE B	Beta	T-Test
DEMAND				
Median income	0.00	0.00	.107	5.38
Rent (%)	0.73	0.05	.208	13.42
No. gov. workers	−0.31	0.62	.007	−0.50
CONSTRAINTS				
True value	0.00	0.00	.184	11.06
Tax bill	0.00	0.00	.043	2.55
Debt	0.00	0.00	.072	5.71
Population	0.00	0.00	.029	1.84
Distance	−0.00	0.00	−.028	−2.02
Density	−0.00	0.00	−.030	−2.04
INTERGOVERNMENTAL FACTORS				
Fed. categorical aid	0.00	0.00	.054	4.35
Gen. revenue sharing	0.00	0.00	.098	7.10
State categorical aid	0.00	0.00	.209	15.40
General state aid	0.00	0.00	.053	3.68
Mandates	−0.00	0.00	−.036	−0.71
Functions	0.03	0.00	.168	9.98
ECONOMIC COMPOSITION				
Manufacturing	0.19	0.06	.061	3.28
Services	0.73	0.18	.082	4.19
Retail	0.24	0.16	.024	1.50
Wholesale	0.35	0.19	.036	1.79
PUBLIC-SECTOR WORK FORCE FACTORS				
Unionization	0.00	0.00	.036	2.35
Pay ratio	−0.00	0.00	−.000	−0.54
COMPETITION				
Borders	−0.00	0.00	−.025	−1.79
S.D. total expenditures	−0.00	0.00	−.042	−1.68
S.D. tax bill	−0.00	0.00	−.045	−1.99
Herfindahl index	−0.30	0.06	−.065	−4.84
TIME				
1977 dummy	−0.15	0.02	−.134	−6.79
1982 dummy	−0.35	0.03	−.303	−10.93
Constant	3.48	1.80		1.92
Adjusted R square, full model,	.58			

NOTES: "Categorical aid" is actually total aid minus the most unrestricted grant money: general revenue sharing.

Number of cases in pooled sample = 2523.

variation in expenditures and taxes. Thus, these three forms of competition consistently limit the size of local government.

The other two indicators of competition, the Herfindahl index and the number of suburbs in a region, are not as well behaved. The number of suburbs in a region does not enter into the equation, because of multicollinearity with the SMSA indicators (see chapter 3). The direction of effect of the Herfindahl index is opposite to that predicted by McGuire et al. (1979): a more concentrated work force is associated with a smaller work force, even after controlling for service responsibility and a host of other intervening factors.

Public Sector Wages

Table 20 showed that larger cities have a larger per capita work force; table 21 shows they also pay significantly higher wages, supporting Hirsch's idea of the diseconomies inherent in the political environment of larger cities. Similarly, wealthier communities pay higher wages than poorer ones. While a greater concentration of renters was associated with a larger work force, renters apparently do not (or cannot) support higher wages for these workers. Higher debt per capita is also associated with higher wages (and a larger work force). Suburban municipalities may be meeting present demands by mortgaging the future—a tactic used earlier (and to disastrous effect) by central cities.

Again there is no evidence of a factor supplier effect, nor is there evidence supporting the notion of a trade-off between the number of workers and their wages: the effect of the number of FTE local workers on wage rates is insignificant.

Unionization is clearly associated with higher wages. Interestingly, the coefficient for the unionization variable is higher in the pay equation than in the size of work force equation. This suggests that unions are in fact more interested in pay rates for their existing members than in expanding the local work force. While the size of the work force was strongly driven by intergovernmental aid, transfer payments from higher levels of government do not increase the local wage ratio. Note the strong effect of the police variable and the significant effect of the index of functional responsibility: functional assignment affects the costs of the local work force.

Over the decade, there was a significant decline in the private/public-sector wage ratio. While Table 19 showed a restoration of the wage ratio by 1982, the results of the multivariate analysis indicate a continuing secular decrease in public-sector wages, *ceteris paribus*.

While three of the four business indicators were associated with

TABLE 21

GOVERNMENT PAY RATIO AS A FUNCTION OF LOCAL COMMUNITY FACTORS,
MARKET FACTORS AND EXOGENOUS CONDITIONS, CONTROLLING FOR SMSA,
POOLED CROSS-SECTIONAL ANALYSIS, 1972, 1977, 1982

Variable	B	SE B	Beta	T-Test
DEMAND				
Median income	0.03	0.00	.178	9.65
Rent (%)	−0.70	1.83	−.005	−0.38
No. gov. workers	2.92	2.51	.020	1.42
CONSTRAINTS				
True value	0.16	0.02	.113	7.18
Tax bill	−0.00	0.00	−.001	−0.08
Debt	0.00	0.00	.056	4.74
Population	0.01	0.01	.143	9.59
Distance	−0.16	0.03	−.068	−5.25
Density	−0.00	0.00	−.017	−1.26
INTERGOVERNMENTAL FACTORS				
Fed. categorical aid	−0.00	0.00	−.001	−0.15
Gen. revenue sharing	0.01	0.02	.009	0.74
State categorical aid	0.00	0.00	.003	0.27
General state aid	0.01	0.01	.016	1.18
Mandates	0.00	0.10	.000	0.01
Functions	0.86	0.11	.118	7.42
ECONOMIC COMPOSITION				
Manufacturing	5.09	1.75	.051	2.90
Services	6.19	5.40	.021	1.14
Retail	3.41	4.66	.011	0.73
Wholesale	−1.63	5.67	−.005	−0.28
PUBLIC-SECTOR WORK FORCE FACTORS				
Unionization	0.07	0.00	.124	8.62
FTE per capita	−24.06	59.32	−.006	−0.40
Police (%)	23.82	1.79	.174	13.30
COMPETITION				
Borders	−0.05	0.10	−.006	−0.51
S.D. total expenditures	−0.00	0.00	−.018	−0.76
S.D. tax bill	−0.00	0.00	−.019	−1.34
Herfindahl index	−12.21	2.04	−.075	−5.97
TIME				
1977 dummy	−9.32	0.73	−.229	−12.61
1982 dummy	−12.42	1.04	−.308	−11.90
Constant	81.29	5.74		14.14
Adjusted R square, .64				

NOTE: Number of cases in pooled sample = 2523.

upward pressure on the size of the local work force, only the size of the manufacturing sector pushes up the wage ratio. Where more opportunities for manufacturing employment exist, especially given the higher wages manufacturing pays, local governments may have to pay more to keep their workers.

Market effects are mostly negligible. Of the four market variables that enter the equation (again the number of suburbs in a region drops out because of problems of multicollinearity), three have no significant effect on the wage ratio. Only the Herfindahl index is significantly associated with the pay ratio and here the effect is similar to that observed elsewhere: a more concentrated work force has a lower wage ratio than a less concentrated one.

Do Politicians Affect Public Sector Labor Practices?

In the next stage of analysis I introduced political variables into the reported equations to see if the conditions politicians face as entrepreneurs change the calculus by which local governments determine their labor practices.

Table 22 reports the analysis of the size of the local work force as a function of local community characteristics, including political variables, and table 23 reexamines the wage ratio. Because of data limitations, this analysis is run for only a subset of suburbs in the sample— only 531 suburbs had complete information including political variables.

First, note that with only minor exceptions the direction and size of the effects of the independent variables in this smaller sample and the larger one are virtually identical. This increases confidence in the empirical estimates produced in the analysis of this subset of cases. Thus, rather than repeating the above analysis, I concentrate only on the market and political variables: the two sets of variables with the most theoretical interest.

Political variables have almost no effect on the number of public workers per capita. Higher turnover in the office of city manager leads to a slightly larger local work force. While the effect is not strong, it may indicate that new city managers have less ability to counter the expansionary demands of long-tenured bureaucrats and entrenched unions.

Of the market variables, the Herfindahl index has no significant effect on the FTE measure. The border variable retains its negative effect as does variation in local taxes (again significant at the .05 level using a one-tailed test). While the measure of variation in expenditures has the

TABLE 22

GOVERNMENT WORKERS (FTE PER CAPITA) AS A FUNCTION OF LOCAL COMMUNITY FACTORS,
MARKET FACTORS, EXOGENOUS CONDITIONS, AND POLITICAL CONDITIONS,
CONTROLLING FOR SMSA, POOLED CROSS-SECTIONAL ANALYSIS, 1972, 1977, 1982

Variable	B	SE B	Beta	T-Test
DEMAND				
Median income	0.01	0.00	.251	7.15
Rent (%)	0.89	0.07	.282	10.97
No. gov. workers	0.23	0.90	.006	0.25
CONSTRAINTS				
True value	0.00	0.00	.159	5.87
Tax bill	0.00	0.00	.036	1.37
Debt	0.00	0.00	.070	3.34
Population	−0.00	0.00	−.027	−1.05
Distance	−0.00	0.00	−.044	−1.94
Density	0.00	0.00	−.010	−0.44
INTERGOVERNMENTAL FACTORS				
Fed. categorical aid	0.00	0.00	.039	1.91
Gen. revenue sharing	0.00	0.00	.149	6.37
State categorical aid	0.00	0.00	.264	12.77
General state aid	0.00	0.00	.120	4.75
Mandates	−0.00	0.00	−.030	−0.36
Functions	0.03	0.00	.210	7.63
ECONOMIC COMPOSITION				
Manufacturing	0.07	0.08	.029	0.94
Services	0.11	0.24	.149	4.15
Retail	0.32	0.22	.039	1.48
Wholesale	0.44	0.34	.046	1.38
PUBLIC-SECTOR WORK FORCE FACTORS				
Unionization	0.00	0.00	.025	0.98
Pay ratio	−0.00	0.00	−.042	−1.40
POLITICAL FACTORS				
Mayor turnover	0.00	0.00	.008	0.36
Manager turnover	0.02	0.00	.052	2.31
Mayor	0.01	0.02	.014	0.60
Partisan	0.03	0.03	.030	1.05
COMPETITION				
Borders	−0.00	0.00	−.025	2.62
S.D. total expenditures	−0.00	0.00	−.035	−1.56
S.D. tax bill	−0.00	0.00	−.063	−1.68
Herfindahl index	−0.10	0.09	−.025	−1.08

Continued on next page

TABLE 22—*Continued*

Variable	B	SE B	Beta	T-Test
TIME				
1977 dummy	−0.21	0.03	−.025	−6.67
1982 dummy	−0.42	0.04	−.044	−9.06
Constant	0.02	0.24		0.11
Adjusted R square, .45				

NOTES: Number of cases in pooled sample = 1593.

The "partisan" and "mayor" variables are dummy variables. See text for complete description.

TABLE 23

GOVERNMENT PAY RATIO AS A FUNCTION OF LOCAL COMMUNITY FACTORS, MARKET FACTORS, EXOGENOUS CONDITIONS, AND POLITICAL CONDITIONS, CONTROLLING FOR SMSA, POOLED CROSS-SECTIONAL ANALYSIS, 1972, 1977, 1982

Variable	B	SE B	Beta	T-Test
DEMAND				
Median income	0.02	0.00	.142	4.80
Rent (%)	−3.38	2.74	−.027	−1.23
No. gov. workers	6.39	30.63	.004	0.20
CONSTRAINTS				
True value	0.20	0.03	.138	6.14
Tax bill	−0.00	0.00	−.003	−0.16
Debt	0.00	0.00	.064	3.66
Population	0.01	0.00	.155	7.10
Distance	−0.09	0.04	−.036	−1.90
Density	0.00	0.00	.019	1.02
INTERGOVERNMENTAL FACTORS				
Fed. categorical aid	−0.02	0.02	−.017	−1.04
Gen. revenue sharing	0.06	0.04	.026	1.35
State categorical aid	−0.00	0.00	−.011	−0.60
General state aid	0.01	0.01	.019	0.89
Mandates	0.15	0.14	.069	1.02
Functions	0.83	0.16	.116	4.99
ECONOMIC COMPOSITION				
Manufacturing	8.37	2.45	.086	3.412
Services	−6.77	7.40	−.026	−0.915
Retail	5.11	6.69	.016	0.764
Wholesale	16.34	9.79	.045	1.669

Continued on next page

TABLE 23—*Continued*

Variable	B	SE B	Beta	T-Test
PUBLIC-SECTOR WORK FORCE FACTORS				
Unionization	0.06	0.01	.128	5.91
Police (%)	25.90	2.77	.178	9.33
FTE per capita	41.95	88.29	.010	0.47
POLITICAL FACTORS				
Mayor turnover	0.08	0.30	.005	0.28
Manager turnover	−0.29	0.29	−.019	−1.01
Mayor	−1.74	0.74	−.047	−2.33
Partisan	−1.49	1.09	−.032	−1.36
COMPETITION				
Borders	0.04	0.15	.006	0.30
S.D. total expenditures	−0.00	0.00	−.040	−1.19
S.D. tax bill	−0.00	0.00	−.027	−0.87
Herfindahl index	−13.15	3.25	−.077	−4.04
TIME				
1977 dummy	−8.61	1.09	−.220	−7.85
1982 dummy	−10.57	1.59	−.273	−6.62
Constant	75.49	8.06		9.36
Adjusted R square, .62				

NOTE: Number of cases in pooled sample = 1593.

appropriate sign, its level of statistical significance falls below the acceptable criterion.

Turning to the pay ratio (table 23), among political variables, only the mayor variable has an effect: cities with mayors pay their public-sector workers marginally *less* than cities with more reformed structures. Reformed governments may be willing to pay higher wages to attract better qualified workers. Of the market indicators, the number of bordering municipalities has no relationship with pay ratio. Both the variation in expenditures and in taxes are negatively associated with the pay ratio, but not at acceptable levels of statistical significance. The Herfindahl index remains significantly and negatively associated with the pay ratio in this smaller sample, replicating previous findings.

CONCLUSIONS

Suburban municipal governments determine the size and wages of their public-sector labor force in a dynamic environment created by the interplay of local actors. But these local policy choices are conditioned by competition in the local market for public goods, by the unequal distribution of wealth, and by changes in the macroenvironment in which municipalities operate.

Wealthy suburbs, as measured by their property tax base and by the income of their citizens, employ more workers and pay them more than do less affluent suburbs. The suburban public work force thus is a normal good: consumption increases with income. This finding is at odds with the results of Stein (1986) and Jones et al. (1977) which suggest the demand for municipal public services *decreases* with income.

This difference in demand is explicable by differences in the distributional implications of the package of goods and services offered by cities and by suburbs. As I argued earlier in the analysis of expenditures, the negative relationship between income and demand found in central cities results to a large degree because a significant share of central city expenditures support redistributive services targeted on lower income residents. Given such redistribution, wealthier residents in a city have incentives to oppose higher service levels, that is, faced with redistribution away from them, higher income residents rationally reduce their demand for local public services. But the typical suburb allocates only a very small portion of its budget to redistributive services; instead, it spends most of its money on the developmental services designed to benefit all residents. Higher income residents in suburbs demand more because they get more.

The response of local decision makers to the demands of their residents is clearly shifted by the demands of public-sector workers. The political power of these workers, especially unionized ones, inflates the size and wages of the public work force beyond the objective demand of local residents. Clearly, political considerations must be added to the analysis of the operations of the Tiebout market, with its emphasis on consumer demand.

But not all potentially important political actors affect responsiveness to local demands. Specifically, there is no strong evidence that the interests of politicians, at least as conditioned by reform and turnover in the executive offices of the local government, significantly affect local policy outputs. Rather than acting as an independent force in the local market for public goods, politicians may maximize their goals by becoming conduits for the demands of other actors.

The results of this chapter reinforce the idea of the polycentric metropolitan market as an open market. Powerful exogenous influences cut across individual local governments and affect local policy decisions. In response to such secular influences, the size and wage rates of the public work force across suburbs track closely together over time.

Of the exogenous influences I identified, among the most interesting are intergovernmental influences on local policy decisions. Intergovernmental transfer payments and the assignment of functional responsibility directly affect the number of local public-sector workers and the wages they are paid. An even more important influence is the assignment of high cost services, such as police, which directly affects the size of the local wage bill. By conditioning labor inputs in the delivery of local services, the general size and cost of local government are driven by the policies of higher level government.

Strong secular trends produced by macro-level changes in the economy and society already limit the independent policy role of suburban cities. Given the growing presence of higher level governments in local decisions, suburban city limits may grow tighter, further constricting and perhaps ultimately redefining the role suburban governments play as service delivery agents in the polycentric metropolitan market.

Finally, the local market for public goods affects the labor policies of local governments. Competition between local communities limits the relative size of the local work force, if not its wages. Where local residents have greater choice in service bundles and tax bills, and where more alternate providers are available, the increased consumer choice and higher levels of information which result pressure politicians to limit their response to bureaucratic and worker demands for a larger work force. Competition in the local market for public goods has a significant, albeit marginal, role enforcing efficiency in public-sector labor policies and in limiting the size of the public work force.

6

THE FLYPAPER EFFECT:
BUREAUCRATS AND RESIDENTS
IN CONFLICT

In this chapter I explore the effects of competition on the ability of local bureaucrats to control a specific community resource, examining the allocation of intergovernmental aid as an indicator of bureaucratic power.

Intergovernmental aid directly increases the income of a local community. As with any increase in income, intergovernmental monies are divided among competing goods and services, including items in both the public and private sectors. At one extreme, every dollar of additional income generated through the intergovernmental system could be used to buy an additional dollar of public goods. In this case, intergovernmental aid would stimulate the public sector, greatly increasing the consumption of public goods. At the other extreme, every dollar of intergovernmental aid could be used to reduce local taxes, allowing for greater consumption of private goods. In this case, intergovernmental aid would be used only for tax relief, and every dollar of aid would substitute for a dollar of locally raised revenues.

Empirically, the use of intergovernmental aid falls between these two extremes: some part of the money supports the purchase of more public goods, some goes to private goods. Given variation in this allocation process, the extent to which intergovernmental aid actually stimulates the purchase of public goods can be used as an indicator of the relative ability of bureaucrats to control local resources.

THE "FLYPAPER EFFECT" AND BUREAUCRATIC POWER

During the 1970s, virtually every local government in the United States received transfer payments from the federal government and from their respective state governments. Intergovernmental aid falls into two major categories: aid for specific projects and less restricted grants such as general revenue sharing.[1] Theoretical expectations vary about how these different types of grants will be used by local governments.

Project grants are specifically designed to increase local government expenditures in designated policy areas by reducing the local price of subsidized projects or services. Using intergovernmental aid as an inducement for local governments to change their behavior, higher level governments seek to achieve their own policy goals or to correct policy failures caused when local governments neglect the more widespread societal implications or externalities of local policy actions. The stimulative effects of categorical project grants are specifically part of the purpose for which the money is granted.

In contrast, unrestricted revenue sharing type grants are not designed to stimulate a specific set of expenditures or to achieve narrowly defined policy goals. Rather, revenue sharing distributes wealth collected at a higher level of government to be used by a lower level government according to *local* preferences and needs. In neoclassical economic theory, given the unrestricted nature of these grants, revenue sharing monies will not stimulate local government purchases to the same degree as categorical project grants. Instead, revenue sharing is analytically identical to any other increase in the private income of community residents and funds will be allocated between private and public goods in the same way as an increase in private income.

Among suburbs, local public goods are normal goods. Therefore unrestricted intergovernmental aid (which increases income) will stimulate public expenditures. But just as a dollar increase in local private income will be allocated to purchase both public and private goods, an increase in local income produced by revenue sharing should also be allocated to both types of goods.

To illustrate: if in a given community, a dollar increase in private income produces a ten-cent increase in public expenditures and a ninety-cent increase in private consumption, a dollar of unrestricted intergovernmental aid should be allocated across public and private goods in the same proportion: ten cents for higher local expenditures on public goods; ninety cents for local tax relief. In contrast, a dollar increase in project grants should be allocated significantly more to public expenditures. To use the terms associated with this phenomenon: unrestricted aid has income effects, while project aid is more stimulative because it has both income and price effects (Chubb 1985; Gramlich 1977; Inman 1979).

Despite these well-developed theoretical expectations, empirical research has consistently demonstrated that unrestricted grants are *not* returned to local citizens at the predicted rate; instead, unrestricted grants are more stimulative of local expenditures than can be explained by income effects alone. This is the "flypaper effect," that is, intergovernmental aid is retained disproportionately for use by local government agencies and not returned at the rate predicted to local citizens for the purchase of more private goods. In the colorful language that explains the origin of the term "flypaper," intergovernmental money "sticks where it hits" (Courant et al. 1979a; Oates 1979; Filimon et al. 1982).

While the flypaper effect has most often been viewed as a problem of intergovernmental relations, I root it in the general theoretical perspective concerning the strategic goals of bureaucrats.

According to neoclassical economic theory, residents of a community will support the allocation of intergovernmental aid to public and private goods in the same proportion to which they have already agreed to allocate their own personal income. And they will oppose any allocation of unrestricted aid to the public sector which is in excess of this "contracted" amount. When intergovernmental aid is allocated in this fashion, the status quo is preserved and local residents have controlled the additional income. By extension, to the extent that intergovernmental aid is less stimulative of local expenditures than is private income, local residents have "rewritten" the local contract and transferred public money to private use. Bureaucrats and residents clearly will be in conflict on this issue. Indeed, bureaucrats will try to retain a disproportionate share of this aid to support a larger public sector. Rather than returning intergovernmental money to residents, allowing them to purchase more private goods, bureaucrats will try to use intergovernmental aid to achieve their own goal of budget maximization.

Filimon et al. (1982) argue that local bureaucrats, as a strategy in this conflict, use their monopoly over information and their agenda setting power to create a fiscal illusion around intergovernmental aid, trying to convince residents that it is not purely an addition to community income, but comes with requirements to support public-sector activities. In short, the flypaper effect is a predictable result of bureaucratic strategies designed to increase agency budgets and reflects a political conflict between residents and bureaucrats, each seeking to increase their own income.

While other actors are also involved in local allocation decisions, the dimensions of conflict are less obvious. Theoretically, the interests of business firms in revenue sharing grants should parallel the interests of any other local tax payer. That is, firms have already helped establish a given community allocation of income to private and public goods and should therefore consent to the same allocation of intergovernmentally generated revenue.

The interests of politicians are more complex. Politicians will clearly favor the receipt of more intergovernmental aid—such grants allow politicians to take credit for more and better services at any given tax rate. If local residents believe that intergovernmental aid comes with greater requirements to support public-sector activities, local politicians will have an even greater ability to use the monies for public-sector activities. Furthermore, intergovernmental monies can be used to buy peace with workers and bureaucrats in the public sector, without incurring higher taxes.

These incentives may push politicians to support "stickier" intergovernmental flypaper. However, politicians are under countervailing pressure from their constituents to lower taxes and unrestricted intergovernmental aid can be used for this purpose. Given these conflicting political forces, it may be safest for politicians simply to go along with the existing consensus and try to allocate new intergovernmental income along the lines of the existing community consensus.

The political cleavages over the allocation of revenue sharing most clearly pit bureaucrats, who want intergovernmental aid to support more public goods, against other community actors who prefer to maintain the existing allocation of intergovernmental aid across private and public consumption. The well-documented flypaper effect testifies *a priori* to the power of bureaucrats to influence the outcome of this conflict.

But the power of bureaucrats to achieve their goals at the expense of other actors is not unlimited; rather, bureaucratic power is relative to the power of other actors in the environment. Specifically, the power of bureaucrats derives directly from their control of information and the inability of local residents to engage in choices in the local market for public goods. Consequently, the ability of bureaucrats to control resources will vary directly with the degree of competition in this market: the absence of competitive choices increases bureaucratic power vis-à-vis other local actors. In more competitive environments, the flypaper effect will be weaker than in less competitive environments.

I test this proposition empirically, by relating measures of competition in the local market to the degree to which the flypaper effect is found. Specifically, I measure the stickiness of intergovernmental flypaper by comparing the stimulative effect of general revenue sharing with the effect of community income on local expenditures. To measure competition, I use the indicators of market choice developed in the previous chapters: the extent of regional variation in consumer choice for expenditures and in the local tax bill (assuming that more consumer choice translates into more competition); the degree of internal competition between agencies within each local community; the number of municipalities bordering each community; and the number of municipalities in the region as a whole (these last two measures assume more communities translate into more information about the possible range of service choices available and reduces the cost of Tiebout-like market mechanisms).

The fundamental question investigated in the following analysis is the degree to which the flypaper effect is contingent upon competition in the local market for public goods: more competition should mean less stickiness because competition limits the ability of bureaucrats to exact rents from their community.

METHODS

Because general revenue monies (GRS) were not delivered until late in 1972 and the Census of Government did not separately report the payments in that year, the three wave panel design used in previous chapters cannot be used here. Instead, I use data only from 1977 and 1982.

The empirical analysis centers on the comparison of two equations which assess the relationship between the structural characteristics of the local market for public goods and the ability of bureaucrats to achieve their strategic goals: competition should limit the extractive capabilities of local bureaucrats, reflected in a smaller flypaper effect:

Omitting subscripts i and t, the first equation is:

(4) Total Expenditures $= f$(Median Income
                                          + General Revenue Sharing
                                          + Other Intergovernmental Factors
                                          + Competition
                                          + Demographic Factors
                                          + Economic Composition
                                          + Fiscal Factors + SMSA).

The second equation duplicates equation 4, but adds a critical set of interaction terms to test contingency effects:

(5) Total Expenditures $= f$(Median Income
                                          + General Revenue Sharing
                                          + Other Intergovernmental Factors
                                          + Competition

+ INTERACTION TERMS
+ Demographic Factors
+ Economic Composition
+ Fiscal Factors + SMSA)

where all dollar measures have been standardized for changes in the cost of living (using the consumer price index) and where:

Total Expenditures are measured per capita for community *i* at time *t* = 1977, 1982.[2]

Median Income = median family income in community *i* at time *t*. I estimated 1977 and 1982 median income using the rate of change in the median income of each community as reported in the 1970 and 1980 Census (see note 6, chapter 3).

General Revenue Sharing = the GRS grant from the Federal government, per capita, at time *t*.

Other Intergovernmental Factors = a vector of three indicators of intergovernmental aid per capita received by community *i* at time *t*: categorical aid from the Federal government; categorical aid from state government; and general aid from state government. The number of state mandates and the level of local functional responsibility are also included here.

Competition = the five measures of competition used throughout this book. Two measures are specific to each community: the number of bordering municipalities and the Herfindahl index of bureaucratic concentration. Three are contextual—every municipality in the same SMSA has the same value for each competition indicator. These are the number of suburban municipalities in a SMSA; the standard deviation of tax bill; and the standard deviation of expenditures.

Demographic Factors = a vector of indicators for community *i* indicating sources of demand for local services, other than income. This vector includes the terms used in the previous chapters: population percent black, percent renters, distance of suburb from central city, and density.

Economic Composition is also measured to control for this source of demand on local budgets.

Fiscal Factors include the tax bill at time *t* (as previously defined) and true value per capita. Recall, these measures are effective measures, adjusted for differences in assessment practices.

In equation 5, I add:

Interaction Terms = a vector of five terms computed by multiplying the General Revenue Sharing term with each of the five indicators of the market. These interaction terms reflect the extent to which the flypaper effect is *contingent* on the structure of the local market.

This design assumes that greater consumer choice as reflected in the market structure variables translates into more competition in the local market for public goods. The design also assumes that the local market is largely defined by consumer choice and competition measured at the regional level, minimizing the importance of mobility and choices of individuals across different SMSAs.

As in previous chapters, to control the contemporaneous effects endemic to pooled cross-sectional analysis I use the Least Squares Dummy Variable approach (Stimson 1985), and introduce SMSA location dummies to account for the well-known fact that patterns of development and patterns of local government responsibility are often regionally specific.

Table 24 reports the results of the first equation, examining total expenditures as a function of income, general revenue sharing, competition and other local factors.

The flypaper effect is evident by comparing the standardized regression coefficients of the median income term with the coefficient of the general revenue sharing (GRS) term.[3] Repeating the result of chapter 3, total expenditures increase with community income: the standardized regression coefficient of community median income is positive (.11) and statistically significant. But the standardized coefficient for the general revenue sharing term is much larger. Indeed, its coefficient (.23) makes it one of the variables most strongly associated with local expenditures.

From neoclassical economic theory, categorical grants should be more stimulative than revenue sharing grants. Surprisingly, the pattern for federal aid is empirically reversed: federal general revenue sharing is, in fact, more strongly related to expenditures than are federal categorical project grants ($\beta = .16$). However, the expected pattern is evident for state aid: state categorical aid ($\beta = .36$) is more directly related to total expenditures than is general state aid ($\beta = .03$). State general aid also does not show the flypaper effect—it is less stimulative of expenditures than is community income. Other community factors affect expenditures in ways previously discussed in chapter 3 and are used only as control variables at this stage of analysis.

As in earlier analyses, the effects of market conditions on expenditures are more complex than anticipated. If the identified forms of competition limited the size of government, all market indicators would be negatively associated with expenditures, controlling for other local conditions. The number of bordering municipalities has the expected negative, and statistically significant, effect. However, the Herfindahl index is not related to expenditures.

At the regional market level, empirically, variation in taxes affects

TABLE 24

THE FLYPAPER EFFECT: A BASELINE EQUATION. TOTAL EXPENDITURES PER CAPITA AS A
FUNCTION OF GRS AND MEDIAN INCOME, CONTROLLING FOR OTHER LOCAL CONDITIONS
AND SMSA, POOLED CROSS-SECTIONAL ANALYSIS, 1977, 1982

Variable	B	SE B	Beta	T-Test
FLYPAPER VARIABLES				
Median income	3.12	0.05	.112	5.45
General revenue sharing	7.04	0.55	.233	12.79
OTHER INTERGOVERNMENTAL FACTORS				
Fed. categorical aid	1.00	0.09	.165	11.06
State categorical aid	1.31	0.05	.361	22.09
State general aid	0.25	0.15	.029	1.62
Mandates	0.86	0.82	.069	1.04
Functions	6.83	0.73	.170	9.34
COMPETITION				
Borders	−0.96	0.77	−.022	−1.25
S.D. total expenditures	0.01	0.01	.017	0.91
S.D. tax bill	−0.04	0.01	−.086	−3.17
Herfindahl index	23.59	15.41	.024	1.53
Control variables				
DEMOGRAPHIC FACTORS				
Rent (%)	34.71	12.39	.055	2.80
Black (%)	23.72	14.49	.026	1.63
Population	0.01	0.00	.034	1.76
Population growth	11.41	9.58	.021	1.19
Distance	−0.03	0.22	−.002	−0.14
Density	−0.02	0.00	−.078	−4.05
ECONOMIC COMPOSITION				
Manufacturing	−6.65	9.27	−.013	−0.71
Services	204.76	26.21	.151	7.81
Retail	25.59	24.42	.018	1.04
Wholesale	109.15	26.70	.086	4.08
FISCAL FACTORS				
True value	2.78	0.42	.172	6.91
Tax bill	2.68	1.58	.039	1.76
Constant	−120.68	46.20		−2.61
Adjusted R square, .68				

NOTE: Number of cases in pooled sample = 1678.

local governments as expected: more variation across suburban municipalities in local taxes generates competitive pressure to keep expenditures low. However, the number of suburban municipalities in a region has no effect on expenditures, nor does standard deviation of expenditure levels.

While the results of table 24 document the flypaper effect in suburban municipalities, the next question of my analysis is theoretically more important: to what extent is the flypaper effect *contingent* on the degree of competition that exists in the local market for public goods?

Table 25 measures contingency effects by the use of interaction terms. Specifically, the table reports the results of equation 5, in which the market measures are augmented with interaction terms computed by multiplying each competition term by a community's receipt of GRS (measured per capita).

In this reestimated equation, the coefficient of the GRS term falls sharply to .05. The reestimated model now fits the prediction of neoclassical economics about the relative impact of categorical grants and

TABLE 25

Contingent Flypaper Effects: Total Expenditures per Capita as a Function of GRS and Median Income, Mediated by Competition and Controlling for Other Local Conditions, Pooled Cross-Sectional Analysis, 1977, 1982

Variable	B	SE B	Beta	T-Test
FLYPAPER VARIABLES				
Median income	3.44	0.05	.123	5.99
General revenue sharing	1.62	1.46	.053	1.11
OTHER INTERGOVERNMENTAL FACTORS				
Fed. categorical aid	1.00	0.08	.165	11.14
State categorical aid	1.30	0.06	.358	21.22
State general aid	0.23	0.15	.027	1.49
Mandates	0.93	0.82	.075	1.13
Functions	7.02	0.72	.175	9.63
COMPETITION				
Borders	−4.52	1.18	−.105	−3.80
S.D. total expenditures	0.01	0.03	.013	0.39
S.D. tax bill	−0.06	0.01	−.125	−3.61
Herfindahl index	7.49	23.74	.007	0.31
CONTINGENCY (INTERACTION) TERMS				
w/ S.D. total expenditures	−0.00	0.00	−.005	−0.16
w/Borders	−0.87	0.20	−.141	3.97
w/Tax bill	−0.07	0.00	−.090	2.29
w/Herfindahl index	5.61	4.97	.045	1.14
w/No. in SMSA	0.01	0.01	.031	0.77

Continued on next page

TABLE 25—*Continued*

Variable	B	SE B	Beta	T-Test
Control variables				
DEMOGRAPHIC FACTORS				
Rent (%)	35.91	12.32	.057	2.91
Black (%)	19.35	14.49	.021	1.33
Population	0.01	0.00	.030	1.55
Population growth	10.50	9.54	.019	1.10
Distance	− 0.00	0.22	.000	− 0.03
Density	− 0.02	0.00	− .079	− 4.13
ECONOMIC COMPOSITION				
Manufacturing	− 16.25	9.41	− .033	− 1.72
Services	214.62	26.21	.159	8.18
Retail	33.75	24.34	.023	1.38
Wholesale	91.05	26.81	.071	3.39
FISCAL FACTORS				
True value	2.57	0.41	.160	6.28
Tax bill	2.67	1.51	.039	1.76
Constant	− 115.92	46.83		− 2.47
Adjusted R square, .70				

unrestricted grants. Table 25 shows that the coefficient of federal categorical grants ($\beta = .17$) is larger than the effect of GRS (the greater importance of state categorical aid relative to state general aid seen in table 24 is repeated).

Note that in this reestimation the effects of the "border" variable and the tax competition variable marginally increase compared to baseline equation 4. But the effects of the other competition variables remain insignificant. Finally, note that two of the five interaction terms, one measuring the effects of GRS contingent on variation in the local tax bill, and the other measuring the effects of GRS contingent on the number of bordering communities, are significantly associated with total expenditures. Other interactions do not reach levels of statistical significance.

More theoretically important, the direction of the coefficients shows that the stimulative effect of GRS is significantly *lower* in regions with greater variation in the taxes paid to local government and in communities with more local governments on their borders.[4]

In short this analysis shows that the flypaper effect varies with the competitive market conditions bureaucrats face: in a more competitive environment, bureaucrats are less able to control unrestricted inter-governmental aid.

CONCLUSIONS

In the baseline estimation of equation 4, general revenue sharing was empirically more stimulative of suburban municipal expenditures than was median income. This "flypaper effect" confirms the power of suburban bureaucrats to exact more resources from their local community than the residents of the community objectively demand. While the flypaper phenomenon has been documented in previous research, the analysis of equation 5 shows that it is contingent on the institutional arrangements of the local market for public goods.

Specifically, where there is more variation in the tax bills levied by local communities and consumers have more choice and information about the costs of local government, the "stickiness" of intergovernmental flypaper declines. Local residents and the sponsors of bureaucrats are clearly sensitive to the price of local government: where providers charging lower taxes are available in a local market, pressure is exerted on bureaucrats to lower their own price for service and return more intergovernmental money to local citizens. This result is congruent with the predicted effects of a competitive market.

Similarly, when communities are surrounded with more bordering communities, the stickiness of intergovernmental flypaper is also reduced. This outcome is again consistent with a model of bureaucratic monopoly: in communities with more low cost information generated by a variety of alternate service providers, the monopolistic power of bureaucrats is reduced and they are less able to "win" their conflicts with local residents over the allocation of local resources, including intergovernmental income. In short, competitive markets limit the exactive capabilities of local bureaucrats.

Part III

THE PURSUIT OF
HIGHER SERVICE/TAX RATIOS

In the local market for public goods, major actors want a higher service/tax ratio. Increasing the quality and range of public services in relation to local taxes provides the opportunity for all actors to increase the likelihood that their other specific goals can be achieved. It allows firms to increase profits and residents to choose among a variety of service levels at a reasonable tax bill. A higher ratio increases the opportunities for bureaucrats to pursue budget maximization without encountering taxpayer resistance. And it allows politicians to increase their likelihood of remaining in office. Given the structure of the local market for public goods, increasing the service/tax ratio is desired by the most important actors in a community. Thus the chapters in this section look at the pursuit by local governments of a largely consensual goal.

In the next four chapters I look at several characteristics that largely define a community's service/tax ratio. First I consider factors that contribute to the local tax base and thereby influence the denominator of the ratio. Chapter 7 studies the distribution of community income levels and the distribution of specific income groups across suburbs over time. Chapter 8 looks at the distribution of economic development as reflected in the number of manufacturing and service jobs in these suburbs. Chapter 9 looks directly at the size of the local tax base, and chapter 10 the receipt of intergovernmental aid. Intergovernmental aid is important to the analysis because it transfers the costs of local services outside the community. This can improve the local service/tax ratio, mostly by influencing its numerator.

In each of these chapters, the argument develops in a manner parallel to the chapters in part 2. First, I briefly review the distribution of benefits and costs of the specific resource across the sets of suburban actors. I then present basic descriptive information outlining the distribution of the particular resource with which the chapter is concerned. Following these descriptive statements, a multivariate analysis of the distribution of the dependent variable is presented.

Each of the variables I examine in part 3 can contribute to the higher service/tax ratio local actors desire. There are many policy tools and strategies that local governments adopt in pursuit of these resources. The ultimate question motivating the analysis is simply put: in the local market for public goods, despite a widely shared desire to pursue a higher service/tax ratio, do local actors actually have the capacity to formulate municipal policies which successfully achieve an outcome they want?

7

LOCAL WEALTH AND PERSONAL INCOME

The structure of the local market for public goods leads communities to enact policies they hope will increase their wealth. Broadly defined, local wealth is a function of the level of personal income in a community, the concentration of businesses, and the size of the property tax base. In this chapter, I analyze the distribution of personal income across communities. I review briefly exclusionary zoning, incorporation, and fiscal/expenditure policies as tools suburbs use to increase local personal income. I then assess empirically the relationship between local budgetary tools and local income.

Exclusionary zoning is probably the policy most frequently used by municipalities in their pursuit of higher income. Using zoning laws, local governments can regulate land availability and minimum lot size. Zoning can also affect the mix of single versus multiple family dwellings, the physical size of housing units, and the amenities associated with each unit. Through these factors, zoning directly influences the cost of housing in a community—and the wealth of the individuals who can purchase it.

The literature critical of zoning is extensive. At the core, critics argue that suburban municipalities use zoning laws to limit the number of available housing units and to increase local housing costs; the overriding goal of exclusionary zoning is to raise the price of entry into a community, and thereby increase the income level of in-migrants. In the extreme, critics argue that local governments use their zoning powers to erect "invisible walls" to "zone out" low-income families (Branfman et al. 1973; Danielson 1976). Furthermore, because purchases in the local market for public goods are made by locational decisions, entry barriers directly affect the quality of public services to which low-income individuals have access. Hill (1974) argues that the overlapping of personal and public resources creates a system of metropolitan government which is "separate *and* unequal."

Because the poor usually cost more in local services than they contribute in taxes, the incentives for any individual community to zone out the poor are clear. But if exclusionary zoning is a "rational" goal for any given locality, critics believe that individual community incentives produce negative results for regional growth patterns and for society at large. However, most attempts to reform exclusionary zoning practices have not been successful, in large part because they run squarely into the fundamental incentives built into the structure of the local market for public goods.

While zoning has been widely studied, there are other means of controlling community income. For example, Miller, in *Cities by Contract* (1981), identifies a fundamental, but less well documented, exclusionary growth strategy in the politics of incorporation. Miller extends the link between government policies and the concern for community income by showing how the very act of creating a suburban city is often driven by an exclusionary impulse. According to Miller, many suburbs in the Los Angeles region incorporated as municipalities primarily to protect their tax base and to limit the number and income of the families sharing it. Miller's findings are not surprising—given the incentive structure of the local market for public goods, we should expect communities to use local policy tools to protect the balance between taxes and services. Miller's contribution is his careful analysis of how the politics of incorporation flow from the incentive system built on the relationship between municipal policies and community wealth.

Of course, the same incentive structure drives Peterson's analysis of the politics of local budgets. Suburbs emphasize developmental programs and policies in order to attract fiscally productive families, and they avoid redistributive policies which they fear will repulse higher income residents and in-migrants.

Thus, a variety of analytic works link the very existence of suburban municipal governments and the exercise of their most basic policy tools, zoning and budgeting, to the desire to enhance local income levels. Underlying the use of these policy tools is the belief that attracting individuals and families with incomes above the existing community median is a rational growth strategy with benefits to the community.[1]

Later in this chapter, I investigate empirically changes in median income and the distribution of affluent and poor families across suburbs. But first I look in more detail at the flow of benefits to the actors in a community. While attracting rich families and increasing median income produces communitywide benefits, the distribution of benefits varies somewhat across sets of actors, which in turn may affect the degree of support they are likely to lend to the pursuit of higher community income.

WHO BENEFITS FROM HIGHER COMMUNITY INCOME?

The Interests of Local Public-Sector Actors

Bureaucrats want larger public agencies and higher public spending. To the extent that increased community income translates into a larger public sector, suburban bureaucrats should support policies designed to increase it. Compared to central cities, the mix of services offered by suburbs may make the propensity of bureaucrats to support such policies even stronger.

While most private goods and services are normal goods, the demand for some municipal services may *decrease* with income. Consequently, some bureaucrats may face a dilemma: greater personal wealth might generate the fiscal resources necessary to support higher levels of public services, but the individuals generating these resources might not want what public bureaucrats are selling.

I argued earlier that a downward sloping demand curve may be an outcome particular to the service mix offered by central cities. Many of their services are designed for low-income residents and consume a significant share of central city budgets although they do not directly benefit the affluent—for example, public hospitals, public health services, public welfare, or public housing. As the number of affluent residents in a city increases, demand may decline because they shift their political support away from redistributive programs to programs which produce benefits for them.

Moreover, given the ethnic and class heterogeneity of central cities, and given that public services once provided are usually open to all residents, the affluent may avoid municipal facilities, such as pools or parks, preferring to substitute private recreation facilities for public ones. When this happens, the affluent could decrease even further their demand for central city services.

Shifts in the demand for services that result from an influx of higher income residents might lead bureaucrats whose careers are built around social service programs to support only weakly or even oppose policies designed to attract the affluent. But in suburbia the absence of strong bureaucracies linked to redistributive programs reduces potential con-flict among public-sector actors and should produce a stronger consen-sus among local bureaucrats in favor of growth.

Politicians Politicians also want rising local income levels, since greater wealth can contribute to their goal of staying in office. Delivering and taking credit for quality public services is a campaign strategy which increases the likelihood of reelection. The appeal of quality services is even greater if they can be provided without increasing local tax rates. This can be accomplished if local wealth rises. Furthermore, to the extent that increased local wealth improves the physical appearance of and the quality of life in the community, incumbent politicians can also benefit.

Some politicians may face risks as the composition of the local com-munity changes. An influx of wealthy new residents may disrupt existing political coalitions and create new groups challenging the electoral base of incumbents. While this may moderate the enthusiasm of politicians for programs aimed at increasing local wealth, most studies show a strong predisposition for local politicians to support pro-development policies (for example, Molotch 1976; Fainstein et al. 1984; Friedland 1983).

Residents Individuals and families clearly benefit when their own income increases. In addition, as aggregate local income rises or as more rich families are found in a community, benefits can spillover into the community as a whole. For example, higher income communities are more likely to attract quality retail establishments and other types of desirable economic growth than are poorer suburbs (Schneider 1986a). Such growth directly benefits individual consumers who gain access to a more attractive array of goods, and it also benefits local residents em-ployed by the new businesses.

In addition, rising income generates collective benefits for the com-munity. A diversification of the tax base, reduced pressure on residential property taxes, an "upscale" image for the community (with higher home values), and a competitive position to attract desirable growth in the future may all accrue to a wealthier suburb. Collective benefits can also flow from the expansion of the local public sector resulting from higher local income. Improved public services may directly match the tastes of wealthier residents, but lower income residents also benefit from access to a better set of services supported by greater local wealth.

In short, residents of communities stand to gain from policies which successfully increase local income, and they should be particularly sup-portive of policies designed to attract higher income in-migrants. In suburbia, this argument is verified by the vehement opposition directed at almost any plan to build subsidized housing to which lower income families will have access. Local opposition to the construction of high cost housing for affluent families is much less frequent and almost always less intense.

Local Businesses Most local businesses should support policies to increase the income of families in the community. Wealthier communities represent stronger potential markets for many businesses, especially for those in the retail and service sectors.

The benefits to local retailers from increased community wealth are clear. Since consumption of private goods increases with income, retail markets are stronger in communities with higher income. Furthermore, a retailer located in a wealthy community has a "good address" which can lure shoppers from a wider geographic market, increasing sales and profits. Empirically, retail firms "shop around" to locate in communities with a wealthier population; as a result, retail growth has been more rapid in suburbs with higher median income than in other lower income communities (Schneider 1986a).

Many service-sector firms also benefit from higher community income. If a local firm specializes in consumer services, it will directly benefit from increased local income. Affluent communities will have more expensive houses, producing higher fees for real estate agents, insurance brokers, and attorneys (see Molotch 1976). Firms providing financial services, such as banks and investment counseling, will also benefit from higher local income. While the rewards for production oriented service firms are less clear, in general, most service firms will likely join with retail firms to provide strong support for policies that increase the wealth of the community.

Manufacturing firms are less likely to be interested in the personal wealth of the local community in which they are located. Their products compete in larger, often national or even international, markets. Manufacturing firms may actually be negatively affected by prosperity in the local community. Wealthier residents may be upset with any environmental degradation associated with manufacturing activity, they may resent the noise and congestion associated with manufacturing processes, and, especially if their income is not directly dependent on local manufacturing firms, they may be willing to support local ordinances regulating manufacturing activity. When these attitudes produce restrictions on the behavior of manufacturing firms, for example by forcing firms to adopt pollution control devices, manufacturers can experience lower profits. Consequently, manufacturing firms may not support policies for increasing local wealth as strongly as will firms in the retail and service sector.[2]

Recent economic changes may strengthen the role of the retail and service sectors in setting local growth policies. These sectors are the fastest growing segments of the suburban economy, while the manufacturing sector is losing ground (see chapter 8). The clout of the expanding sectors and the congruence of their interests with other major actors in the local community can lead to their participation in coalitions formed around policies designed to attract the wealthy.

LIMITS ON LOCAL GOVERNMENTS

Increasing the number of affluent people and the median income in a community is a goal upon which most local actors can agree. However, achieving that goal using the policy tools available to local governments is difficult, if not impossible. The distribution of personal wealth across communities is highly stable and changes in this distribution are influenced by large scale economic, social, and demographic forces, which may be beyond the control of local government. Local actors may agree to pursue a policy goal which they cannot achieve.

The ability of local policies to increase community income is directly limited by changes in the national and international marketplace, driven by innovations and transitions in the demand for private sector goods and in the technologies of their production. The ongoing "restructuring" of the world economy affects the success of local governments in accumulating wealth and is beyond the control of local government policies (Norton and Rees 1979; Noyelle and Stanback 1983; MacKenzie 1979; Kasarda 1980).

In concrete terms, between 1970 and 1980, the national economy and the economies of different regions in the United States were affected by large scale events such as the energy crisis (caused by political problems in the Middle East) and the resulting spurt in demand for the development of domestic energy sources; the collapse of heavy industry, such as steel and autos (caused largely by the evolving export economies of Asian countries); and the boom in high-tech and service industries. Throughout the 1970s, these economic changes were reflected in the relative economic stagnation of the Northeast and North Central regions and growth in the "Sunbelt." However, in the mid 1980s, worldwide market forces changed radically, and the previously booming areas of Texas, Louisiana, and other parts of the south declined while the economies of many northeastern metropolitan regions revived.

The fate of regions is linked to the national and international economy, and the fate of localities is linked to the fate of their region. While individual communities may be relatively more or less successful than their neighbors, all communities in a region share a common fate, which imposes limits on just how well an individual community can do.

Within these regional parameters, strong demographic and ecological forces further restrict the success of individual communities. Empirical studies of suburban development document high stability in the social status of suburbs for periods as long as fifty years (Farley 1964; also see Guest 1978). Persistence is rooted in basic ecological patterns of metropolitan growth and implies further limits on suburban policies. While political factors and the incentives of the local market for public goods can affect the distribution of income (see, Logan 1978; Logan and Schneider 1981; Schneider and Logan 1982a), policy effects are often quite small compared to the importance of demographic factors. While communities clearly enact fiscal policies to increase local income, just as clearly they face stringent limits on the success of their policies.

To explore these limits more fully, I turn briefly to an examination of patterns of persistence and change in median income. I then examine the effects of individual community characteristics on change in median income and the relative standing of communities vis-à-vis their neighbors.

Regional Patterns of Changing Income 1970–1980

Communities want to increase local personal wealth, but the external world does not necessarily oblige. I have already noted that regional patterns affect the fate of individual communities. This is clearly seen in the data presented in table 26. Among the most important regional trends evident in these data are the relatively rapid growth in the income of suburbs in western and southern metropolitan regions (especially those in the West South Central SMSAs) and the stagnation of income growth in the New England, Mid-Atlantic, and North Central regions. In these "older" regions, the collapse of heavy industries, such as steel and autos, sent shock waves through entire local economies, limiting the growth of community income (Buss and Redburn 1983).

Other macroeconomic factors affected local income. Inflation in the 1970s was so intense that, on the average, the real median income of

TABLE 26
MEDIAN INCOME AND PERCENT CHANGE IN MEDIAN INCOME
IN 1452 SUBURBS, BY REGION

	Mean 1970	Mean 1980	Mean Change
New England	$10,611	$20,715	93%
Mid-Atlantic	12,804	26,153	106
East North Central	13,278	27,804	109
West North Central	12,175	26,492	118
South Atlantic	10,372	21,195	104
East South Central	9,553	20,872	119
West South Central	10,956	26,458	143
Mountain	9,728	21,021	116
Pacific	12,719	27,185	110
All suburbs	12,380	26,155	112

suburbs actually eroded over the decade. Between 1970 and 1980, the Consumer Price Index increased by over 125 percent; however, among the suburbs in this sample, median income increased by only about 110 percent, from approximately $12,000 in 1970 to slightly more than $26,000 in 1980. The consequent erosion in real income helped set off the numerous tax revolts of the 1970s and set local governments scampering in search of policies designed to increase local wealth, to diversify the local tax base, and to ease the growing budget constraints caused by stagnation in growth of the real income of their residents.

In analyzing changes in the distribution of community income, Collver and Semyonov (1979) argue that local income can be decomposed into at least two distinct dimensions: changes in absolute wealth, such as reported in table 26, and changes in *relative* levels of community income, which can be measured by the correlation in median income over time. The high correlation ($r = .85$) between community median income in 1970 and 1980 across the suburbs in this sample is evidence of stability in relative income.

Persistence and regional patterns of change in community income define the boundaries within which local governments operate. To assess the effectiveness of local budgetary and fiscal policies, I turn to an analysis of change in absolute median income and in relative wealth as a function of community characteristics, controlling for regional patterns of change. The following analysis addresses a simple question: can local policies affect either the absolute or relative income in a community?

Individual Community Effects on Local Income

My analysis proceeds in two steps. First, change in absolute levels of individual suburban median income is investigated, instituting controls for differences in region using a set of dummy variables representing SMSA location. To account more fully for regional patterns, I specifically investigate change in community income relative to other suburbs in its region. In this "positional analysis," all variables are transformed into Z-scores based on SMSA means and standard deviations (Collver and Semyonov 1979).

I use the following equation to analyze change in absolute community median income:

(6) Median Income $1980_i = f($Median Income 1970_i
$$+ \text{SMSA}$$
$$+ \text{Demographic Factors}_{i,1972}$$
$$+ \text{Intergovernmental Factors}_{i,1972}$$
$$+ \text{Economic Composition}_{i,1972}$$
$$+ \text{Expenditures}_{i,1972}$$
$$+ \text{Fiscal Factors}_{i,1972}).$$

The following equation examines change in relative position:

(7) Standardized (Z-score) Median Income $1980_i =$
$$f(\text{Z-score Median Income } 1970_i$$
$$+ \text{Z-score Demographic Factors}_{i,1972}$$
$$+ \text{Z-score Intergovernmental Factors}_{i,1972}$$
$$+ \text{Z-score Economic Composition}_{i,1972}$$
$$+ \text{Z-score Expenditures}_{i,1972}$$
$$+ \text{Z-score Fiscal Factors}_{i,1972}).$$

Following Markus (1980), these lagged endogenous variable regressions are interpreted as the analysis of the effects of the independent variables, measuring community conditions at time t-1 on *change* in the dependent variable. Thus, equation 6 assesses the causes of change in absolute community median income; while equation 7 analyzes the causes of change in standing relative to neighboring communities.[3] Z-scores further reduce the statistical effects of the exogenous and unmeasured factors over which local governments have no control— the results of equation 7 focus more fully on what local governments can do within the overall limits imposed by regional location.

The variables in these equations represent a mix of geographic, economic, demographic, and policy characteristics of a local community. Since almost all have been previously defined, just a brief summary statement is necessary:

Median Income 1980, 1970 = median income of each suburb as reported in the 1980 and 1970 Census of Population.

SMSA = a series of dummy variables, coded 1 for location in a specific SMSA, 0 otherwise.

Demographic Factors = a set of community conditions, including density, percent black, and percent renters. I also include median home value to reflect the quality of the local housing stock. Distance reflects the community life cycle hypothesis central to ecological theories of growth.

Intergovernmental Factors = total federal grants and total state grants per capita in 1972.[4] Intergovernmental payments can reduce the costs of services directly borne by local residents. A community with a large number of intergovernmental grants may present an attractive benefit/ cost ratio. However, intergovernmental transfer payments, especially those from the federal government, are notoriously unstable. Furthermore, intergovernmental grants may force local governments to spend not only the intergovernmental monies they receive but their own revenues on services not desired by local residents. The overall effects of intergovernmental aid on the attractiveness of local communities are thus difficult to predict.

Economic Composition = the size of the work force in the retail, wholesale, manufacturing, and service sectors relative to the size of the local population in 1972.[5]

Expenditures = per capita budgetary outlays in each of Peterson's three categories of expenditures: developmental, redistributive, and allocational. These are the policy variables over which local governments have the most control and following Peterson (1981) should have direct effects on the pattern of local growth.

Fiscal Factors = two indicators of fiscal conditions prevailing in a suburb: the tax bill and true value per capita.[6]

RESULTS

Table 27, which reports the analysis of the rate of change in community income between 1970 and 1980, shows that the factors most strongly determining changes in community median income are beyond the immediate control of local budgetary policies.[7] Most basically, persistence in the distribution of community income limits the policy space of local governments.

In a simple equation in which community median income in 1980 is regressed against median income in 1970, the following results were obtained:

Median Income 1980 = $1108 + 2.00*(Median Income 1970)
R square = .768

Persistence is clearly evident: more than three quarters of the variance in 1980 community median income is explained by median in-

TABLE 27

Change in Median Income, 1970–1980, as a Function of Demographic, Intergovernmental, Economic, Budgetary, and Fiscal Factors, Controlling for SMSA and 1970 Lagged Value

Variable	B	SE B	Beta	T-Test
LAGGED VALUE				
Median income 1970	1.50	0.06	.659	23.89
DEMOGRAPHIC FACTORS				
Rent (%)	−3326.35	1351.10	−.047	2.46
Black (%)	−510.82	1407.90	−.005	0.13
Home value	205.95	23.04	.251	8.61
Distance	26.52	20.69	.020	1.64
Density	−264.28	0.46	−.009	0.31
INTERGOVERNMENTAL AID				
Federal aid	−9.01	11.39	−.010	0.62
State aid	−1.35	8.44	−.003	0.02
ECONOMIC COMPOSITION				
Manufacturing	−1139.41	690.71	−.026	1.64
Service	−3096.69	3868.79	−.013	0.64
Wholesale	−973.82	4952.05	−.002	0.03
Retail	−1697.27	2584.61	−.010	0.43
PER CAPITA EXPENDITURES				
Distributive	12.27	9.01	.022	1.85
Allocational	2.64	13.31	.003	0.03
Redistributive	−5.66	8.09	−.009	0.48
FISCAL FACTORS				
True value	10452.38	3146.50	.071	3.32
Tax bill	541.23	164.28	.081	3.29
Constant	899.99	3379.76		0.26
Adjusted R square, lagged value,	.76			
Adjusted R square, + SMSA,	.78			
Adjusted R square, full model,	.80			

NOTE: Number of cases = 864.

come in 1970.[8] Adding the SMSA dummy variables increases the variance explained to .784 percent. Combining strong persistence in the distribution of income with regional patterns, the possible effects of individual community characteristics, including local government policies, can be only limited.

Of individual community factors, higher home value is most strongly associated with increased community income. In contrast, a concentration of renters is associated with slower income growth. As a development strategy, many suburban governments use zoning and building codes to increase the costs of local housing and to exclude rental units. These exclusionary growth policies clearly constitute a rational policy choice for any individual community—exclusionary growth patterns are linked empirically to the desired goal of higher community income.

Some local fiscal conditions marginally affect change in community income. According to Peterson (1981), controlling for service levels, a higher tax bill should reduce a community's attractiveness for mobile high income families. But empirically a higher tax bill is associated with *more* rapid growth in median income. High local taxes may act as a constraint on the in-migration of low-income families (Jackson 1975:11). In a perfect market, tax capitalization will drive down housing prices to compensate for higher taxes (Oates 1969). Yet in the imperfect market of the real world, complete tax capitalization does not occur and higher taxes increase the carrying costs of a house, erecting entry barriers to low-income families.

Perhaps more important, a stronger tax base is associated with more rapid growth in community income. A strong tax base represents a positive externality for all members of a rich community and allows a municipality to compete more effectively for wealthier mobile families.

Local budgetary allocations do not affect the rate of change in local income. Thus, the investment decisions and budgetary instruments most controllable by the local government have no visible impact on changes in community wealth.

Positional Change in Income

Table 28 reports change in the *relative* income of communities using Z-scores. Regional patterns are controlled by the method of transformation, so that SMSA dummy variables are no longer necessary. Paralleling earlier results, table 28 shows high stability in the relative standing of communities over time (note that since all variables are standardized, the intercept is 0 and the unstandardized and the standardized regression coefficients are the same). A simple regression of relative position, measured by Z-scores, in 1980 against relative position in 1970 produces the following result:

$$\text{Position } 1980 = .856 * (\text{Position } 1970)$$
$$\text{R square} = .733$$

High stability in relative position is again evident. Adding community level indicators increases the explained variance to just over .77 percent—some local factors matter. Among these factors, both a concentration of rental units and higher density lead to lower future

TABLE 28

CHANGE IN RELATIVE MEDIAN INCOME, 1970–1980, AS A FUNCTION OF DEMOGRAPHIC, INTERGOVERNMENTAL, ECONOMIC, BUDGETARY, AND FISCAL FACTORS, CONTROLLING FOR SMSA AND 1970 LAGGED VALUE, Z-SCORES

Variable	Beta	SE B	T-Test
LAGGED VALUE			
Std. median income 1970	.574	0.023	24.35
DEMOGRAPHIC FACTORS			
Std. rent (%)	−.070	0.018	3.99
Std. black (%)	−.008	0.014	0.34
Std. home value	.305	0.022	13.52
Std. distance	−.003	0.000	0.07
Std. density	−.040	0.015	2.44
PER CAPITA EXPENDITURES			
Std. distributive	.021	0.014	1.44
Std. allocational	.012	0.015	0.70
Std. redistributive	−.007	0.014	0.29
ECONOMIC COMPOSITION			
Std. manufacturing	−.004	0.000	0.10
Std. service	−.003	0.000	0.07
Std. retail	−.020	0.014	1.48
Std. wholesale	−.015	0.000	1.29
INTERGOVERNMENTAL FACTORS			
Std. federal aid	−.004	0.000	0.05
Std. state aid	.022	0.000	1.36
FISCAL FACTORS			
Std. true value	−.003	0.000	0.07
Std. tax bill	.016	0.014	1.26
Adjusted R square, .77			

NOTE: All variables are Z-scores standardized by SMSA means and standard deviations.

position. In contrast, higher home value is strongly associated with increases in a community's relative position. These results again show that exclusionary growth strategies are rational choices for individual communities.

The composition of the local economy does not affect the rate of relative change; neither do budgetary allocations. In the positional analysis, the tax bill and true value per capita do not significantly affect change in relative position.

There is obviously strong persistence in the relative wealth of suburban communities. Exclusionary growth policies in which local governments manipulate the quality and composition of their housing stock will change a community's wealth relative to its neighbors, but budgetary policies do not.

The Movement of Affluent and Poor Families

Two distinct processes contribute to changes in local community income, and they may be differentially amenable to manipulation by local policies. First, the income of present residents may increase ("incumbent upgrading"), pushing up the median income of the community. The level of community income will also be affected by the income level of new migrants.

The process of incumbent upgrading is subject to strong constraints. For example, the occupational distribution of local residents and the stage they are in their careers will affect the rate at which their income changes over time. Communities with a larger concentration of young families will be more likely to experience increases in median community income as wage earners climb their career ladders. Conversely, a community with a large number of older residents might experience declining median income levels as wage earners leave the job market and collect retirement benefits lower than their previous wages. These factors may be well beyond the control of local government.

Change in local income is also dependent on the income of in-migrants, and here local government policies might have a greater impact. I thus analyze separately the change in concentration of affluent and poor families in communities between 1970 and 1980. The concentration of the affluent is measured by the proportion of families in a community whose income was more than 150 percent of the *SMSA* median income in 1970 and in 1980. Conversely, low income families are those with incomes less than 50 percent of the SMSA median. This method adjusts for differences across SMSAs in costs of living and for inflation in the 1970s (see Schneider and Logan 1981).[9] The percent affluent and the percent poor in 1970 and 1980 are substituted for the median income terms in equations 6 and 7.

Attracting the Affluent

Table 29 reports changes in the concentration of the affluent as a function of previous population composition, regional location, and individual community characteristics. The simple regression of the percent affluent in a community in 1980 against percent affluent in 1970 yields the following result:

Percent Affluent 1980 = .01 + .657*(Percent Affluent 1970)
R square = .597

Compared to median income, there is lower persistence in the distribution of the affluent: only about 60 percent of the variance in community affluent 1980 is explained by the 1970 value, compared to over 75 percent of the variance in median income. Also note the unstandardized regression coefficient is less than 1.0: large concentrations of the rich in 1970 do not automatically lead to greater concentrations in 1980. The affluent are more likely to move around producing change in their distribution across metropolitan communities.

Regional patterns are strong: adding SMSA to the equation increases the explained variance from about 60 percent to over 80 percent. Adding individual community level indicators increases the explained variance to almost 88 percent. Of such community factors, higher median home value at time *t*-1 most strongly attracts affluent families. In contrast, a concentration of rental units reduces a community's attractiveness to the affluent, as does higher density.

Among local fiscal conditions, a higher tax bill is associated with a greater concentration of the wealthy in 1980—again this may indicate that local taxes act as a barrier to entry. Not surprisingly, higher true value per capita increases the concentration of the affluent. Again, there is no evidence of budgetary effects: in no budgetary category do per capita expenditures affect change in the concentration of the affluent.

Substituting Z-scores for absolute percentages, we see that the relative position of suburbs in their concentration of the affluent is highly stable. (See table 30.) Regressing the Z-score of each community in 1980 on its Z-score in 1970 yields:

Position Affluent 1980 = .88*(Position Affluent 1970)
R square = .780

The individual community characteristics affecting change in position are predictable: suburban municipalities with more rental units and higher density lose position over time. Note that there is a positive relationship between the service ratio and concentration of affluent, but the manufacturing ratio has no effect. Paralleling the previous results, no budgetary effect is evident.

TABLE 29

CHANGE IN CONCENTRATION OF THE AFFLUENT, 1970–1980, AS A FUNCTION OF
DEMOGRAPHIC, INTERGOVERNMENTAL, ECONOMIC, BUDGETARY, AND FISCAL FACTORS,
CONTROLLING FOR SMSA AND 1970 LAGGED VALUE

Variable	B	SE B	Beta	T-Test
LAGGED VALUE				
Percent affluent 1970	0.42	0.02	.502	19.54
DEMOGRAPHIC FACTORS				
Rent (%)	−0.06	0.01	−.062	3.97
Black (%)	0.05	0.01	.040	3.46
Home value	0.00	0.00	.558	22.09
Distance	0.00	0.00	.014	0.97
Density	−0.01	0.00	−.039	4.83
INTERGOVERNMENTAL FACTORS				
Federal aid	−0.00	0.00	−.000	0.00
State aid	0.00	0.00	.004	0.08
ECONOMIC COMPOSITION				
Manufacturing	−0.00	0.00	−.013	1.28
Wholesale	−0.05	0.05	−.010	0.95
Retail	−0.04	0.03	−.019	1.59
Service	0.07	0.04	.021	1.46
PER CAPITA EXPENDITURES				
Distributive	0.00	0.00	.011	0.82
Redistributive	0.00	0.00	.010	0.95
Allocational	−0.00	0.00	−.009	0.41
FISCAL FACTORS				
True value	1.15	0.00	.052	3.82
Tax bill	0.00	0.00	.037	1.92
Constant	−0.03	0.00		1.93
Adjusted R square, lagged value,	.59			
Adjusted R square, with region,	.81			
Adjusted R square, full model,	.87			

TABLE 30

CHANGE IN RELATIVE CONCENTRATION OF THE AFFLUENT, 1970–1980,
AS A FUNCTION OF DEMOGRAPHIC, INTERGOVERNMENTAL, ECONOMIC, BUDGETARY, AND
FISCAL FACTORS, CONTROLLING FOR SMSA AND 1970 LAGGED VALUE, Z-SCORES

Variable	Beta	SE B	T-Test
LAGGED VALUE			
Std. affluent (% 1970)	.479	0.021	22.203
DEMOGRAPHIC FACTORS			
Std. black (%)	.038	0.012	3.45
Std. rent (%)	−.041	0.015	2.51
Std. density	−.044	0.012	3.88
Std. distance	−.004	0.000	0.13
Std. home value	.461	0.020	24.89
INTERGOVERNMENTAL FACTORS			
Std. federal aid	−.006	0.000	0.15
Std. state aid	.042	0.000	2.61
PER CAPITA EXPENDITURES			
Std. redistributive	−.002	0.011	0.03
Std. distributive	.029	0.012	2.46
Std. allocational	.003	0.012	0.09
ECONOMIC COMPOSITION			
Std. manufacturing	−.000	0.000	0.00
Std. wholesale	−.010	0.011	0.77
Std. retail	−.010	0.012	0.79
Std. service	.035	0.000	3.35
FISCAL FACTORS			
Std. true value	.012	0.000	1.08
Std. tax bill	−.006	0.012	0.25
Adjusted R square, .848			

NOTE: All variables are Z-scores standardized by SMSA means and standard deviations.

The Location of the Poor

Just as communities seek to attract the more affluent, they want to exclude less affluent families. And success seems to breed success (or failure to breed failure): the location of the poor is highly stable over time. A simple regression of the percent poor in 1980 against the percent poor in 1970 yields the following results:

Percent Poor 1980 = .068 + 1.07*(Percent Poor 1970),
R square = .515

Stability in the distribution of the poor over time is evident, although lower than for other community income indicators. The unstandardized regression coefficient of 1.07 shows communities with concentrations of the poor in 1970 were more likely to have even greater concentrations in 1980.

Regional patterns of the concentration of the poor are statistically significant: adding the SMSA dummies increases the explained variance to .693 percent. Adding individual community factors increases the variance explained to .774 percent. (See table 31). Not surprisingly, the factors affecting change in the concentration of the poor are mirror images of those conditions attracting the affluent. The poor are more likely to concentrate in communities with more rental housing, of higher density, and with lower valued housing. Suburbs with larger concentrations of blacks accumulate more poor families.

TABLE 31

CHANGE IN CONCENTRATION OF THE POOR, 1970–1980, AS A FUNCTION OF DEMOGRAPHIC, INTERGOVERNMENTAL, ECONOMIC, BUDGETARY, AND FISCAL FACTORS, CONTROLLING FOR SMSA AND 1970 LAGGED VALUE

Variable	B	SE B	Beta	T-Test
LAGGED VALUE				
Percent poor 1970	0.63	0.04	.427	15.81
DEMOGRAPHIC FACTORS				
Rent (%)	0.14	0.01	.184	8.48
Black (%)	0.13	0.01	.131	7.41
Home value	−0.00	0.00	−.292	12.32
Distance	−0.00	0.00	−.033	1.92
Density	0.01	0.00	.054	2.96
INTERGOVERNMENTAL FACTORS				
Federal aid	0.00	0.00	.020	1.34
State aid	0.00	0.00	.003	0.02
ECONOMIC COMPOSITION				
Manufacturing	0.00	0.00	.007	0.17
Services	−0.05	0.04	−.023	1.25
Retail	0.04	0.03	.022	1.34
Wholesale	0.13	0.05	.034	2.28
PER CAPITA EXPENDITURES				
Distributive	−0.00	0.00	−.026	1.54
Redistributive	0.00	0.00	.007	0.24
Allocational	0.00	0.00	.025	1.32

Continued on next page

TABLE 31—*Continued*

Variable	B	SE B	Beta	T-Test
FISCAL FACTORS				
True value	− 0.78	0.00	− .048	2.12
Tax bill	− 0.00	0.00	− .033	1.26
Constant	0.21	0.04		4.93
Adjusted R square, lagged value,	.51			
Adjusted R square, with region,	.69			
Adjusted R square, full model,	.77			

Budget allocations do not affect changes in the concentration of the poor. But poor families are more likely to be excluded from suburbs with a strong tax base. Note that the coefficient on the tax bill, while not significant, is negative: higher local taxes deter the poor.

Persistence is also evident in the positional analysis of communities with respect to their concentration of the poor:

Position Poor 1980 = .79*(Position Poor 1970)
R square = .624

As table 32 shows, communities with large concentrations of blacks, with higher density, with more rental units, and with cheaper valued housing increase their concentration of the poor relative to their neighbors.

Of budgetary factors, local communities spending more on infrastructure are less likely to increase their relative concentrations of poor families. However, higher suburban municipal expenditures for social services do not increase a community's attractiveness to the poor.

TABLE 32
CHANGE IN RELATIVE CONCENTRATION OF THE POOR, 1970–1980,
AS A FUNCTION OF DEMOGRAPHIC, INTERGOVERNMENTAL, ECONOMIC, FISCAL AND
BUDGETARY FACTORS, CONTROLLING FOR SMSA AND 1970 LAGGED VALUE, Z-SCORES

Variable	Beta	SE B	T-Test
LAGGED VALUE			
Std. poor (% 1970)	.473	0.025	18.89
DEMOGRAPHIC FACTORS			
Std. rent (%)	.150	0.021	6.92
Std. black (%)	.142	0.017	8.49

Continued on next page

TABLE 32—*Continued*

Variable	Beta	SE B	T-Test
Std. home value	−.218	0.020	10.51
Std. distance	−.006	0.000	0.14
Std. density	.117	0.017	6.86
ECONOMIC COMPOSITION			
Std. manufacturing	−.001	0.000	0.00
Std. service	.036	0.000	2.51
Std. wholesale	.048	0.016	2.79
Std. retail	.010	0.016	0.40
PER CAPITA EXPENDITURES			
Std. distributive	−.049	0.016	2.76
Std. allocational	.009	0.017	0.28
Std. redistributive	.009	0.016	0.35
FISCAL FACTORS			
Std. true value	.013	0.000	0.69
Std. tax bill	.014	0.016	0.71
INTERGOVERNMENTAL FACTORS			
Std. federal aid	.014	0.000	0.40
Std. state aid	.000	0.000	0.00
Adjusted R square, .711			

NOTE: All variables are Z-scores standardized by SMSA means and standard deviations.

CONCLUSIONS

Given the present organization of the local market for public goods, actors in suburban communities want to increase the level of personal wealth found in their community. The flow of benefits is extensive: direct benefits accrue to the residents receiving higher income; programmatic benefits are likely to accrue to members of the public sector; electoral benefits are likely to accrue to politicians; and higher profits accrue to many local businesses.

If the increase in personal wealth occurs by attracting new residents whose income level is higher than existing median community income, this growth will have added benefits: new higher income residents generate a fiscal surplus paid to present residents (Buchanan 1981).

Consequently, it is easy to generate community consensus to use the powers of local government to attract higher income residents. Yet the constraints are severe. The distribution of income across suburban communities is highly stable and there is little evidence of success resulting from the manipulation of local budgetary policies. Further constraints are rooted in macroeconomic forces, reflected in regional patterns of change. In the 1970s, suburbs in the South and West experienced faster growth in personal wealth than did those in the North as the demand for goods and services shifted to the Sunbelt.

Some local growth policies are enacted to attract the affluent by appealing to their taste in housing. Through zoning laws and building codes, suburbs try to create a more attractive and more expensive housing stock. Given the rewards for attracting the affluent and increasing the level of community income, this is a rational growth strategy.

However, the fiscal and budgetary policies most directly under the control of local governments have only marginal impact on changes in the distribution of wealth.

While local property taxes increase entry costs into a community and subsequently increase its level of wealth, the extent to which a community can raise its taxes to erect such barriers is limited. Increased taxes raise the location costs borne by present residents and by incumbent businesses, weakening their appeal as entry barriers. Convincing residents that higher taxes may benefit them in the long run through possible increases in community income levels is not an argument local politicians would enjoy making.

The consistent relationship between true value, class specific migration patterns, and the level of local wealth is particularly important. Affluent families tend to locate in communities with a stronger tax base, while poor families are more likely to be excluded from such suburbs. Given the importance of local taxes in financing services, the tax base of a local community is a critical factor determining the level of community services and the associated tax bill. Communities with a strong tax base have the *option* of choosing high services, which can be paid for without high taxes, or they can have lower service levels and even lower tax rates. Communities with a weak tax base do not have these options: they have lower services *and* a high tax rate.

This pattern of local fiscal benefits and costs makes a strong tax base a positive externality for all members of the local community. While no single set of expenditures appears to attract the more affluent, by moving into communities with a strong tax base, the affluent are purchasing an extended set of policy options and are more likely to experience a better balance between taxes and services. Communities with a strong tax base have a competitive advantage in attracting desirable growth and more affluent families use their greater purchasing power to buy entry into these attractive places.

Suburbs will also use their budget authority to design service/tax bundles they hope attract the affluent. But the distribution of community income is highly stable and the movement of the affluent across communities is largely determined by factors other than local budgetary policies. What change does occur is largely driven by strong external forces related to changing economic conditions and life style choices made largely without regard to the interests and inducements of local government.

8

ECONOMIC DEVELOPMENT
OF LOCAL COMMUNITIES

Economic development became increasingly attractive to suburbs during the 1970s and 1980s. The failure of local income to keep pace with inflation and the growing resistance to the higher taxes necessary to meet the escalating costs of public services forced communities to look for ways of diversifying their tax base in order to support local services without higher taxes. Economic growth became an attractive way to accomplish this.

Beginning as early as the 1920s, and accelerating rapidly in the 1950s, changing technologies and evolving demographic patterns made suburban location increasingly attractive for a variety of economic activities. The creation of a national economic marketplace, resulting from improvements in transportation and communications systems, made suburbs as convenient as central cities for economic activity. Suburbs began to present a desirable labor pool, cheap land, and the infrastructure necessary to support business activity. The need of suburban communities to enhance their tax base thus coincided with the interests of business firms that wanted the smooth and profitable decentralization of business activity.

Local support for economic development was made easier by changes in the nature of the American economy. Early patterns of economic decentralization usually meant the decentralization of manufacturing. This was often a dirty business because heavy manufacturing generated negative side effects for host communities. Not surprisingly, suburbs with high levels of economic activity were often the "industrial suburbs" described by Schnore: high-density, low-income communities with a poor housing stock (Schnore 1961). More recently, however, as the U.S. economy has evolved, manufacturing has come to encompass lighter and cleaner industries. Moreover, economic decentralization now involves other sectors of the economy besides manufacturing: retail and service firms have moved to suburbia in large numbers (Schneider 1986a; Schneider and Fernandez 1989). There is even evidence that firms have moved their headquarters, long thought to be firmly anchored in central cities, to suburbia (for example, Muller 1982; Leinberger and Lockwood 1986). As a result, it may now be possible for a local community to attract economic growth without sacrificing environmental quality or otherwise radically diminishing desirable qualities of community life.

If the costs of economic growth decline, as they did during the 1960s and 1970s, the net benefits of development increase. In turn, policies favorable to business can more easily attract wide support. Politicians can advocate such policies to gain the support of local residents and to curry favor with business groups (and, in the process, increase their chances of reelection). Bureaucrats can push economic development to provide the tax base for expanding their agencies. Residents can support economic growth to shift tax costs to business property. Business groups, especially those local business actors whose economic well-being is contingent upon the value of local property, can advocate economic development to increase markets and profits. These incentives created the fertile soil for the "growth machine" (Molotch 1976).

INTERNAL PROBLEMS IN THE GROWTH MACHINE

As long as the costs of economic development remain low in relation to its benefits, support for growth is a formidable political force. However, tensions may now be emerging in the growth machine, weakening its cohesiveness and undermining its appeal. Much of this tension emerges as economic development comes into conflict with local amenities and the quality of local life. In their study of such conflicts, Molotch and Logan (1984) argue that the growth machine emphasizes the "exchange value" of land, treating land as a market commodity from which to draw maximum profits. Conflict emerges if a significant number of local residents discount the exchange value of land by questioning the benefits of economic growth. This can happen if residents begin to emphasize the present use of local land—for example, by valuing the noneconomic benefits of open space. The "use value" of land can reduce its exchange value: some development may not take place and some profits may be eschewed in favor of preservation of the amenities flowing from non-development.

Rapid suburbanization can exacerbate such conflict, undermining the amenities and the very life style suburbanites sought when moving into their communities. Facing the destruction of desirable life styles, coalitions of residents can form to block new growth. The most well known conflicts have emerged in California, where no-growth coalitions throughout the state, and in the San Francisco and Los Angeles metropolitan regions in particular, have attracted nation wide attention (see, for example, Molotch and Logan 1984; Logan and Molotch 1987; Hartman 1984). In New York City, strong neighborhood opposition to a proposal to build a massive building on the southern tip of Central Park forced a total revision of the project. A key issue was the adverse effects of the building's huge shadow on Central Park. Interestingly, the proposed project was strongly supported by the city government, which hoped to gain significant revenues from the deal. Other large-scale projects in New York (such as Donald Trump's Television City) and in other presently prosperous northeastern cities, notably Boston, have also encountered opposition from neighborhood groups.

Because attitudes toward growth are rooted in an evaluation of the benefits of growth compared to its costs, opposition may become more common, given new corporate styles which decrease the local benefits of development. According to Molotch and Logan (1984), large corporations (which are often multinational) no longer draw their suppliers, their managers, or even their workers from the local community. Such firms also do not interact with local cultural or educational institutions to the extent smaller, more locally based, companies did in the past. This new form of economic development decreases the local benefits of economic growth while continuing to impose costs. As benefits weaken in relation to costs, the appeal of continued growth also weakens, providing the basis for the politics of no-growth.

It appears that a propensity to opt out of the growth machine has developed among some actors in local politics. While the literature on no-growth politics documents deviation from the pro-development bias described in earlier studies, in fact both the pro-growth and the no-growth literatures share the common view that support for growth policies is ultimately driven by the benefit/cost ratio of development. The underlying theme is that for at least some actors in some situations the benefit/cost ratio of growth has changed—perceived costs have escalated while benefits have not. This change is most evident among residential groups representing neighborhoods that have been adversely affected by continued growth or fear the impact of future growth. In many fights over development, such as the one noted above in New York City, neighborhood groups have dropped out of the growth machine and have come into conflict with other local actors who still believe in growth.

Clearly, this conflict means that support for growth will be more selective in the future. But selectivity will be easier to maintain in regions where businesses want to locate. Given high demand for entry into a community, local actors can select among alternative projects, choosing the best and rejecting the worst. In contrast, given low demand, policy options are limited (Rubin and Rubin 1987; Fischel 1975). Thus the politics of limited growth are most evident and most successful in booming regions, such as California, because the demand for location is so strong. But most communities do not have the luxury of "excess demand" and must continue to attract economic development using an array of policies so rich and so varied that suburbs resemble a "well stocked candy store" (Gray and Spina 1980).

If the politics of local economic growth are intimately linked to the demand for location in a given community, the demand for entry is largely beyond the control of local communities. Demand is primarily the product of macroeconomic changes over which local communities have little control. The relative weakness of local public policies can be seen in recent regional patterns of economic change. Consider the policy "lessons" embedded in the boom and bust of Texas communities and the mirror-image pattern of bust and boom of northeastern cities during the 1970s and 1980s.

When the economies of cities and towns in Massachusetts were teetering on the edge of bankruptcy and the cities in the Dallas and Houston regions were booming, the policy lesson was that local taxes deter economic development. It was "evident" that the low taxes of Texas were attracting firms which were steering clear of "Taxachusetts." By the mid 1980s, however, Boston and its suburbs had among the lowest unemployment rates in the United States, and the economies of Dallas and its suburbs were in virtual depression. The "new" policy lesson (as clearly evident as the earlier message on taxes) was that investment in infrastructure (especially education) was important.

The underlying truth is that local policies in the two regions did not much change, but rates of regional economic growth were nonetheless radically different. This hints at the ultimate conundrum of the local politics of economic growth. While the debate about the value of economic development swirls and theoretical debates emerge comparing the politics of growth and the politics of no-growth, the true irony is not that the costs and benefits of growth keep changing. The real problem for local governments is that regardless of the intensity of the desire for economic growth, local communities are ultimately limited in their ability to attract development. The pursuit of economic growth using local policies may be as successful as the pursuit of the Holy Grail.

To show more systematically the relative inability of local policies, particularly fiscal and budgetary ones, to affect economic development, I examine growth in two sectors of the suburban economy, manufacturing and services. I chart the distribution of economic growth in these sectors across suburbs and then investigate the degree to which the characteristics and policies of suburban municipalities affect such growth.

A TALE OF TWO SECTORS: MANUFACTURING AND SERVICES

The recent history of the manufacturing and service sectors, and their prospects for future growth, are radically different. In terms of employment, the manufacturing sector historically has been the largest source of jobs in suburbia, but a sector in decline. Among the suburbs in this sample, manufacturing jobs represented over 45 percent of employment in 1972; just over 40 percent in 1977; and around 30 percent in 1982.[1]

In contrast to the decline of manufacturing employment, the rise of the service economy in the nationally has been widely heralded. Rapid growth in the share of suburban employment in services is evident. Among the suburbs in this sample, in 1972, service jobs accounted for only 12 percent of local employment. In 1977, this increased to 15 percent; and in 1982 over 22 percent of all jobs were in the service sector.

To give an idea of how dramatically the relative importance of these two sectors changed over the course of the 1970s and early 1980s, I computed a measure of the ratio of manufacturing to service jobs in each community and then report the average manufacturing/service ratio over time by region and by SMSA. (See table 33.)

The relative change in the size of the two sectors is striking. In 1972 across this sample of suburbs there were almost 13 manufacturing jobs for every service job. In 1977, the ratio narrowed to under 7 manufacturing jobs for every service job. But in the following five years, the change was even more spectacular: in 1982, there was an average of less than 2.2 jobs in manufacturing for every service job.[2] The increasing importance of the service sector vis-à-vis manufacturing could not be more clearly documented.

There are distinct regional patterns evident in the distribution of the manufacturing/service ratio. Suburbs in New England, the Mid-Atlantic, the East and West North Central regions have the highest ratios—but, not surprisingly, these ratios fell dramatically during the 1970s and early

1980s. Outside the northeastern quadrant of the United States, the manufacturing/service ratio tends to be lower.

TABLE 33
MANUFACTURING/SERVICE EMPLOYMENT RATIO IN 952 SUBURBS

	1972	1977	1982	N
NEW ENGLAND	7.83	6.78	2.71	21
Boston	4.64	3.81	1.78	16
Providence	18.03	16.28	5.69	5
MID-ATLANTIC	13.64	7.07	2.42	288
Allentown	31.06	21.91	7.54	12
Buffalo	11.68	6.53	1.97	17
Newark	11.74	6.73	2.28	30
New York	4.41	2.47	0.69	61
Paterson	6.06	4.83	2.91	56
Philadelphia	13.73	9.18	2.97	42
Pittsburgh	25.30	9.91	2.68	60
Rochester	17.80	5.99	1.82	10
EAST NORTH CENTRAL	19.74	7.03	2.78	291
Chicago	30.92	7.66	4.11	84
Cincinnati	7.78	6.53	2.26	31
Cleveland	12.23	6.50	2.28	51
Columbus	3.97	4.30	1.42	8
Davenport	5.42	12.09	6.34	3
Detroit	19.00	5.96	1.11	55
Gary	4.90	2.48	0.87	1
Grand Rapids	11.86	10.49	4.42	12
Indianapolis	6.76	6.45	2.55	10
Milwaukee	15.48	7.96	3.59	34
Peoria	7.08	2.53	0.52	2
WEST NORTH CENTRAL	8.52	5.91	1.27	83
Minneapolis	7.66	3.90	1.35	44
St. Louis	9.16	8.19	1.14	39
SOUTH ATLANTIC	3.49	2.48	1.27	26
Atlanta	3.37	1.47	1.16	8
Baltimore	2.66	2.56	1.44	5
Ft. Lauderdale	0.90	0.80	0.75	6
Tampa	1.71	1.65	1.60	3
Wilmington	9.25	7.56	1.84	4
EAST SOUTH CENTRAL	16.53	5.98	3.05	12
Birmingham	10.22	6.96	3.74	8
Louisville	29.94	4.03	1.84	4

Continued on next page

TABLE 33—*Continued*

	1972	1977	1982	N
WEST SOUTH CENTRAL	7.84	3.58	0.91	81
Dallas	4.99	5.77	1.64	23
Houston	14.10	3.53	1.06	28
New Orleans	1.17	0.86	0.43	3
Oklahoma	1.64	1.13	0.15	13
San Antonio	1.08	1.09	0.23	7
Tulsa	4.92	4.80	0.51	7
MOUNTAIN	3.44	2.97	1.27	25
Denver	1.98	1.62	1.27	7
Phoenix	3.13	2.78	1.74	6
Salt Lake	5.03	3.87	1.11	12
PACIFIC	3.91	4.22	1.94	125
Anaheim	3.87	3.04	1.58	17
Los Angeles	4.37	5.34	2.72	53
Portland	9.83	7.93	2.00	7
San Francisco	2.30	3.05	2.03	26
Seattle	2.12	2.59	0.70	18
Tacoma	5.37	2.77	1.04	4
All suburbs	12.94	6.29	2.22	952

INDIVIDUAL COMMUNITIES AND THE DISTRIBUTION OF ECONOMIC GROWTH

Competition between communities for economic development takes place in a market with at least two levels. At one level, local economic development can be viewed as driven by the constant "restructuring" of the national and international market (see, for example, Norton and Rees 1979; MacKenzie 1979; Kasarda 1980; Rees 1979; Yago et al. 1984). From this perspective, the economic fate of communities is largely beyond their individual control: the economic fate of regions is determined by large-scale macroeconomic forces. Regions move up or down depending on the demand for the resources they control and the changing demand for the goods and services they produce. Communities in any region are pulled up or dragged down along with their neighbors. The oil based economies of Texas communities did well during the 1970s because of energy shortages induced by OPEC. These same local economies lag now because of the weakness of the OPEC cartel and declining energy prices, and not because of any changes in local policies.

Despite the importance of extralocal forces, the desire to gain the benefits of economic growth forces localities into the market for economic growth. Local officials emphasize the importance of policies designed to maximize the attractiveness of their individual communities to desirable business firms. Politicians and bureaucrats design and promote programs to lure business and to create jobs. They then seek credit for the decisions of business firms, even if the decisions were driven by market considerations and the demand for local resources rather than by the policies of the local government. Such behavior in effect emphasizes a "lower level" market in which each locality represents a particular (and, by implication, controllable) combination of factors defining its attractiveness to mobile economic resources and affecting its rate of economic growth.

In this local market, the effects of several types of community factors on business location have been subject to previous analysis. The factors most widely studied include tax rates, public service levels, market demand characteristics, and locational factors such as density and agglomeration effects. These conditions vary in the degree to which they have been found empirically related to economic development and in the degree to which they can be manipulated by local government.

Local Fiscal Policies and the Location of Firms   Because they are the most visible local government policies, the effects of local taxes and expenditures on business location have been widely investigated. However, there has been little consensus about the actual impact of these policies on the behavior of firms.

Early studies consistently failed to find significant effects of taxes on the location decisions of firms, and for a time the issue seemed dead (see the reviews by Oakland 1978, and, especially, Scott 1982). More recent studies reopened the question. This research suggested that the effects of local tax policies varied by sector and that local taxes have more impact on the location of manufacturing firms, whose products must compete in a larger market, than on firms in other sectors, such as retail, more tied to limited local markets (see Fox 1981; Wasylenko 1980, 1981; Charney 1983; Schneider 1985). According to this argument, the failure of previous work to find an effect of local taxes resulted from methodological errors, most notably the failure to investigate economic sectors separately.

The role of local expenditures on the location decisions of firms has also been widely studied. Original expectations were that expenditures on business related services would attract economic growth, while social welfare expenditures would slow growth. This argument is, of course, central to Peterson's work (1981; see Hansen 1965; Holland 1975; also Wasylenko 1980, 1981; Fox 1981; Moriarity 1980). While the link between local expenditures and economic growth has been widely accepted as theoretically sound, empirical research results based on both econometric models and survey data have, in general, not confirmed an empirical relationship between expenditures and local economic growth (Schmenner 1982; Wasylenko 1980; Fox 1981; Scott 1982; Humberger 1983; Schneider 1985, 1986).

These waters have been muddied even further by the analysis of the links between local expenditures and economic growth undertaken by "critical" analysts, such as Smith (1984), Fainstein et al. (1984), Saunders (1981), O'Connor (1973), and Friedland (1983). Providing the foundations for the recent analysis of the politics of no-growth, these critics argue that local government expenditures that encourage business simply represent subsidies to private capital and, in the long run, can adversely affect a community.

Clearly, the politics and efficacy of local taxes and budgets have attracted considerable attention and have ignited debates conducted on both theoretical and empirical grounds. The theoretical debates focus on tax and expenditure policies, but other community fiscal characteristics which have been less studied in this literature also affect economic growth. For example, businesses might be sensitive to local fiscal conditions, such as high debt levels or high reliance on intergovernmental transfer payments, which may increase uncertainty about future taxes and service levels.

The Local Market for Private Goods   Local communities present locational advantages and disadvantages to firms in addition to the set of public goods and services. They represent a bundle of demographic characteristics that define a local market for private goods. In assessing the effects of public policies on the decisions of business firms such conditions must be controlled.

Perhaps the most important factor is the income of the community: higher income communities represent a stronger market for retail goods and consumer services. Racial characteristics may also matter: a large black population can depress the local market because blacks generally have lower incomes than whites. In addition, black suburbs are usually less prestigious than white ones and consumer-oriented firms may avoid them, fearing that the wrong address will discourage shoppers.

The desirability of a local market can also be affected by certain physical characteristics. As is evident in table 33, growth of the local market will be affected by trends in the regional economy. In addition, specific locational characteristics of individual communities can potentially affect growth. For example, a suburb's distance from its central city may help determine attractiveness by influencing transportation costs and defining access to the larger markets represented by central cities and by large inner suburbs.

Local density can affect economic growth in two ways. First, communities with higher population density may have less land available and at higher cost. But balancing this, communities with higher population density may represent a more compact market where there are more potential customers.

Finally, the locational behavior of firms may be affected by agglomeration factors reflected in the number and type of other firms in a community (Scott 1982; Moses and Williamson 1967; Czamanski and Czamanski 1977). For example, wholesale and manufacturing firms may need to locate near one another. Conversely, the community characteristics that appeal to manufacturing firms—large roads, good accessibility to highways, and so on—may be characteristics that make a community undesirable to upper-income residents and the retail and service firms that cater to them.

To assess the effects of individual community factors, especially local budgetary policies, on the growth of employment in the service sector and the manufacturing sector,[3] I follow the procedures I used in earlier chapters, treating the sample of suburban municipalities as a panel with community factors measured at one or two points in time and indicators of the size of the specific sector measured at three points of time.

I began with the following equation, which is estimated separately for the manufacturing and service sectors:

(8) $\text{Employment}_{i,t} = f(\text{Employment}_{i,t-1}$

$+ \text{Demographic Factors}_{i,t-1}$

$+ \text{Expenditures}_{i,t-1}$

$+ \text{THFiscal Factors}_{i,t-1}$

$+ \text{Intergovernmental Factors}_{i,t-1}$

$+ \text{Agglomeration Effects}_{i,t-1}$

$+ \text{SMSA}_i).$

Where:

Employment i,t = the number of manufacturing or service employees in community i in 1977 and 1982. Similarly, Employment $(i,t-1)$ is the number of manufacturing or service employees in community i at time $t-1$.

Demographic Factors = the set of demographic characteristics for community *i* used throughout this book, including size of population, percent population black, percent renter, median income, density, distance, and population growth.

Expenditures = local per capita outlays for developmental, allocational, and redistributive services.

Fiscal Factors = local true value per capita and the local tax bill. Debt per capita is also included here, since business firms may be sensitive to the fiscal security of a local community.

Intergovernmental Factors = total federal and state aid per capita, since these payments can affect local costs for public goods and services.

Agglomeration Effects = the number of workers in the three sectors of the local economy not measured in the dependent variable: for the service sector equation—retail, wholesale and manufacturing workers; for the manufacturing equation—retail, wholesale, and service workers.

SMSA = a set of dummy variables representing community location in a specific SMSA.

Employment data are from the various censuses of business conducted in 1972, 1977, and 1982. I excluded from analysis those suburbs for which the census does not report information because of confidentiality problems related to a small number of jobs or firms. This restriction means that the municipalities studied are participants in the "supply side" of the market for jobs, avoiding the criticism of the sample used in some previous work (Wasylenko 1980, 1981).

As in previous chapters, to increase the efficiency of the estimates of the effects of community factors on economic growth, I wanted to pool the two panels. After appropriate tests, I pooled observations from the two time periods, adding a time variable (time = 1 for 1977–1982 observations, 0 otherwise). I also used the set of SMSA dummy variables to ameliorate problems in the error terms.

After pooling, omitting the subscript *i*, and noting that the equations were run separately for each of the two indicators of employment, I had the following "full model":

(9) $EMP_t = \alpha + \beta EMP_{t-1} + \beta X_{72} + \beta X_{77} + \beta SMSA + \beta Time + Error$

where X represents the vector of community indicators previously described and EMP represents either the number of manufacturing or the number of service jobs in a community, estimated in separate equations. After imposing restrictions to force the slopes of each variable in the X vector to be equal across time, and using the Chow test, I found that the effect of each independent variable on change between 1972 and 1977 was not statistically different from its effect on change between 1977 and 1982. This yielded the final restricted model:

$$(10) \quad EMP_t = \alpha + \beta EMP_{t-1} + \beta X + \beta SMSA + \beta Time + Error$$

This final model is used to investigate directly the effects of local fiscal and budgetary policies on economic development. I turn first to the analysis of change in manufacturing employment, then to change in service employment.

RESULTS

Change in Manufacturing Employment

The ability of communities to attract manufacturing jobs is limited. Changing regional patterns in the distribution of manufacturing jobs are one source of limits. Regional location explains about 13 percent of the variance in the number of manufacturing jobs in suburbs. But more important, the distribution of manufacturing employment is highly stable. When the number of manufacturing jobs in a community lagged five years is added to regional location, the variance explained jumps to 89 percent. Indeed, stability across the entire ten-year period is almost as high as estimated when using five-year intervals. For example, regressing the number of manufacturing jobs in a community in 1982 against the number in 1972 (and adding region), the explained variance is 80 percent. The coefficients on the time dummy variables show time effects are also important: less growth took between 1977 and 1982 than in the earlier five year period. (See table 34.)

TABLE 34

Change in Number of Manufacturing Jobs as a Function of Local Conditions and Previous Number of Jobs, Controlling for SMSA, Pooled Analysis, 1972–1977 and 1977–1982

Variable	B	SE B	Beta	T-Test
LAGGED VALUE				
Man. jobs$_{(t-1)}$	0.84	0.01	.853	64.99
DEMOGRAPHIC FACTORS				
Median income	−0.01	0.01	−.015	−0.95
Rent (%)	267.92	371.29	.007	0.72
Black (%)	−145.03	471.13	−.007	−0.30

Continued on next page

TABLE 34—*Continued*

Variable	B	SE B	Beta	T-Test
Population	0.01	0.00	.076	3.75
Population growth	69.75	99.23	.001	0.70
Distance	6.09	6.25	.012	0.97
Density	−0.27	0.14	−.029	−1.88
PER CAPITA EXPENDITURES				
Developmental	4.19	3.20	.012	1.30
Allocational	−5.01	3.47	−.014	−1.44
Redistributive	−1.19	2.62	−.008	−0.45
FISCAL FACTORS				
Debt	0.37	0.27	.019	1.36
True value	59.74	11.35	.078	5.26
Tax bill	−141.67	46.28	−.041	−3.06
INTERGOVERNMENTAL FACTORS				
Federal aid	−2.55	2.37	−.013	−1.07
State aid	2.33	1.58	.019	1.46
EMPLOYMENT IN OTHER SECTORS				
Service	−0.02	0.04	−.003	−0.51
Retail	0.01	0.04	.006	0.31
Wholesale	0.14	0.06	.035	2.21
TIME				
1977 dummy	−186.56	88.31	−.021	−2.11
Constant	−177.10	344.63		−0.51
Adjusted R square, SMSA dummies,			.13	
Adjusted R square, + lagged manufacturing employment,			.88	
Adjusted R square, + local characteristics,			.89	

NOTE: Number of cases in pooled sample = 1722.

These empirical results show that the policy space of local govern-ments is clearly limited by stability in the distribution of jobs and by both secular and regional trends. But there is still a marginal impact of local conditions on change in employment. For example, growth in manufacturing employment is faster in less dense communities, where more land is available. Larger communities also experience more rapid expansion in manufacturing jobs, perhaps because of the availability of labor. But community population growth is not associated with faster job expansion in manufacturing. Finally, growth in manufacturing employment is marginally faster in communities with a relatively larger concentration of wholesale workers.

Central to my investigation are the effects of fiscal variables. The tax

bill indeed matters: communities with higher tax bills experience marginally slower growth in the number of manufacturing jobs. This is
consistent with the idea that manufacturing firms must sell their products in competitive markets and must be sensitive to the relative costs of
inputs into their production process.

Note too that manufacturing jobs are attracted to communities with
a stronger fiscal base. In contrast, the number of manufacturing jobs
does not respond to the local income of community residents: there is
no relationship between median income of the community and change
in the number of manufacturing jobs—the wealth in which manufacturing firms are interested is tax base, not personal income.

There is no impact of local expenditures on the creation of jobs in
manufacturing. As predicted by Peterson, allocational expenditures do
not affect economic development in the manufacturing sector. But, contrary to Peterson, manufacturing jobs are not created in response to
greater investments in infrastructure; nor are they avoiding communities with higher expenditures on social services.[4]

Thus, there is some evidence that the creation of manufacturing jobs
is sensitive to fiscal conditions. Manufacturing firms create more jobs
in communities with lower tax bills and a stronger tax base. But the
creation of manufacturing jobs is not responsive to local expenditure
policies.

Changes in the Service Economy

Compared to stagnation in manufacturing employment, the service
sector in suburbia has experienced rapid growth. But even these jobs are
distributed across regions and communities in a stable manner. Regional patterns account for about 15 percent of the variance in the
distribution of service jobs. Adding the number of service jobs in a
community lagged five years increases the variance explained to almost
88 percent. Like the pattern for manufacturing, the value of service
employment lagged ten years, when combined with region, explains
fully 81 percent of the variance in 1982 service employment. Thus, even
in this dynamically expanding sector of the economy, local governments
face high stability, which imposes limits on the effects of local policies.
Note also the strong time effects: expansion of the service sector was
much faster in the second half of the decade than in the first half. Again,
macroeconomic factors clearly affect local economic growth.

Replicating the analysis of manufacturing employment, table 35
reports the results of a pooled regression analysis of change in service
jobs. One local condition stands out as the most strongly related to

growth in the service sector: the size of the retail sector (measured by employment) in a community five years earlier. There is a clear affinity between retail jobs and service jobs. Similarly, there is a positive, but much weaker, relationship between wholesale jobs and growth in the

TABLE 35

CHANGE IN NUMBER OF SERVICE JOBS AS A FUNCTION OF LOCAL CONDITIONS
AND PREVIOUS NUMBER OF JOBS, CONTROLLING FOR SMSA,
POOLED ANALYSIS, 1972–1977 AND 1977–1982

Variable	B	SE B	Beta	T-Test
LAGGED VALUE				
Service jobs$_{(t-1)}$	1.21	0.02	.755	54.36
DEMOGRAPHIC VARIABLES				
Median income	0.04	0.00	.066	5.17
Rent (%)	280.03	171.07	.014	1.63
Black (%)	−107.47	217.08	−.005	−0.49
Population	−0.00	0.00	−.043	−2.70
Pop. growth	133.96	45.72	.022	2.93
Distance	−0.94	2.88	−.007	−0.32
Density	−0.02	0.06	−.002	−0.41
PER CAPITA EXPENDITURES				
Developmental	0.86	1.47	.001	0.58
Allocational	0.80	1.60	.007	0.50
Redistributive	−0.26	1.20	−.004	−0.22
FISCAL FACTORS				
Debt	0.00	0.12	.009	0.04
True value	−17.01	5.23	−.048	−3.25
Tax bill	−49.38	21.32	−.035	−2.31
INTERGOVERNMENTAL FACTORS				
Federal aid	0.20	1.09	.004	0.18
State aid	−0.76	0.73	−.014	−1.03
EMPLOYMENT IN OTHER SECTORS				
Manufacturing	−0.01	0.00	−.034	−2.59
Retail	0.24	0.01	.222	12.67
Wholesale	0.17	0.03	.073	5.63
TIME				
1977 dummy	−437.97	40.69	−.090	−10.76
Constant	−477.02	158.79		−3.00
Adjusted R square, SMSA dummies only,		.14		
Adjusted R square, + lagged service employment,		.87		
Adjusted R square, + local characteristics,		.90		

service sector. Thus these three sectors of the economy seem to complement one another, and indeed, some analysts classify jobs in all three sectors as "service jobs" (for example, Noyelle and Stanback 1983). But note the negative coefficient on the manufacturing term: service-sector growth is repelled by a larger local manufacturing sector. Thus, communities cannot maximize growth across all economic sectors—choices may have to be made among them.

Tax considerations affect the growth of the service sector: higher taxes lead to slower job growth. But note that a stronger tax base does not attract service firms. In contrast, community median income is positively related to service growth. Service firms and manufacturing firms respond to different dimensions of community wealth when choosing to expand the number of jobs in a locality. Service firms want to be near a wealthier population, which is more likely to purchase their services, and service firms choose not to be near manufacturing firms.[5]

Turning finally to the effects of budgetary policy, no effects of allocational, redistributive, or developmental expenditures are found.

CONCLUSIONS

The fiscal and budgetary policies of suburban communities do not strongly influence the growth of local economies, at least as reflected in employment patterns.[6] In contrast, regional location clearly affects local economic development. Moreover, the process of creating local jobs is wide open to secular trends generated by changing macroeconomic conditions. Between 1972 and 1982, there was a clear decrease in the creation of manufacturing jobs and a rapid increase in service jobs. Suburbs were more strongly affected by such secular and regional trends than by any of the policies which they more directly control.

But even given these strict limits, some local actions do matter, for example, tax policies. On the margin, both manufacturing and service firms avoid creating jobs in jurisdictions with higher taxes. Given the difference in the size of the markets in which their products compete, it is not surprising that the relationship was much stronger in the manufacturing sector than in the service sector.

While taxes matter, local budgetary expenditures do not. In the competitive market for economic development, firms shop around for the package of goods and services that best suits their individual needs. No *single* combination of taxes and services dominates the location decisions of firms: rather than presenting a general budgetary package to businesses, local governments may have to enter into separate negotiations with different firms to fashion a package of goods and services the firm wants. In this light it is understandable why manufacturing firms locate in communities with a stronger tax base: it allows local governments more latitude to design attractive service/tax bundles. Thus the tax base becomes a crucial factor because it increases the policy options of local governments in their dealings with manufacturing firms.

The combination of relatively weak policy effects, high stability in the distribution of jobs, and strong "macromarket" effects severely restricts the policy options available to local governments in their attempts to attract economic development. The item most under their control—their budget—does not seem to be of interest to firms.[7] As a result, suburban city limits are severe and the desire of many actors in suburban municipal government to increase local wealth by using local policies to lure economic development may remain unrealized.

9

MAXIMIZING THE LOCAL TAX BASE

The desire for more services without higher local taxes or for the same services at lower taxes clearly motivates the behavior of key actors in communities. Because a stronger tax base improves the local service/tax ratio, the pursuit of tax base emerges as a core goal in local politics. Its importance traces directly to the uneven distribution of property wealth across communities and to the centrality of the property tax in the generation of local revenues: it accounts for over 75 percent of local tax collections and about half of total revenues (ACIR 1985: table 39).[1]

Inequalities in the distribution of the tax base directly affect the relationship between local tax rates and service levels and largely explain the unequal capacity of local governments to generate revenues.[2] With a strong property tax base, a community can support high local service levels without necessarily imposing high property taxes—a low rate applied to a large base can produce revenues sufficient to support quality services. Alternately, a community with a strong tax base can choose to offer fewer services, with even lower taxes. Thus, a strong property tax base allows a community wide latitude in framing attractive service/tax bundles. In contrast, given a weak property tax base, even high tax rates cannot yield high revenues.[3] Ultimately, the pursuit of local property wealth fuels the growth machine.

Fiscal zoning, economic development tools, and a host of other strategies are used to pursue tax base. Budgetary allocations have more recently become a focal point in the study of the politics of growth. According to Peterson (1981), municipal governments invariably emphasize expenditures on infrastructure because investments in this area are believed to lead to a stronger local property tax base.

However, as I demonstrated in previous chapters, cities are limited in their ability to attract wealth. The logic of Molotch's growth machine and of Peterson's model of local budgetary politics are process-oriented, not result-oriented: in these models, local governments are compelled to take certain actions, but these actions do not necessarily produce desired outcomes.

The limits explored in previous chapters are ultimately reflected in limits on the ability of local governments to maximize their tax base. For example, the local property tax base is clearly affected by the income of the families within its borders. A local government can undertake policies to increase the likelihood that wealthy families will choose to live in that community, but as shown in chapter 7, the extent to which local policies actually affect the level of community wealth is limited.

Similarly, actions designed to attract business firms to boost the local tax base have only a limited relationship to rates of business formation and local job creation. While some firms may respond, on the margin, to local budgetary policies, many more are influenced by national and international economic trends (which are beyond the control of local governments), by the demographic conditions of a local community (which are themselves highly stable), and by regional economic trends. Thus despite the ardent desire of most suburbs for economic development, the tools at their disposal are of limited effectiveness.

The incentives of the local market for public goods and the policy tools to achieve these goals are therefore not congruent. In the polycentric market, because variation in the local property base directly affects the costs of local services and the fiscal well-being of local residents, competition forces local governments to invest in services they hope will maximize local property wealth. However, given the severe limits on the effectiveness of suburban municipal policies, there is a considerable disjuncture between what suburbs hope they are "buying" with their budgetary investments and what they actually get. In this chapter, I specifically investigate the relationship between the tax/expenditure bundles of suburban municipalities and the development of local property tax base, assessing the efficacy of local government fiscal policies in attracting property wealth.

METHODS

To test directly the effects of local service/tax bundles on the size of the local property base, I measure the size of the local property tax base as true value per capita in 1972, 1977, and 1982 and analyze the effects of local service bundles on change in true value, controlling for other community conditions. Paralleling the analysis of community income reported in chapter 7, this analysis is undertaken both for absolute levels of the local property tax base and then in terms of community property wealth relative to other communities in its regions. Paralleling the methods of earlier chapters, I pool observations over time.

I begin with the following lagged endogenous variable equation:

(11) True Value per Capita$_{i,t}$ = f(True Value per Capita$_{i,t-1}$
+ Demographic Factors$_{i,t-1}$
+ Economic Composition$_{i,t-1}$
+ Expenditures$_{i,t-1}$
+ Fiscal Factors$_{i,t-1}$
+ Intergovernmental Factors$_{i,t-1}$
+ SMSA).

I also estimated a second equation in which the variables of equation 11 are transformed into Z-scores based on SMSA means and standard deviations. In both equations, all dollar measures are standardized by the CPI. As in earlier chapters, I interpret these equations as the analysis of the effects of the independent variables, measuring community conditions at time t-1, on change in the dependent variable.[4]

Thus, equation 11 assesses the causes of change in the absolute value of local true value per capita. The parallel equation using Z-scores is an analysis of positional change—it analyzes how a community has changed its standing relative to neighboring communities in its region. Z-scores control further the effects of many of the exogenous variables over which local governments have no control—the analysis using Z-scores more fully focuses on how local governments can affect their tax base within the overall limits of economic and regional change.

The variables used in this analysis have all appeared in earlier chapters. Briefly, they are:

True Value per Capita (i,t) = the true value per capita of each municipality in the sample in 1977 and 1982.[5]

True Value per Capita (i,t-1) = true value per capita of each suburb lagged five years.

Demographic Factors (i,t-1) = a set of community characteristics including: percent black 1972 and 1977; percent renters 1972, 1977; median income 1972, 1977; population growth; distance; and density.

Economic Composition (i,t-1) = indicators of the make-up of the local economy, including the number of firms and the relative number of workers in the wholesale, retail, service and manufacturing sectors. These data come from the various censuses of business in 1972 and 1977.[6]

Expenditures (i,t-1) = a vector of indicators of the service bundle offered by the local community, including per capita expenditures on developmental, allocational, and redistributive services. In addition, I employ several other indicators of local fiscal policies which might also affect the locational choices of fiscally desirable resources.

First, I measure each municipality's construction expenditures per capita. Higher investment in the construction of public facilities may parallel the hypothesized effects of operating expenditures for infrastructure services—that is, capital investments may indicate the development of facilities for more efficient economic activity and hence encourage the accumulation of the local property tax base.

Construction expenditures directly affect outstanding long-term debt per capita. Local debt is highly correlated with construction expenditures, so it may share a positive impact on the accumulation of local wealth. However, higher debt may also imply a higher percentage of expenditure devoted to debt service that could detract from the support of other services. Higher debt may also imply future fiscal problems potentially deterring the location of mobile resources.

Fiscal Factors $(i, t\text{-}1)$ = the effective tax bill in each community in 1972 and 1977. These tax data are from the same source as the true value data.[7] Also included here is long term debt per capita, the effects of which were discussed above.

Intergovernmental Factors = the total level of state and federal transfer payments per capita received by local governments.

SMSA = a set of dummy variables representing the specific SMSAs in which communities are located.

In the positional analysis, all variables have been standardized using regional means and standard deviations. The SMSA dummy variables are not included in that equation, since regional effects are canceled by the standardization procedure.

As in other chapters, in order to increase the efficiency of the estimates of the effects of community factors on growth of local property wealth, I wanted to pool the two panels. I ran each equation separately for 1972–1977 and for 1977–1982. After appropriate tests, observations from the two time periods were pooled and a time variable added (time = 1 for 1972–1977 observations, 0 otherwise).[8] After appropriate tests for the stability of slopes over time, omitting the subscript i I had the final model:

(12) $\text{TVCAP}_t = \alpha + \beta\text{TVCAP}_{t-1} + \beta X_{t-1} + \beta\text{SMSA} + \beta\text{Time} + \text{Error}$

and for the standardized analysis:

(13) $\text{ZTVCAP}_t = \alpha + \beta\text{ZTVCAP}_{t-1} + \beta Z_{t-1} + \beta\text{Time} + \text{Error}$

where, in equation 12, X represents the vector of community characteristics described above and, in equation 13, Z represents the same
measures standardized by SMSA patterns.

RESULTS

Table 36 presents the results of the regression analysis using unstandardized variables. Not surprisingly, as with other sources of local wealth,
there is high stability in the distribution of tax base across communities
over time. Over 75 percent of the variance in true value per capita at
time t is explained by true value per capita at time t-1. Moreover, SMSA
location accounts for about 30 percent of the remaining variance in
changing true value over time.[9] Clearly, a community's geographical
location affects how well it fares in the competition for new wealth.
Finally, note the time dummy has a statistically significant effect on the
change in true value. Between 1972 and 1977, local property tax base
grew faster across the nation than between 1977 and 1982. Again the
size of this coefficient reflects secular trends in the face of which local
governments are relatively powerless.

Among local community demographic characteristics, growth in the
property tax base is associated with a wealthier population. In contrast,
there is no relationship between a community's concentration of blacks
and change in the tax base. But tax base did increase faster in communities which were less densely settled.

Several economic conditions affected the rate at which the property
tax base accumulated. The relative size of the work force in the retail
sector is associated with a faster increase in property wealth; in contrast,
the number of retail firms is negatively associated with increase in the
tax base. This may indicate that communities housing shopping malls
with large department stores are faring better than communities with
"strip" development of small retail operations. A similar pattern obtains
for the wholesale sector, although the negative relationship between the
number of wholesale firms and tax base is not significant. Somewhat
surprisingly, the size of the manufacturing sector is not significantly
related to change in property wealth.

After controlling for these conditions, fiscal policies have a statistically significant impact on the rate of change in the local tax base.
Developmental expenditures further the growth of the local property tax
base. Note too that higher tax bills are associated with a slower accumulation of tax base (with the appropriate one-tailed t-test, the negative relationship is significant at the .03 level).

Contrary to Peterson, there is no relationship between redistributive expenditures and change in true value. But note that, consistent with Peterson, allocational expenditures have no effect on growth in the local tax base. Higher debt levels are marginally associated with faster growth of local property tax base, although, somewhat surprisingly capital investments do not share this positive role.[10]

TABLE 36
CHANGE IN SUBURBAN MUNICIPAL TRUE VALUE PER CAPITA AS A FUNCTION OF
LOCAL CONDITIONS AND PREVIOUS TRUE VALUE, POOLED ANALYSIS,
1972–1977 AND 1977–1982

Variable	B	SE B	Beta	T-Test
LAGGED VALUE				
True value$_{(t-1)}$	0.67	0.02	.654	29.21
DEMOGRAPHIC FACTORS				
Median income	1.43[a]	2.91[b]	.091	4.92
Rent (%)	−0.20	0.67	−.005	−0.30
Black (%)	−0.29	0.81	−.005	−0.36
Population	0.23	0.46	.004	0.49
Population growth	−0.63	0.17	−.054	−3.66
Distance	0.00	0.01	.004	0.32
Density	−6.65[a]	2.61[a]	−.042	−2.54
ECONOMIC COMPOSITION				
Workers/1000 Population				
Manufacturing	−0.37	0.52	−.012	−0.72
Service	1.87	2.27	.015	0.82
Retail	2.62	1.33	.028	1.96
Wholesale	4.34	2.27	.040	1.90
NUMBER OF ESTABLISHMENTS				
Manufacturing	0.00	0.00	.037	1.74
Service	0.00	0.00	.060	2.11
Retail	−0.00	8.39[a]	−.073	−2.49
Wholesale	−0.00	0.00	−.022	−0.94
PER CAPITA EXPENDITURES				
Developmental	0.02	0.00	.080	5.15
Allocational	0.00	0.00	.015	0.87
Redistributive	−0.00	0.00	−.007	−0.57
Construction	0.00	0.00	.013	0.75

Continued on next page

TABLE 36—*Continued*

Variable	B	SE B	Beta	T-Test
FISCAL FACTORS				
Debt	9.86[a]	5.04[a]	.029	1.95
Tax bill	−0.15	0.08	−.032	−1.82
INTERGOVERNMENTAL FACTORS				
Federal aid	−0.00	0.00	−.013	−0.89
State aid	−0.00	0.00	−.051	−2.88
TIME				
1972 dummy	1.58	0.15	.137	10.08
Constant	−3.36	0.59		−5.67
Adjusted R square, SMSA dummies,	.303			
Adjusted R square, full model,	.784			

NOTES: Number of cases in pooled sample = 1678.
a. Coefficient multiplied by 10**4.
b. Coefficient multiplied by 10**5.

Positional Change

Table 37 reports the analysis of positional change. Recall that the SMSA dummy variables are not included in this analysis since regional effects are partialled out by the standardization procedure. Recall, too, that all variables in the equation are standardized, so that the unstandardized "B" regression coefficients and the standardized beta coefficients are identical.

Paralleling the results of table 36, high stability in the relative ranking of communities is evident—in the final equation, the regression coefficient for the lagged variable is .51 and fully 62 percent of the variance of regional position at time t is explained by position at time t-1.

Paralleling the unstandardized results, some demographic variables affect the relative position of communities. Increases in relative position are associated with higher median income and with a "whiter" population living in a less densely settled community.

Controlling for demographic and economic conditions, there is again evidence of rational benefit/cost considerations in the location of the resources that increase relative tax base. Suburbs with higher tax bills lose position over time. In contrast, higher relative investments in infrastructure are associated with a marginal increase in position. But, despite Peterson's argument that allocation expenditures should be neutral with regard to the accumulation of wealth, higher relative allocational expenditures are more strongly associated with gain in position than relative infrastructure investments. Finally, in neither the positional nor the unstandardized equations is there a negative effect of redistributive expenditures—in fact, redistributive expenditures are not related at all to change in true value. Paralleling the earlier results, debt is positively associated with increases in property wealth, but intergovernmental aid has a negative association with such increases.

TABLE 37
CHANGE IN TRUE VALUE PER CAPITA AS A FUNCTION OF LOCAL CONDITIONS
AND PREVIOUS TRUE VALUE, POOLED ANALYSIS, 1972–1977 AND 1977–1982, Z SCORES

Variable	B	SE B	T-Test
LAGGED VALUE			
Std. true value$_{(t-1)}$	.514	0.022	23.16
EMOGRAPHIC FACTORS			
Std. median income	.244	0.019	12.43
Std. rent (%)	.020	0.017	1.16
Std. black (%)	−.029	0.014	−2.01
Std. population	−.008	0.019	−0.42
Std. population growth	−.058	0.015	−3.69
Std. distance	.003	0.016	0.23
Std. density	−.100	0.017	−5.61
ECONOMIC COMPOSITION			
Workers/1000 population			
Std. manufacturing	.075	0.019	3.83
Std. service	.138	0.020	6.72
Std. retail	.008	0.016	0.50
Std. wholesale	.001	0.018	0.08
NUMBER OF ESTABLISHMENTS			
Std. manufacturing	.013	0.021	0.62
Std. service	−.072	0.032	−2.21
Std. retail	−.004	0.030	−0.14
Std. wholesale	.054	0.028	1.91
PER CAPITA EXPENDITURES			
Std. developmental	.031	0.015	2.01
Std. allocational	.031	0.015	2.03
Std. redistributive	−.001	0.013	−0.10
Std. construction	.014	0.014	0.96
FISCAL FACTORS			
Std. debt	.027	0.014	1.82
Std. tax bill	−.050	0.024	−2.29

Continued on next page

TABLE 37—*Continued*

Variable	B	SE B	T-Test
INTERGOVERNMENTAL FACTORS			
Std. federal aid	−.025	0.013	−1.85
Std. state aid	−.030	0.014	−2.08
TIME			
1972 dummy	.038	0.026	1.46
Adjusted R square, full model, .697			

NOTES: Number of cases in pooled sample = 1678.

CONCLUSIONS

In the polycentric system of metropolitan government in the United States, wealth is unequally distributed across municipalities. Given the role local governments play in providing and funding many public goods, service quality and tax costs are directly affected by the unequal distribution of property wealth. Given present institutional arrangements, actors in local governments rationally want to maximize the local tax base. While fiscal zoning is the "traditional" strategic tool for achieving this, recent attention has focused on the role of budgetary and fiscal policies.

Suburban municipalities face severe limits on the efficacy of their fiscal and expenditure policies in the competition for tax base. But within these limits, local budgets marginally affect both the rate at which property wealth accumulates and the position of suburbs relative to their neighbors.

As expected, growth in local property wealth is inversely related to the local tax bill. Further, higher expenditures on infrastructure, both in absolute terms and relative to the expenditures of neighboring communities, encourage more rapid growth in the local property tax base. These findings are consistent with a model of competition for fiscally productive resources driven, on the margin, by benefit/cost considerations.

However, redistributive social expenditures do not deter the accumulation of local property wealth; but this may be because such expenditures represent only a small share of suburban municipal budgets. Also not congruent with Peterson's version of the competitive model, the relative tax base of suburbs is sensitive to the support of local "housekeeping" functions. This may indicate that Peterson's model does not fit into the suburban context where local governments provide only relatively low redistributive expenditures and where there may be substantial variation across neighboring communities in the level and quality of their housekeeping functions.

"Critical analysts" of local expenditure policies, including O'Connor (1973), Friedland (1983), Smith (1984) and Fainstein et al. (1984), argue that investments in infrastructure and other local public investment tools designed to attract mobile economic resources are often not productive for communities, since the costs of such investments often exceed the benefits to the community. Other analysts, such as Peterson and Holland (1975), argue that, to the contrary, these investments are in the city's interests since they increase local property wealth, with positive spillovers to all community residents. This disagreement has been central to the recent study of local budgetary politics and even more central to the study of community growth politics.

The evidence developed in the last several chapters shows that local fiscal policies can affect the accumulation of local wealth—but the impact is, at best, marginal. The location of businesses, wealthy families, and tax base are all part of a highly stable distribution of wealth that changes only slowly. The institutional arrangements of the local government system are also highly stable. Attempts radically to restructure the service delivery role of local governments have been noted mostly for their failure. Given this stability, wealthy suburbs remain wealthy, poor communities remain poor, and their services remain unequal. Exogenous factors, such as macroeconomic conditions, the shared fate of communities in a region, and strong demographic and ecological forces, all limit the ability of local policies to affect the distribution of wealth.

Within the limits of the existing system, communities that manipulate their fiscal policies to offer a better benefit/cost ratio to mobile, fiscally productive resources can marginally increase their local wealth.[11] Some firms do respond to local service levels and tax bills; wealthy families do shop around for a good tax base. These factors all marginally affect the distribution of local wealth. There are probably enough pay-offs to local communities and local actors to keep most of them aggressively pursuing growth and development. Indeed, given the incentives of the system, they cannot easily do otherwise.

But in fact the stability of the distribution of wealth in the local market for public goods is overwhelming. If we emphasize this stability, local government policies designed to increase community wealth must be viewed as ineffective—systemic constraints and inertia overwhelm any marginal impact they may have. From this standpoint, local fiscal and budgetary policies do not much improve a community's welfare.

And these investments may represent an unwarranted subsidy to business and the wealthy as local governments compete with one another to attract them.

The specific "city limits" Peterson identified constrain the behavior of suburbs as much as they constrain the behavior of the central cities with which he was most directly concerned. But there are city limits additional to those identified by Peterson. In his analysis, cities are limited in that the structure of the local market for public goods forces them to undertake certain kinds of expenditures and ignore others. But suburban municipalities are already doing exactly what Peterson suggests local government must do. They invest in developmental and allocational expenditures rather than redistributive services. But even while pursuing this strategy, suburbs face other limits on the degree of success their budgetary and fiscal policies can achieve: both local policy tools and local policy successes are limited.

10

INTERGOVERNMENTAL AID
AS A LOCAL RESOURCE

In the previous chapters, I examined the distribution of community income and economic development, factors which affect the local tax base and help define the relationship between local public goods and local tax costs. In this chapter, I analyze another resource which affects the relationship between local services and taxes, by augmenting local revenues and shifting the cost of services outside the community.

Monetary transfers between different levels of government are fundamental to the practice of federalism in the United States and affect local policies and consumption patterns. By decreasing the local costs of subsidized services relative to the costs of nonsubsidized ones, transfer payments induce local governments to buy more of a subsidized good than they would otherwise. This effect is inherent to a federal system: higher level governments often give aid to local governments for the express purpose of changing local practices to make them more in tune with national priorities.

However, the way in which intergovernmental grants have been delivered during the most recent period of fiscal federalism has caused many behavioral and policy changes which are more problematic than a simple theory of federalism would predict. Changes in the level and type of intergovernmental aid has affected the value local actors assign to aid and the enthusiasm with which they pursue it.

In the American system of federalism, local-state relations are much more developed, long-standing, and stable than is the relationship which has developed between the federal government and local governments. State aid has historically represented a larger share of local budgets than federal aid and, more important, has been a more stable addition to local revenues. Many studies have found that local governments are relatively secure in the continued flow of these monies and are likely to rely on state aid to fund on-going policies and activities.

In comparison, the flow of federal monies has been erratic. Since the mid 1950s, federal aid has grown to represent a significant component of local revenues. But there have been wide swings in the amount of federal aid available, in the form in which it is made available, and the purposes for which it can be spent (Wright 1982; and Walker 1980, present excellent summaries of these trends; also see Bowman 1981).

Consequently, local governments are often uncertain about federal aid and they are reluctant to treat federal grants as secure revenue. Instead, these grants are often spent on "big ticket" items, such as large scale construction projects or expensive equipment, which will not disappear with changes in the flow of aid (Nathan et al. 1982; Schneider 1986c). While it is a reasonable local strategy to minimize budgetary disruptions caused by an irregular flow of federal dollars, this defensive practice can severely distort local budgeting and policy priorities.

Lessons learned by local governments in the most recent era of fiscal federalism likely insure that they will continue to be suspicious of federal aid. During the early and mid 1970s, after almost two decades of caution, federal aid flowed so freely into local coffers that many cities began to treat it as a permanent addition to their revenues, incorporating transfer payments into their ongoing operating budgets. Most dangerously, local governments began to hire new staff, expecting to cover relatively permanent (and expensive) personnel costs with free-flowing federal intergovernmental dollars (Stein 1984).

Ironically, just as many local governments began to overcome their suspicion of aid, the federal government, facing its own growing fiscal problems and succumbing to a new conservative ideology of small government, began sharply to reduce intergovernmental transfers. These reductions, beginning in 1978 and continuing ever since, produced painful consequences for many local governments (Ellwood 1982; Stein 1984). The basic lesson was simple: relying on intergovernmental aid, particularly from the federal government, can be dangerous to local fiscal health.

Despite these problems, intergovernmental funds allow a local government to offer services without raising local taxes. Given the incentive structures of the actors in the system of local government, intergovernmental aid remains a tempting source of income. To explore the flow of aid and some of the attendant issues in more detail, I review the benefits and costs of intergovernmental aid to local actors. I then review recent historical patterns of intergovernmental aid, and look in detail at the flow of aid to suburban municipalities.

THE FLOW OF BENEFITS FROM INTERGOVERNMENTAL AID

Local Public Sector Actors and Intergovernmental Aid

Intergovernmental aid is appealing because it allows communities to offer goods and services at a discount. However, as I demonstrated in chapter 6, the benefits disproportionately accrue to public-sector actors, by leading to "extra" large increases in public-sector agency budgets, the size of the local public work force, and public wages. The size of these benefits is dependent on the political organization and the arrangement of the service delivery mechanisms in a region. It is also dependent on whether aid is in the form of categorical grants or less restricted revenue sharing grants.[1]

Both project and revenue sharing grants raise local income and stimulate public purchases—an "income effect." But by reducing the local price of the projects or services, project grants stimulate public purchases even more. This "price effect" of categorical intergovernmental aid is above and beyond the income effect (Chubb 1985). Furthermore, project grants often have maintenance-of-effort provisions, preventing local governments from using the money to lower taxes or reduce the size of local contributions to services. Categorical aid clearly stimulates the local public sector.

Revenue sharing grants are less restricted and do not subsidize the local price of specific services. Theoretically, they should have only income effects, and be allocated between public and private goods in a manner virtually identical to an increase in private income (Chubb 1985; Gramlich 1977; Inman 1979). However, we know that unrestricted grants are *not* returned to local citizens at the predicted rate. Instead, because of the "flypaper effect," even revenue sharing grants are disproportionately retained by local government agencies.

Given the benefits they receive, bureaucrats provide a strong constituency for the pursuit of intergovernmental money.

Politicians To the extent that intergovernmental aid increases the level of local services without increasing local taxes, politicians benefit from its receipt. Moreover, given that intergovernmental aid is disproportionately retained in the public sector, it can allow local politicians to gain the support of bureaucrats and public-sector workers in the community by providing larger budgets, new equipment, travel, and other perks. In turn, public-sector workers represent a major voting block which can reward politicians at reelection time (Courant et al. 1979b; Frey and Pommerehne 1982; Spizman 1980).

Politicians also benefit if the capital projects supported by intergovernmental aid attract business growth and increase the profitability of existing firms. The resulting economic development benefits politicians by diversifying the local tax base and relieving pressure on residential taxes.

While these benefits make intergovernmental aid attractive to local politicians, there are attendant risks, many stemming from the irregular and unpredictable flow of funds. Intergovernmental aid is subject to the slowness of both legislative decision processes and administrative red tape, and it often arrives later than anticipated. In turn, budgeting around intergovernmental aid can be risky: politicians must establish their budgets with uncertain commitments from a major revenue source. This uncertainty is bad enough when intergovernmental aid is expanding; but cutbacks in aid can force politicians into the much more uncomfortable position of reneging on promised expansion of services, reducing present services, or firing workers who were subsidized by intergovernmental money (Stein 1984; McInturff 1980; Fitzgerald 1979; Kim 1982; Schneider 1986c).

Local politicians also resent intergovernmental interference in community decision making. Surveys commonly find that local political leaders believe the restrictions on the use of intergovernmental aid are confusing and that they distort local policies. As a result, they often discount the net benefits of intergovernmental aid (ACIR 1984: 187).

Intergovernmental aid is thus a mixed blessing for local politicians, who reap maximum benefits from a secure and guaranteed flow of unrestricted grants. In the present system of fiscal federalism, this translates into a preference for revenue sharing grants over project grants and a preference for stable intergovernmental commitments over fluctuating ones. But the flow of aid has not often matched these preferences.

Local Residents   Within limits, residents will favor intergovernmental aid for their community. Specifically, it is rational to support the pursuit of aid which reduces the cost of a service the resident would choose to have even without the intergovernmental subsidy. For example, if a resident is willing to spend $10 of income on a service, any intergovernmental transfer that reduces the cost below $10 would be welcome.

However, if intergovernmental grants force a local government to deliver services a resident does not want, the decision calculus is more difficult. When a higher level of government provides extensive funding for a service, minimizing the local contribution, resistance should be low; a program entirely paid for by a higher government may even be considered free. Yet truly free programs are rare, and most intergovernmental grants require the use of some local funds. The local resident must then decide whether or not the subsidized "bargain price" for a service he or she may not really desire is attractive enough to support.

Of the types of intergovernmental grants available, residents, like their local political representatives, should prefer revenue sharing grants to project grants, because they are more likely to be spent on programs wanted by the local population. This preference is reflected in action: many suburbs, particularly affluent ones, which did not participate in categorical aid programs, took advantage of the General Revenue Sharing program adopted in the early 1970s. While categorical programs supported projects of little or no interest to many suburbs (even at a bargain basement price), revenue sharing grants were used to upgrade recreational facilities and other amenities, or to provide tax relief, making these grants attractive to local residents of virtually every community, even the most affluent.

Businesses Intergovernmental aid will also be of interest to local business firms. When transfer payments support better services without raising local taxes, they represent a potential boost to profitability. If they pay for infrastructure, providing sewers, water mains, or utilities, local businesses may especially benefit. However, if intergovernmental aid forces local governments to expand their support of social services at the expense of infrastructure, the local business community can suffer.

Since intergovernmental aid is not a reliable source of income, business leaders should prefer secure revenue sharing grants or intergovernmental aid spent on capital projects that outlast intergovernmental grant cycles.

Intergovernmental aid is a significant source of revenues which can improve the local service/tax ratio. It thus appeals to local actors. But benefits flowing from aid vary across actors depending on the form in which it is given. Compared to local bureaucrats, who stand to gain more from narrow purpose and highly stimulative project grants to their specific agencies, the interests of residents and politicians are maximized when intergovernmental aid is unconditional. Because most intergovernmental aid has been categorical in nature, it has tended to match the interests of bureaucrats. On the other hand, the interests of all local actors are served when aid is stable. Historically, however, intergovernmental aid, especially from the federal government, has not often met this condition.

FLUCTUATING INTERGOVERNMENTAL AID

Between 1955 and the mid 1970s intergovernmental aid from the federal government increased dramatically, paralleled by a rapid increase in state aid (some of which was federal money being "passed through" state agencies). Taking advantage of these expanding fiscal resources, local governmental reliance on intergovernmental aid expanded sharply.

Table 38 reports general trends of federal and state aid to all cities in the nation. (Later I present comparable data for the suburbs in this sample for the years 1972, 1977, and 1982.) The growth and decline of federal aid is evident. Before the New Deal, the federal intergovernmental role was limited by constitutional doctrine and historical practice (Walker 1980; Wright 1982). Although the Great Depression planted the

TABLE 38

INTERGOVERNMENTAL AID TO ALL CITIES, SELECTED YEARS, 1955–1982 (IN $ MILLIONS), AND AS PERCENT OF GENERAL MUNICIPAL OWN-SOURCE REVENUES

	Federal Aid		State Aid	
	$	Percent of Own-Source General Revenues	$	Percent of Own-Source General Revenues
1955	121	1.9	1,236	19.4
1960	256	2.8	1,868	20.1
1965	557	4.5	2,745	22.1
1970	1,337	7.1	6,173	33.0
1972	2.538	10.8	8,434	35.9
1975	5,844	19.3	13,052	43.2
1977	8,880	24.2	14,236	38.7
1978	10,844	25.8	14,482	36.5
1982	10,998	18.4	18,947	31.7

SOURCE: ACIR, 1985: 62.

seeds of a growing federal role, federal intergovernmental transfers represented less than 2 percent of municipal own-source revenues in 1955, less than 3 percent in 1960, and less than 5 percent in 1965. While Lyndon Johnson's "Great Society" increased the role of the federal government, it was actually under a relatively conservative president, Richard Nixon, that the federal presence mushroomed.

The explicit goal of the Nixon administration was to limit the direct policy role of the national government in local affairs and, following a traditional theme of conservatives, to return power to local government, the level "closest to the people." To accomplish this goal, it sought to reduce categorical project grants and increase the flow of relatively unrestricted grants.

The Nixon administration called for both general and special revenue sharing programs. In 1972, a program of General Revenue Sharing (GRS) was enacted, in which general purpose local governments became *entitled* to grants, the amount of which was formula driven (Nathan et al. 1975). This made GRS a "right" rather than an award given to the most deserving or needy communities. The revenue sharing program spread federal aid to thousands of local governments, many of which had never received federal aid before. Most of these new participants were suburbs.

The Nixon administration also proposed a series of "special revenue sharing" programs, allowing local governments freedom to allocate their monies across programs within a single policy area, such as education or community development. The two most important programs actually adopted, the Comprehensive Employment and Training Act of 1973 (CETA) and the Community Development Block Grant program (Title 1 of the Community Development Act of 1974), allowed suburban governments to participate in formula-driven entitlement programs previously targeted on central cities.

Not surprisingly, the shift to less restricted grants was enthusiastically received by suburban governments. But the central cities that were already receiving large federal grants wanted assurances that the new monies would not come from a reduction in existing funding levels. This created a dilemma for the administration, which wanted to reward its constituents in the suburbs and in the cities of the South and West without unduly alienating the still powerful political interests in the older cities of the North, the primary recipients of existing intergovernmental programs. In the short run, the easiest solution was to pump new money into the system. Between 1972 and 1978, the peak of federal involvement, local governments received a dramatic infusion of new funds.

By the late 1970s, however, inflation, the fiscal problems of the federal government, and a new fiscal conservatism reversed the expansion of federal intergovernmental aid: taking account of inflation, by 1982 real federal dollars flowing to local governments decreased dramatically. Thus, federal aid went through a wild expansion and an almost equally large contraction in the space of just ten years.

Compared to this erratic pattern, levels of state aid have been relatively stable and considerably higher than federal aid. Moreover, while federal aid has historically concentrated on central cities, state aid is more widely distributed; suburbs have a much longer history of participation in the state system.

GENERAL TRENDS OF INTERGOVERNMENTAL AID TO SUBURBS: 1972–1982

To more fully document how these trends in intergovernmental aid affected suburbs, I begin with a simple review of levels of funding and reliance on intergovernmental aid in 1972, 1977, and 1982. For the suburbs in this sample, I report intergovernmental aid per capita and as a percent of total local revenues for the suburbs grouped into the nine geographic regions defined by the census.

Tables 39–42 show that while aid to suburbs in this sample followed the same temporal swings as aid to all municipalities, intergovernmental aid to suburbs is significantly lower than aid to central cities.

Furthermore, rates of suburban participation in some types of intergovernmental aid are low. In 1972, before general revenue sharing came fully on line, only 28 percent of the suburban municipalities in this sample received any aid at all from the federal government. However, in both 1977 and 1982, almost every suburb received federal intergovernmental aid, mostly because of the availability of general revenue sharing. Rates of suburban municipal participation in non-GRS programs are much lower than in GRS. While over 97 percent of suburbs received GRS funds in 1977 and 1982, in 1977, only 61 percent of the suburbs received other forms of federal aid. In 1982, reflecting the collapse in federal aid, suburban participation in non-GRS aid dropped to 42 percent.

Moreover, in both 1977 and 1982 about 80 percent of federal aid dollars the average suburb received came through general revenue sharing. For many suburbs, it was the only form of federal aid they received:

in 1977, about 40 percent of suburbs received *only* GRS from the federal government; in 1982, 55 percent. In current dollars the average per capita grant increased to $21, up from $18 in 1977. However, since the consumer price index increased by almost 60 percent during the same five-year period, the value of federal aid declined considerably. Moreover, since so many suburban governments were drawn into the system of federal aid through general revenue sharing, their real problems may just be emerging with the recent demise of GRS.

TABLE 39
AVERAGE FEDERAL AID IN CURRENT DOLLARS RECEIVED
BY SUBURBAN MUNICIPALITIES (PER CAPITA)

	1972	*1977*	*1982*
New England	$9.17	$85.36	$90.44
Mid-Atlantic	1.86	18.78	14.99
East North Central	2.26	17.16	21.58
West North Central	3.18	13.86	15.63
South Atlantic	2.32	18.06	26.98
East South Central	1.80	20.70	17.17
West South Central	1.82	14.84	22.79
Mountain	3.78	23.11	27.53
Pacific	2.96	19.23	23.12
All suburbs	2.44	18.56	21.05

TABLE 40
FEDERAL AID AS PERCENT OF SUBURBAN MUNICIPAL TOTAL REVENUES

	1972	*1977*	*1982*
New England	1.8%	11.4%	8.6%
Mid-Atlantic	0.9	10.1	5.3
East North Central	1.1	7.0	5.1
West North Central	1.6	7.2	4.7
South Atlantic	1.7	7.8	6.7
East South Central	2.3	10.0	6.0
West South Central	1.6	7.8	6.1
Mountain	2.3	10.5	7.7
Pacific	1.7	5.2	5.4
All suburbs	0.9	7.6	5.1

TABLE 41

AVERAGE STATE AID IN CURRENT DOLLARS RECEIVED BY
SUBURBAN MUNICIPALITIES (PER CAPITA)

	1972	1977	1982
New England	$67.74	$133.03	$235.65
Mid-Atlantic	12.43	22.42	49.98
East North Central	26.11	42.26	52.63
South Atlantic	11.87	26.46	32.34
East South Central	10.08	19.91	28.71
West South Central	4.68	4.45	24.03
Mountain	12.42	31.03	43.11
Pacific	27.58	51.54	48.62
West North Central	15.23	29.22	43.27
All suburbs	18.79	34.27	49.64

TABLE 42

STATE AID AS PERCENT OF SUBURBAN MUNICIPAL TOTAL REVENUES

	1972	1977	1982
New England	17.0%	18.8%	24.1%
Mid-Atlantic	10.2	8.9	13.7
East North Central	19.7	18.9	14.6
West North Central	17.7	15.3	12.4
South Atlantic	12.4	12.3	9.5
East South Central	11.0	12.0	10.2
West South Central	4.8	1.9	6.9
Mountain	11.6	14.3	10.7
Pacific	23.6	21.9	13.1
All suburbs	14.3	14.9	15.4

State Aid to Suburban Governments

State aid to suburbs has been more widely dispersed than federal aid. In 1972, 90 percent of the suburbs in this sample received state aid of some type (compared to the 28 percent which received federal aid). The percentage of suburbs receiving state aid increased to 95 percent in 1977 and 96 percent in 1982.

Using the Census of Governments category "General State Aid" to reflect the extent to which state grants are relatively unrestricted, another difference between state and federal aid is evident.[2] While most federal aid going to the average suburb was revenue sharing money, only about one-third of the dollars in state intergovernmental transfers are general aid. A gradual shift toward more general state aid is evident. In 1977, this type of aid represented about 30 percent of state aid dollars for the average suburb; by 1982 this was up to almost 40 percent.

Not only do more suburbs get state aid, they also receive more money from the states than from the federal government. In 1972, the average suburb received almost $19 from their respective state governments, compared to less than $3 from the federal government. Between 1972 and 1977, total state aid to the average suburb grew by almost 90 percent, an increase about twice the change in the consumer price index. Coupled with a similar steep increase in federal aid, the years between 1972 and 1977 were the "golden years" of fiscal federalism.

However, such beneficence was short lived—between 1977 and 1982, intergovernmental revenues from states increased an average 41 percent (from $34 to just less than $50 per capita). This was less than the rate of inflation. Combining the sharp decline in real federal aid and the more modest, but still very real, decline in state aid, local governments engaged in "cutback management." They also turned back to their own revenue sources: the ACIR found that in the early 1980s, the local property tax, the "work horse" of local government revenue systems, reversed a long term decline as a source of revenue (ACIR 1985).

INDIVIDUAL COMMUNITY EXPERIENCES WITH INTERGOVERNMENTAL AID

In the rest of this chapter, I identify the individual community characteristics associated with the receipt of intergovernmental aid. I look specifically at the relationship between individual suburban characteristics and local receipt of total federal aid per capita and total state aid per capita.[3]

As in other chapters, I treat the data base for this analysis as a three wave panel design measuring community characteristics and intergovernmental aid in 1972, 1977, and 1982. I pool these cross sections using Least Squares Dummy Variable (LSDV) method.

The following model of intergovernmental aid was estimated:

(14) $IG_{i,t} = f(+ \text{ Demographic Factors}_{i,t}$
$+ \text{ Economic Composition}_{i,t}$
$+ \text{ Expenditures}_{i,t}$
$+ \text{ Functional Responsibility}_{i,t}$
$+ \text{ Fiscal Factors}_{i,t}$
$+ \text{ Time } + \text{ SMSA}$
$+ \text{ Political Factors}_i).$

Where:

IG = total federal aid per capita and total state aid per capita analyzed separately.

The other indicators, which have all been defined in previous chapters, include:

Demographic Factors = a set of indicators of local residential demands and needs of the community: percent black, percent poor,[4] percent renters, population, median home value, median income, density, and distance from the central city.

Economic Composition = the relative size of employment in the manufacturing, service, retail and wholesale sectors. Also included is a measure of the ratio of government jobs in the municipality to population. Since government workers are primary beneficiaries of intergovernmental aid, this measure reflects their relative concentration in a community and hence their potential power.

Expenditures = per capita expenditures for developmental, redistributive, and allocational services. In addition, a measure of expenditures per capita on construction projects was computed. A strong relationship between intergovernmental aid and construction projects should be found because some intergovernmental aid programs are designed to support large scale capital projects and because local governments prefer to use intergovernmental aid for such projects.

Functional Responsibility = three indices of functional responsibility, paralleling expenditure domains (developmental, redistributive, allocational).

Fiscal Factors = true value per capita and the local tax bill.

Time = two dummy variables; the first is recorded 1 for observations in 1977, the other recorded 1 for observations in 1982.

SMSA = a vector of dummy variables for SMSA location.

Political Factors = two indicators to represent conditions of the local political environment which might affect the interests of politicians. First is a dummy variable in which a community with a city manager is assigned a value of 1; 0 otherwise. City managers may be more professionally trained than mayors and may therefore be potentially more capable of fulfilling the technical requirements inherent in the competition for many categorical aid programs. Second, is the extent of turnover in the executive offices of the local government, adding together the number of different city managers and the number of different mayors each city has had between 1972 and 1982. Faced with higher turnover, local political executives may have incentives to augment the flow of aid. On the other hand, higher turnover in executive leadership might weaken the staff and technical support capabilities of the local government in its competition for intergovernmental aid.

Given the limitations on the availability of these political data (see chapter 5), I report in detail the results of the analysis in the larger sample, then briefly note the results of reestimating these equations in the smaller sample that results when the two political variables are added. In general, the coefficients in the equations do not change across subsamples.

Following the procedure used in other chapters, I initially ran a model in which each variable was allowed to have its own slope in each of the three years. By imposing restrictions across panels and using the Chow test, with a few important exceptions, I found the relationships between most independent variables and the dependent variables did not vary significantly across time. When variation was found, I report separate coefficients.

Patterns of Federal Aid

Table 43 estimates total federal aid per capita as a function of suburban municipal characteristics. Federal aid is a national system: SMSA location is relatively unimportant, explaining only about 7 percent of the variation in the receipt of federal aid. When I add individual community characteristics to the model, the variance explained increases from 7 percent to about 35 percent.

The local characteristic that most affects federal intergovernmental aid is the extent to which a local government is undertaking capital improvements and construction projects.[5] This is not surprising since many federal grants are available specifically to help underwrite these types of projects. Further, given the erratic history of federal aid, local governments rationally allocate federal aid for construction projects.

A redistributive component of federal aid emerged over the course of the 1970s. In 1972, neither the concentration of low income families nor blacks affected the flow of federal aid. However, after 1972, communities with more blacks and with more poor people received higher aid. Note

TABLE 43

Total Federal Aid as a Function of Local Conditions and Time, Controlling for SMSA, Pooled Cross-Sectional Analysis, 1972, 1977, 1982

Variable	B	SE B	Beta	T-Test
DEMOGRAPHIC FACTORS				
Median income	−0.01	0.01	−.046	−1.21
Poor (% 1972)	5.14	9.61	.023	0.53
Poor (%)	20.09	5.37	.169	3.73
Black (% 1972)	6.76	6.60		1.02
Black (%)	12.45	3.54	.079	3.51
Rent (%)	−0.93	2.81	−.003	−0.33
Home value	−0.00	0.00	−.012	−0.40
Population	0.00	0.00	.008	0.00
Distance	0.03	0.04	.013	0.82
Density	0.00	0.00	.047	1.72
ECONOMIC COMPOSITION				
Manufacturing	2.57	1.92	.034	1.33
Services	−0.12	6.22	.002	−0.02
Retail	2.73	5.01	.012	0.54
Wholesale	−9.41	6.01	−.037	−1.56
Government	−142.08	94.23	−.059	−1.50
PER CAPITA EXPENDITURES				
Distributive	0.01	0.02	.019	0.65
Allocational	0.14	0.02	.164	6.40
Redistributive	0.03	0.01	.032	1.73
Construction	0.21	0.00	.413	23.56
FUNCTIONAL RESPONSIBILITY				
Distributive	0.62	0.38	.034	1.61
Allocational	−0.44	0.46	−.015	−0.95
Redistributive (1977)	1.28	0.59	.059	2.16
Redistributive	0.20	0.46	.019	0.42
FISCAL FACTORS				
True value	−0.02	0.08	−.008	−0.32
Tax bill	0.05	0.25	.006	0.20
TIME				
1977 dummy	3.38	1.61	.094	2.08
1982 dummy	−1.03	1.69	−.028	−0.60
Constant	−3.05	3.28		−0.92
Adjusted R square, SMSA only,	.07			
Adjusted R square, full model,	.34			

NOTE: Number of cases pooled sample = 2517.

too that total federal aid is negatively (although not significantly) related to median income. Similarly, in 1977, there is evidence that communities providing a larger number of social services received more federal aid. But this is a small effect, and not evident in other years.

Finally note the significant effect of the 1977 time variable: *ceteris paribus,* total federal aid in 1977 was higher than in either 1972 or 1982.

In the equation with political data (see table 44), the two political variables do not affect the flow of total federal aid. While, in this smaller subsample, there are stronger general time effects and the effects of race and the concentration of the poor do not vary across time periods, in

TABLE 44
TOTAL FEDERAL AID AS A FUNCTION OF LOCAL CONDITIONS,
TIME, AND POLITICAL FACTORS, CONTROLLING FOR SMSA, POOLED
CROSS-SECTIONAL ANALYSIS, 1972, 1977, 1982

Variable	B	SE B	Beta	T-Test
DEMOGRAPHIC FACTORS				
Median income	−0.02	0.01	−.083	−1.56
Poor (%)	17.19	4.80	.169	3.57
Black (%)	10.69	3.67	.086	2.91
Rent (%)	−5.22	2.62	−.074	−1.99
Population	0.00	0.00	.000	0.30
Home value	−0.00	0.00	−.020	−0.57
Distance	−0.04	0.03	−.023	−1.02
Density	0.00	0.00	.000	0.09
ECONOMIC COMPOSITION				
Manufacturing	2.05	1.76	.031	1.15
Services	−3.06	5.32	−.024	−0.57
Retail	3.76	4.93	.026	0.76
Wholesale	−0.55	6.50	−.008	−0.08
Government	25.73	92.55	.013	0.27
PER CAPITA EXPENDITURES				
Distributive	0.03	0.02	.036	0.86
Allocational	0.05	0.02	.083	2.49
Redistributive	−0.00	0.01	−.000	−0.23
Construction	0.08	0.00	.268	10.23
FUNCTIONAL RESPONSIBILITY				
Distributive	0.53	0.34	.041	1.53
Allocational	0.23	0.45	.017	0.52
Redistributive	0.84	0.36	.064	2.28

Continued on next page

TABLE 44—*Continued*

Variable	B	SE B	Beta	T-Test
FISCAL FACTORS				
True value	0.16	0.06	.091	2.31
Tax bill	0.02	0.21	.002	0.10
TIME				
1977 dummy	5.92	0.65	.270	9.08
1982 dummy	2.00	0.81	.093	2.47
POLITICAL FACTORS				
Turnover	0.28	0.20	.048	1.43
Manager	0.02	0.67	.002	0.04
Constant	− 4.08	2.83		− 1.44
Adjusted R square, SMSA only,	.08			
Adjusted R square, full model,	.30			

NOTE: Number of cases in pooled model = 1401.

general, effects are in the same direction and of the same magnitude as in the larger sample.

Patterns of Total State Aid

Table 45 reports the pooled cross-sectional analysis of the receipt of total state aid. SMSA location explains 25 percent of the variation in the distribution of state aid, a substantially stronger regional effect than evident in the distribution of federal aid. While federal intergovernmental aid is part of a national system of fiscal federalism, patterns of state aid vary depending on state laws and practices. After controlling for SMSA, other characteristics explain about an additional 20 percent of the variance.

Levels of total state aid are associated with several types of local expenditures. As with federal aid, communities with higher construction expenditures receive more state aid. Suburbs spending more on allocational services also receive more aid from their states, as do suburbs with higher expenditures on developmental expenditures.

But note that there is no relationship between social expenditures and aid from the state government. Peterson argues that local governments which spend more on social services are penalized in the growth game—these data on the flow of state aid further suggests that suburbs are not even rewarded by states for doing more in this policy area. The incentives for redistributive expenditures are clearly low.

TABLE 45
TOTAL STATE AID AS A FUNCTION OF LOCAL CONDITIONS AND TIME, CONTROLLING
FOR SMSA, POOLED CROSS-SECTIONAL ANALYSIS, 1972, 1977, 1982

Variable	B	SE B	Beta	T-Test
DEMOGRAPHIC FACTORS				
Median income	−0.00	0.00	−.024	−0.77
Poor (%)	12.87	8.50	.044	1.51
Rent (%)	−2.44	4.50	−.012	−0.54
Black (%)	1.91	5.09	.006	0.37
Population	0.00	0.00	.058	2.94
Home value	−0.00	0.00	−.024	−0.83
Distance	−0.17	0.07	−.045	−2.42
Density	0.00	0.00	.024	1.18
ECONOMIC COMPOSITION				
Manufacturing	7.05	3.09	.046	2.27
Services	−29.14	9.99	−.065	−2.91
Retail	−3.66	8.02	−.008	−0.45
Wholesale	7.32	9.66	.017	0.75
PER CAPITA EXPENDITURES				
Developmental	0.21	0.03	.125	5.90
Allocational	0.31	0.03	.190	9.05
Redistributive	0.01	0.02	.010	0.65
Construction	0.34	0.01	.370	23.30
FUNCTIONAL RESPONSIBILITY				
Developmental	−1.12	0.62	−.036	−1.79
Allocational	0.24	0.74	.005	0.32
Redistributive	0.88	0.66	.027	1.31
FISCAL FACTORS				
True value	−0.14	0.13	−.028	−1.05
Tax bill	1.78	0.40	.092	4.38
TIME				
1977 dummy	2.39	1.19	.039	2.00
1982 dummy	−0.27	1.45	−.004	−0.18
Constant	0.69	4.83		0.14
Adjusted R square, SMSA only,	.46			
Adjusted R square, full model,	.71			

NOTE: Number of cases pooled sample = 2175.

Total state aid is less directly redistributive than federal aid. Racial makeup is not associated with higher aid, and neither is the concentration of the poor in a community. But states do reward communities making a strong local tax effort.

The economic composition of a community has some impact: communities with a greater concentration of manufacturing activities attract somewhat greater state aid, while communities with a greater concentration of service jobs get less. Finally, time has an effect, with a secular increase in total state aid evident between 1972 and 1977 and a decline in 1982 back to 1972 levels.

Reestimating this equation in the smaller subsample including political variables (see table 46), I find that turnover in the executive office of local governments is significantly associated with lower aid. Apparently, turnover can disrupt the expertise, contacts, and knowledge base necessary to develop ties with state granting agencies. In contrast, cities run by mayors were no less likely to get state aid than were manager cities.

TABLE 46

TOTAL STATE AID AS A FUNCTION OF LOCAL CONDITIONS, TIME, AND POLITICAL
FACTORS, CONTROLLING FOR SMSA, POOLED CROSS-SECTIONAL ANALYSIS, 1972, 1977, 1982

Variable	B	SE B	Beta	T-Test
DEMOGRAPHIC FACTORS				
Median income	−0.00	0.00	−.051	−1.17
Poor (%)	16.69	12.48	.050	1.33
Black (%)	14.28	9.39	.037	1.52
Rent (%)	−6.67	6.76	−.031	−0.98
Population	0.00	0.00	.001	0.04
Home value	−0.00	0.00	−.026	−0.66
Distance	−0.29	0.10	−.070	−2.90
Density	−0.00	0.00	−.008	−0.30
ECONOMIC COMPOSITION				
Manufacturing	−2.89	4.61	−.016	−0.62
Services	−19.92	13.86	−.043	−1.43
Retail	−5.32	12.81	−.010	−0.41
Wholesale	−9.99	16.95	−.018	−0.59
PER CAPITA EXPENDITURES				
Developmental	0.34	0.05	.196	6.63
Allocational	0.28	0.05	.146	5.24
Redistributive	0.04	0.03	.024	1.18
Construction	0.51	0.02	.536	25.05

Continued on next page

TABLE 46—*Continued*

Variable	B	SE B	Beta	T-Test
FUNCTIONAL RESPONSIBILITY				
Developmental	−1.31	0.89	−.039	−1.46
Allocational	1.32	1.17	.025	1.12
Redistributive	0.30	0.95	.008	0.31
POLITICAL FACTORS				
Manager	1.42	1.74	.022	0.81
Turnover	−1.54	0.52	−.079	−2.94
FISCAL FACTORS				
True value	−0.33	0.18	−.064	−1.88
Tax bill	1.71	0.56	.075	3.02
TIME				
1977 dummy	3.86	1.69	.058	2.27
1982 dummy	−2.41	2.09	−.035	−1.15
Constant	12.43	7.24		1.71
Adjusted R square, SMSA only,	.127			
Adjusted R square, full model,	.513			

NOTE: Number of cases in pooled sample = 1383.

CONCLUSIONS

Intergovernmental transfer payments represent a significant revenue source for local communities. In the peak year of 1977, federal aid represented about 8 percent of the revenues of the suburban municipalities in this sample, and state aid represented an additional 14 percent. Thus, in 1977 more than one-fifth of suburban revenues were generated by higher levels of government.

Intergovernmental aid is attractive to local governments. At its best, it reduces the local costs of goods and services, effectively easing local budget constraints and allowing the consumption of more public goods. Alternatively, intergovernmental money can provide tax relief for local residents, allowing greater consumption of private goods.

Despite these benefits, intergovernmental aid has risks. One of the most significant problems is the degree to which funding fluctuates. Relying on intergovernmental aid to pay for on-going services can be a dangerous fiscal strategy, and local governments often hesitate to incorporate intergovernmental grants, particularly federal ones, into their operating budgets. Instead, these monies are often used to support construction projects which will not disappear when intergovernmental support evaporates. Not surprisingly, of all local characteristics, the relationship between construction projects and intergovernmental aid is the strongest.

Another major disadvantage of intergovernmental aid is that while it may be cheap it is usually not free. In fact, the local costs of intergovernmental aid may be rapidly increasing. The federal government, in particular, has used its aid to leverage policy commitments from recipient local governments (ACIR 1984). Thus even though federal aid represents but a small share of local budgets, it is often large enough to cause fiscally strapped local governments to change priorities to meet federal preferences.

Despite such drawbacks, local actors can still benefit from intergovernmental grants. However, the factors determining the level of intergovernmental aid available to communities and its allocation across categorical versus general revenue sharing programs are largely exogenous to the wishes of local actors. This is clear in the effects of time on the level of aid. These effects reflect the policy decisions made by federal and/or state officials driven by the changing economy, and by the changing ideological, budgetary, and revenue climate of the federal and individual state governments.

Time effects clearly are related to the policy changes enacted during the 1970s, as both state and national governments sought to shift their aid programs toward unrestricted aid. In 1977 and 1982, federal general revenue sharing was fully operational and attracted large-scale suburban participation. There was also an increase in the availability of general state aid. As relatively unrestricted aid became more available, the willingness of suburbs to participate increased correspondingly: revenue sharing grants much more closely match the preferences of most local actors, especially politicians and residents, than do categorical grants.

However, the decision to allocate money into categorical or general aid programs is often made independently of local wishes. General revenue sharing and the federal block grant programs were the result of a particular congruence of liberal and conservative interests at a point in time and were enacted only after long and intense deliberations in the Congress and the executive branch. But the rewards flowing to politicians at the national level from unrestricted grants to local governments are relatively low, and a process of "recategorization" began almost immediately in which national policymakers instituted more and more controls over the use of "unrestricted" grants. The payoffs of different forms of aid to national politicians and local politicians vary, and national politicians control the purse strings (see Conlon 1981; and Kettl 1980).

Equally telling, the federal government, because of its own fiscal problems, has terminated the general revenue sharing program, a decision made despite the wishes of local politicians. Compared to the widespread use of GRS funds, suburban participation in other federal grant programs is limited. But even among categorical aid programs, shifts in the availability of funds, determined by federal, not local, politicians drive the system. For example, when faced with recession in the mid 1970s, the federal government decided to increase the availability of compensatory aid programs (Wu 1986). Thus in 1977 and 1982 communities with more poor families received more federal aid. But in 1972, before the *federal* government made that policy decision, local income levels did not affect the level of federal money flowing into communities.

In short, the system of federal intergovernmental aid is a system driven by forces largely exogenous to local communities. While local actors lobby Congress and the executive branch to attend to their interests, local success is sporadic and federal aid seems largely beyond local control.

State intergovernmental aid is only somewhat more amenable to local influence. While less erratic than federal transfer payments, state aid has also fluctuated over the past years, often in tune to changing state ideologies or changing budgetary problems at the state level.

Together, state and federal aid represented over one-fifth of suburban municipal income in 1977 and 1982. But it seems likely that the amount of money pumped through the system of intergovernmental aid will decline, although the mandates and regulations imposed by higher level governments will not. Thus, the system of intergovernmental relations may ultimately produce ever tighter limits on local budgets and local policy.

Part IV

CONCLUSION

11

LOCAL MARKETS AND THE
FUTURE STUDY OF LOCAL POLITICS

Using a market perspective, I have developed a parsimonious model of local politics to explain local budgets and the pursuit of wealth. The general model identified areas of conflict and cooperation in local politics and generated a set of expectations which were tested empirically using a set of suburban communities, whose demographic, fiscal, budgetary, and political conditions were measured over the course of the period 1970–1982.

The model identifies four sets of actors as critical to local politics: residents and business firms—who are the "buyers" of local public goods; and politicians and bureaucrats—who dominate the "sell" decision. Each set of actors has diverse preferences and goals, and each has a diversity of resources and strategies by which to pursue them. On the one hand, conflict is a fundamental outcome of the diverse preferences, goals, and strategies of these actors. On the other hand, actors share a desire to increase the benefits of membership in a community in relationship to the costs.

I define benefits in terms of local expenditures and costs in terms of the local property tax bill. This formulation clearly oversimplifies the decision calculus of real people. Many of the benefits that make a community attractive—its physical amenities, proximity to employment, availability of housing, and so forth—are neglected in the decision rules of the model. Similarly, the focus on the local tax bill oversimplifies the costs of locational choice. In addition to taxes, there are other "disamenities" associated with location in any given community. Even in the realm of local governmental costs, communities levy a variety of taxes and charges to pay for the services they deliver. Nonetheless the centrality of the property tax is easily seen. This tax is the single largest source of local government revenue, and it is a tax which is unavoidable once the decision to locate in a community is made. While a resident can forego a fee for the use of a municipal swimming pool or local beach by not using the facility, nonpayment of the property tax will eventually mean the loss of a home. Thus, the tax bill represents the unavoidable membership dues for living in a community.

These dues can vary widely across neighboring communities, and the benefits of membership vary widely in relationship to taxes paid. The resulting variation in the expenditure/tax (or benefit/cost) ratio is rooted in the unequal distribution of the property tax base. In turn, variation in the tax base and in the relationship between taxes and services is central to the operation of my model.

The works of Charles Tiebout, William Niskanen, and Paul Peterson underlie much of my argument. Tiebout provides the core concepts underlying the analysis of local politics from a market perspective. There are, however, clear limitations in his model. Most importantly, Tiebout's analysis was consumer-oriented and not sufficiently concerned with the independent role of municipalities as producers in the local market for public goods. In the case of pure competition, producers are relatively powerless in the face of the omnipotent and omnipresent "invisible hand" which drives the market. But given the limited competition in the local market for public goods, producers assume a more central role.

In a competitive market, producers must be profit maximizers, they must be efficient, and they must develop marketing strategies and other mechanisms to attract consumers. Even given such actions, producers are ultimately price takers, not price givers, and they cannot manipulate the market. In the model of pure competition, the freedom of any individual or group of producers is constrained by the multiplicity of alternate producers, the substitutability of goods, the availability of information, and the rationality of consumers. Under competitive conditions, the strategies and incentives of producers may be interesting from a management perspective, but not necessarily from a market one.

By analogy, when Tiebout developed his "pure theory of public goods," municipalities as producers received short shrift. His local market for public goods was driven by the actions and incentives of citizen/consumers: citizen/consumers seek to locate in the municipality offering a package of goods and services most closely reflecting individually held preferences. When coupled with interjurisdictional mobility (the ability to "vote with their feet"), a competitive local marketplace resulted. In the Tiebout market an independent role for municipal governments as producers was not analytically critical.

Peterson's argument in *City Limits* is, among other things, a simple yet powerful elaboration of the Tiebout model. Peterson introduces the politics and policies of local government into the world of Tiebout, arguing that the political incentives and strategies of local governments are central to the understanding of the local market. Compared to the original Tiebout formulation, in Peterson's analysis, the local market for public goods is affected by the interests and strategies of sellers, namely, local governments. I especially rely on Peterson's insight that it is the relationship between the above-average income community member and the local benefit/cost ratio which informs the interests of local governments. Note too that this logic is independent of whether a "member" is a person, a family or a business firm.

THE DEMAND SIDE OF THE LOCAL MARKET FOR PUBLIC GOODS

In my model, residents and business firms are the key sources of demand in the local market. Both want to increase the service benefits they receive while minimizing their tax costs. Consequently, they support strategies, such as exclusionary zoning, to maximize the flow of benefits they receive.

But "residents" and "firms" are not homogeneous groupings. For example, the interests of business firms will vary according to the sector of the economy in which they operate. Business firms in different sectors assess the desirability of communities and prospective new members differently. Most clearly, manufacturing firms seek entry into communities with a larger tax base and lower tax rates and appear to be relatively indifferent to levels of personal income in a community. Since a larger tax base increases the likelihood that a community can offer a set of services desired by the firm at a reasonable tax rate, this logic of locational choice is understandable. Given the larger market in which manufacturing firms compete, minimizing local tax costs is basic to higher profitability. In contrast, consumer-oriented firms, such as those in the service and retail sector, are more interested in communities with higher personal income. For these firms, the size of the local tax base is less important than location near a wealthier clientele, more likely to create an "up-scale" market with higher potential profits.

These differences can produce conflict among firms in the policies they want from local government. At the extreme, in order to protect the local tax base, manufacturing interests may seek to exclude residential development—as is the case in Industry City, California. This development strategy would be a disaster for a consumer-oriented firm. On the other hand, retail and service firms may oppose local government expenditures to prepare infrastructure attractive to manufacturing—the affluent people these business want tend to avoid communities with concentrations of manufacturing.

The "tastes" of residents also vary along measurable lines. Upper and lower income residents of the same community will place different value on particular services. Homeowners and renters will be in conflict over how they value local services in relationship to tax costs. Renters experience a fiscal illusion—they do not perceive the true costs of services because the property tax bill is a hidden cost of rent.

Despite such internal cleavages, business firms and residents play a major role in setting the level and composition of local budgets. Their importance is empirically evident in the ability of the demand models, which are based on measures of the composition of the local economy and residential population, to explain a large share of the variance in most types of local expenditures. The notable exception to such robustness is found in the analysis of expenditures on redistributive services, which, while of theoretical interest from Peterson's perspective, account for only a small proportion of local expenditures in most suburbs.

The local market for public goods is responsive to the demands of consumers. However, this does not mean a model can neglect the incentives and strategies of producers. There are clearly identifiable limitations in the local public marketplace which require modifications to a model of the local market driven purely by incentives and strategies of citizen/consumers.

THE LACK OF COMPETITION AND THE SUPPLY SIDE OF THE LOCAL MARKET FOR PUBLIC GOODS

By far, the most basic limitation in the local market for public goods derives from the lack of competition. Municipal providers are spatial monopolists who control a "piece" of metropolitan space. Consequently, the "buy" decision by consumers requires moving across a limited number of jurisdictions at considerable cost.

The mobility requirement underlying the purchase of alternate public goods and services in the local market makes consumer choice more expensive and disruptive than purchase decisions in the private market. In the private market, a consumer can purchase Tide instead of Fab detergent by walking a few more feet down an aisle in a supermarket. Most consumers can even change supermarkets by driving a few extra minutes. The costs of changing these private consumption decisions are relatively small. In contrast, if a consumer doesn't like the bundle of goods, services, and taxes offered by his or her community, exercising the Tiebout move option is more expensive and more difficult.

Furthermore, consumption decisions about local public goods take place at a highly aggregated level—it is impossible to pick and choose among a large number of separable goods as is the case in a private market. Instead, choice is limited to a relatively few bundles of public goods and services offered by a small set of municipal providers. Moreover, restraints on consumption decisions are coupled with the fact that entry of new providers into the local market for public goods is highly regulated. Incorporation as a new municipal provider is often a difficult procedure regulated by state governments. The entry of alternate non-municipal providers can also be a complicated procedure, regulated and controlled (as in the case of contracting out for services) by municipalities themselves. Baumol (1982) has argued that "contestable" markets produce many of the benefits of competitive ones. But a regulated market dominated by spatial monopolists and characterized by high entry costs meets neither the conditions of competition nor of contestability.

As a result of limited competition, more attention must be paid to the incentives, goals, and strategies of the providers of local services. I view the provision decisions of local governments to be the result of the incentives of bureaucrats and the needs of local politicians. In particular, the body of research built on the model of budget maximizing bureaucrats provides a perspective by which to understand the policy decisions of local governments.

Bureaucrats seek to maximize their agency budgets and they have powerful resources at their command to achieve this goal. Most notable is their monopoly over information and subsequent agenda control. From this perspective, bureaucrats use these powers to drive up local expenditures beyond the objective needs of the local population. However, the ability of bureaucrats to maximize budgets is not absolute—rather, it is contingent upon their relative power vis-à-vis other actors, which is in turn a function of the degree of competition in the local market for public goods.

Bureaucratic success in budget maximizing is measurably lower in more competitive environments. In part 2, I demonstrated that competition was associated with lower expenditures, a reduced ability of bureaucrats to control intergovernmental aid, and a smaller and less highly paid public-sector work force.

Two structural conditions reflecting competition in the local market for public goods were most consistently related to restraints on the size of local government. First, the local public sector tends to be smaller in municipalities bordered by more municipalities. As the number of proximate neighbors increases, so does the level of information about alternate costs and service delivery patterns in the local environment. More information reduces the major source of bureaucrats' power in their drive for budget maximization. Furthermore, where there are more proximate providers, moving costs, which increase with distance, are lower, facilitating the exercise of the Tiebout mechanisms enforcing responsiveness and efficiency.

Among the other market conditions I investigated, variation in tax price was more consistently related to smaller government than was variation in expenditures. Given the complexities of public goods and the diversity of the bundles of goods and services provided, this is an understandable result.

Shoppers in the local market for public goods are faced with pre-assembled packages of goods and services rather than a large number of discrete choices. The various combinations encompass complex trade-offs between parks, libraries, parking facilities, street lights, and the other services local governments provide. There is also significant slippage between the expenditures of local government and the quality of the services actually delivered, weakening the relationship between benefits and expenditures.

Such complexity dilutes the role of consumer choice across expenditure levels as a competitive force in the local market for public goods. In contrast, the local tax bill is palpable, indeed, often painful. Knowing tax bills in neighboring communities are lower increases the incentives for citizen/consumers to monitor the behavior of their own local government and impose constraints, by voice or by exit, on the budget maximizing behavior of their own bureaucrats.

THE ROLE OF POLITICIANS

Politicians are the last set of actors in my model. Theoretically, politicians should play a significant role in determining municipal supply decisions because of their institutional role as sponsors of bureaucrats and their strategic position in local budgetary processes. And theoretically politicians have clear incentives to manipulate budgetary decisions to further their own careers.

The abstract identification of the strategic interests of politicians is simple—we can postulate that politicians seek to maximize the likelihood of reelection and engage in credit-seeking activities to do so. However, despite the logical clarity of this position, the empirical identification of the *independent* role of local politicians in the policy process has been a task in which analysts of local governments long have been engaged without much success.

I identified several political factors which reflect the structural characteristics of the local political environment and which should affect the ability and incentives of local politicians to act as independent policy entrepreneurs in budgetary and policy decisions. However, wherever I introduced such political factors into empirical analysis, an independent role for local politicians was virtually impossible to identify. These negative results duplicate a large body of work using a diversity of research perspectives across a range of issue areas.

Perhaps we should *not* expect local politicians to act as an independent force in the determination local policies. Given the median voter model, for example, one could argue that politicians maximize their probability of reelection simply by reflecting the interests of residents and not by staking out independent policy positions. From this perspective, a rational politician will act as a conduit of the demands of others, eschewing an independent policy role. The empirical findings presented in this book can be interpreted in this vein. Local politicians are logically an important (perhaps only mediating) component of the market for public goods, but empirically their independent role is small.

THE FUTURE STUDY OF LOCAL MARKETS

The concept of competition in this market model of local public goods allowed the synthesis and expansion of several important theories of local politics. At this point I want to suggest two avenues by which we can increase our understanding of local politics viewed from a market perspective.

Clearly markets matter in the delivery of local public goods. Part 2 of this book presented consistent empirical evidence documenting theoretically interesting effects of competition. However, this empirical analysis was based on a highly simplified model of the local market for public goods, emphasizing the role of competitive market forces. Yet

I have argued that the local market for public goods is *not* a competitive market. Rather it is a heavily regulated market in which there are relatively few suppliers, the most important of which, municipalities, are spatial monopolists. In contrast to the operation of competitive markets, which is well documented, the characteristics and outcomes of noncompetitive markets, such as the local market for public goods, are among the most difficult markets fully to understand and to model.

While my empirical analysis showed that competition is a tool by which to explore local services, a more complete examination of the local market for public goods will likely require a mode of explanation which, at least in the short run, moves away from the *empirical* investigation characteristic of this book. Specifically, formal theory, especially game theory, by focusing on the interrelationships among producers, has proved useful to understanding the operation of limited oligopolistic markets. Ideas generated by game theory are important because the decisions of individual producers in an oligopolistic market are dependent on and driven by the decisions of other producers. In truly competitive markets, producers can be viewed as independent actors and, as I have argued above, to some extent can actually be ignored. This makes modeling of competitive markets easier than modeling the interdependencies of oligopolistic ones.

Where such formal work may ultimately move the study of the local market for public goods is unclear, although researchers, many associated with Elinor Ostrom, have begun to explore that direction. Moreover, a very simple formal logic underlies the argument of Peterson's, *City Limits* and Gary Miller's *Cities by Contract.* But work applying the economic concepts of oligopoly may produce the breakthroughs of the future.

There is another quite different line of research that can augment the model I use and which can be equally fruitful for future research. There are other mechanisms besides mobility which increase the responsiveness and efficiency of markets. Using Hirschman's terms, the "exit" or mobility option which underlies the Tiebout model must ultimately be viewed in conjunction with the "voice" option of local politics. While future formal models will rely increasingly on economic terms, measuring and developing the concept of "voice" is a traditional area of expertise in political science.

The Role of Voice

As Hirschman argued, markets are driven by a combination of exit, voice, and loyalty. The Tiebout model emphasizes the exit option—and clearly exit provides a powerful force in the local market for public goods. But local politics and citizen participation also affect local policy decisions—the voice option counts.

The importance of voice is already clear in one important strand in the evolving work on local growth politics. Emphasizing only the exit option, and following the work of Peterson, we would expect local governments to pursue wholeheartedly and singlemindedly the maximization of the tax base. As I have argued, this is a core consensual goal around which local actors can coalesce, because, if achieved, all actors benefit.

Thus, it is no surprise that the pursuit of the tax base through economic development and through the attraction of the wealthy is a major goal of local governments. But a number of cases have already been documented where coalitions of residents and neighborhood groups have emerged to protest new economic development which they perceive as detrimental to the local quality of life. Using concerted voice, these groups have forced local governments to impose growth controls. In such incidences, the voice option has overridden, at least in the short run, the imperatives of the exit option. These cases of voice-driven antigrowth politics are still the exception, but, because they have been concentrated in the wealthiest and most visible metropolitan regions (especially in California), they have attracted research and media attention.

Clearly community organization and individual political participation affect the operation of the local market for public goods. Integrating individual and group level political data into models of the market can lead to important insights into its operation. However, a major pitfall lies in merging the exit and the voice perspectives. The Tiebout model, based primarily on the exit option, is a model of a *market*—an aggregate "entity" created through individual and collective processes. The aggregate level data presented in this book and in other places suggest the Tiebout market actually works. But one could argue that such Tiebout processes are based on assumptions of *individual* level behavior and that the model assumes individual rationality and knowledge of the alternate packages offered by municipalities in the local market.

Compared to research at the Tiebout market level, research using the "voice" perspective is much more likely to be rooted in empirical work investigating individual behavior, attitudes and information. As Elaine Sharp has already demonstrated in her excellent work on exit and voice in local government, survey evidence shows that most residents do not have the information necessary to operate in a "Tiebout rational" manner and even if they do have it, they don't consistently act on it.

While Sharp cautiously explores the links between aggregate and individual level data, individual level data will inevitably be used to argue that the Tiebout model is wrong, and that since citizen/consumers do not have high levels of information, the Tiebout-like results observed in aggregate level analysis must be produced from some processes other than those specified in market models.

This argument has face validity and raises the fundamental and interesting problem of linking market ("macro") and individual ("micro") level concepts and data. Not surprisingly, debate about this linkage is evident in economics. Economists have studied a wide range of markets and in many of their explorations, market theories based on rational assumptions find little support in individual-level survey data. Therefore, the failure of survey data regarding "voice" to support market models based on "exit" should not be surprising.

Economists have already identified the terms of the debate which urban researchers in political science and the other social sciences will have to face (but hopefully not duplicate) as they explore market models integrating exit and voice. To oversimplify a complex literature, there are several perspectives in the debate on this linkage.

Certainly the approach of the economists at the University of Chicago (akin to "damn the torpedoes, full speed ahead") must be considered. They stress the role of entrepreneurs who do have the information and rationality to behave as the macro market dictates and who provide the missing macro-micro link. Following this school of thought, and drawing on the work of interest group theorists such as Terry Moe or Mancur Olson, we might search for policy entrepreneurs in local government who provide the information and alternatives to mobilize local citizens or to otherwise pressure local bureaucrats and politicians into making "appropriate" budgetary decisions. The role of what Terry Clark has called the "new fiscal populists" may be an example of such policy entrepreneurs, individuals who emerged when municipal government drifted too far away from the efficient and responsive provision of services.

Alternately, the work of experimental economists such as Charles Plott or Vernon Smith may ultimately provide evidence to solve this macro-micro link. Other behavioral decision theorists working from a variety of perspectives share the underlying concern for the role of limited information in rational decision making: that is, given limited information, what constitutes rational behavior and what effect do such limits have in the operation of markets. Experimental work has emerged in political science, and formal theorists, such as Peter Ordeshook, now use experimental techniques to investigate deductively derived models.

While traditional market models assume high levels of individual information and rationality, one must also consider the role of "rational ignorance": it often makes sense to ignore information because the costs of gathering it are too high. This may explain why the information levels "predicted" by the Tiebout model are not found in survey research: at any given time, most people are not moving and are not contemplating moving. Therefore, most residents of a community have few incentives to gather the information about tax costs and service levels that drives the individual rationality implied by the Tiebout model. Given high information costs, nonmovers (the bulk the population) are rationally ignorant. But this does not mean that when an individual is contemplating moving or is searching for a new residence, he or she does not gather information about services and tax costs. In other words, if movers or potential movers have the information upon which the Tiebout model (at the individual level) rests, they might play the role necessary to produce the outcomes evident in the aggregate market analysis—they may be among the "entrepreneurs" who drive the system.

In short, there are clear avenues by which to expand the model of the local market for public goods. Formal theory may help us understand better the oligopolistic setting of that market. Research at the individual and group level may help us understand political competition and its role in affecting demand. Both lines of future research will move in fits and starts, and, undoubtedly, like lines of earlier research they will generate conflicting models and results. But future research should produce more realistic (and more complex) models of the operation of competition in the local market for public goods. I hope that these models will also provide the means to introduce more fully an independent role of politicians and political forces into market models.

CONSENSUS AND SUBURBAN CITY LIMITS

The model I developed in this book identifies cleavages in local policy decisions, but it also predicts consensus around the pursuit of community wealth. Consensus is based on the importance of the local service/ tax ratio to the individual well-being of the actors in the model. This aspect of my argument is clearly indebted to Peterson's insights in *City Limits*. However, Peterson's concept of limits is too limited—he has identified only a small set of the constraints cities actually face.

It is easy to demonstrate that local actors benefit from an improved service/tax ratio: residents can receive more services at any given tax rate; business firms can increase profits; bureaucrats can increase agency budgets; and politicians can make claims that increase the likelihood of reelection. The importance of the service/tax ratio is built into the very structure of local government. In particular, local autonomy and local responsibility for financing services lead to wide variation in the service/tax ratio across neighboring communities. Because such variation affects the real well-being of local actors, the pursuit of a higher service/tax ratio is a fundamental characteristic of the politics of the local market for public goods.

Ultimately, the local service/tax ratio is the product of other factors which affect the local tax base. In my analysis, I investigated empirically the distribution of family income and of jobs as two inputs into the size of the local fiscal base. I then investigated directly the distribution of the true value of community property.

These inputs were studied both cross-sectionally and longitudinally as a function of local demographic, economic, fiscal, and budgetary characteristics, and as a function of "higher level" macroeconomic forces reflected in regional location and secular trends. The most consistently important empirical patterns demonstrated the stability of the distribution of local resources, the inability of local government policies to affect this distribution, and the openness of local communities to secular changes in the economy.

In Peterson's analysis, city limits emerge because, given the present structure of local government, the ability of cities to invest across the full range of local services is highly constrained—cities are limited in their ability to invest in services other than developmental ones. Cities taking a different budgetary course are penalized in the competition for future resources. But the suburban cities I studied are already "Petersonian." They invest only small sums in redistributive services and developmental services consume the bulk of their budgets. Yet there is little evidence that such investment decisions really improve their relative well-being. At the bottom line, local government policies are relatively ineffective in producing the outcomes local actors want. Yet, despite such evidence, local governments continue to compete for wealth, and they use a wide range of budgetary and fiscal tools in attempts to attract wealthy individuals and new economic development.

This situation may be fruitfully explored in the future as a prisoner's dilemma game. Local governments are forced to invest in developmental goods and services, offer tax abatements, enter into exclusionary zoning practices, and otherwise promote growth, even though the benefits from these activities may not actually be sufficiently high to justify their costs. As in any prisoner's dilemma, total benefits may be improved if a cooperative solution could be reached. However, the structure in which local governments operate makes a cooperative solution difficult, if not impossible. No single local government can opt out of the competition—all are prisoners of the structure—and the benefits of cooperation escape them.

This dilemma highlights a contradiction in the local market for public goods which affects citizen/consumers. The fragmentation of the local market increases the efficiency and the responsiveness of the market. Fragmentation creates competition between providers, which keeps government small and reduces the economic rents collected by bureaucrats. On the other hand, the same fragmented structure means that local government expenditures may be wasted in a futile pursuit of goods which are intended to increase community well-being but which can not be bought with local resources. Fragmentation is thus a two-edged sword and the real limits cities face in trying to maximize community welfare are more complex and extended than in Peterson's analysis.

Intergovernmental aid adds yet a further dimension to the idea of city limits. Intergovernmental aid can improve a community's well-being by transferring the costs of services outside the community. By supplementing locally raised revenues, intergovernmental aid allows more services to be delivered at any given local tax rate. Local governments benefit most from a secure flow of intergovernmental aid, and local interests are best served by unconditional revenue sharing type grants. However, historically the flow of intergovernmental aid has been erratic and the role of the federal government in the system of fiscal federalism uncertain.

During the last several decades, the federal government first expanded and then dramatically contracted the flow of intergovernmental funds. This left local governments with policy commitments they could ill afford absent federal aid. Moreover, Congress has shown little inclination to allow local governments the freedom to spend federal aid as they, the locals, desire. Instead, congressmen, given their own desire for reelection, engage in credit-taking activity by manipulating federal intergovernmental aid. Thus, Congress "recategorized" block grant programs and terminated the general revenue sharing—programs which provided greater flexibility to local politicians—in favor of aid for which federal officials could take greater credit.

Coupling such fiscal machinations with the growing use of inter-governmental mandates, which force cities to undertake specific policies in a prescribed manner, the limits on local government policy space are clearly growing. Thus the intergovernmental system of shared fiscal and service responsibility adds further complexity to the concept of city limits.

CONCLUSION

The structure of local government in the United States produces a market for public goods. The recognition of such a market produces opportunities for new research and provides a testing ground in which many of the most exciting developments in social science research can be employed.

Given the extensive variation within and across metropolitan markets, rigorous empirical analysis of a variety of political, social, and economic theories and propositions is possible. Viewing the metropolitan service delivery system as a market characterized by actors with definable utility functions, identifiable goals, and derived strategies, and also characterized by theoretically interesting structural conditions, such as oligopolistic or monopoly competition, prisoner's dilemmas, and links between market level and individual level phenomena, presents an arena in which to enrich the traditional concerns and methods of political science with concepts drawn from game theory and microeconomics.

At one time, analysts bemoaned the "lost world of municipal research." In fact, this world can provide a rich environment for rigorous theoretical and empirical social scientific analysis.

APPENDICES
NOTES
REFERENCES
INDEX

APPENDIX 1

METHODOLOGY

In each chapter, the number of cases upon which the descriptive analysis and the multivariate analyses are based varies: in general, the descriptive analysis will be based on more cases than any of the multivariate analyses, and the number of cases in any given multivariate analysis may vary from the number of cases in others. This variation results from the distribution of missing data and from my decision to base each individual empirical analysis on the maximum number of cases for which all data are available.

Most of the data are drawn from different census sources, including the Census of Population, 1970 and 1980; the Census of Governments, 1972, 1977, and 1982; and, the individual census reports on the wholesale, retail, service and manufacturing sectors in 1972, 1977, and 1982. Fiscal data on tax rates and tax base are not reported for smaller cities in any census document (the Census Bureau has only begun to report tax data for cities with population greater than 25,000). As a result, fiscal data were obtained from a variety of state, county, and local sources. These data were corrected for variation in assessment practices to compute estimates of effective tax rates and the true market value of local property.

Variation in the number of cases used in the analysis results from differences in the availability of data. As described in Appendix 2, I began with a sample of 1492 incorporated suburban municipalities with population greater than 2,500 in 1970. These municipalities were located in more than fifty metropolitan regions, which were among the 100 largest SMSAs in the United States in 1970. Suburbs from no more than three SMSAs from any given state were included. For the data drawn from the Census of Population, almost all information is available for almost every suburb.

Collecting fiscal data presented more problems than did census data. Repeated and extensive efforts to collect fiscal data from a variety of sources eventually led to complete data for slightly more than 1,100 municipalities. Consequently, a number of cases "fall out" of the analysis whenever fiscal data on are used.

The Census of Manufacturing was the second major limitation on data. The

Census Bureau employs a set of confidentiality restrictions on the release of business data. These restrictions had particularly severe implications for data on the distribution of manufacturing activities—many suburbs have fewer than the five manufacturing firms required for inclusion in census reports. The confidentiality rule had only small effects on the availability of data on other economic sectors (services, retail, and wholesale). Because of the restrictions on manufacturing, only about 1,000 suburbs have complete data on their economic base.

In chapter 5, I introduce another data set on local political structure and elections. This data set was by far the most difficult to assemble, requiring repeated mail and telephone queries to city clerks, mayors, and local politicians. Political data for only about 700 suburbs were collected.

Given the perversity of empirical social science work, the missing data were not always from the same communities—some communities were missing manufacturing data, but not fiscal data; some communities reported their political data but not their fiscal data. As a result, the *joint set* of suburbs upon which most of the multivariate empirical analysis is based totals 800 to 900 cases depending on the exact analysis in question. In chapter 5, the introduction of political variables reduces the number of cases in some analyses to just above 530, and in chapter 10 the number falls even lower. However, because I use a pooled cross-sectional design, the number of cases upon which the empirical results are based is usually 3 times the number of cases for which all data were available—that is, by pooling observations for the approximately 900 communities across three years (1972, 1977, and 1982), the number used to estimate a set of coefficients in a multivariate analysis is about 2,700 (900 cases*3 panels).

Suburban actors want to maximize their service/tax ratio; social scientists want to maximize the cases upon which they report their results. My strategy was to base every analysis on the maximum number of suburbs for which all the necessary data could be assembled. Thus as any given empirical analysis included more variables—especially fiscal or manufacturing data—the number of cases upon which it is based declined. To check the robustness of the results which I report, I reran many of the equations dropping the variables which led to the reduction in the number of cases. I could then compare the coefficients for the variables reported in the equations based on the small number of cases with the equation based on the larger number of cases. Almost without exception the direction of the coefficients, their significance, and their relative strength was replicated across subsamples. This provided a check on the validity of my strategy and testified to the robustness of the results I report.

APPENDIX 2

DISTRIBUTION OF SUBURBS ACROSS SMSAs

There were a total of 1492 suburban municipalities in the full sample. However, as noted, each empirical analysis may be based on a slightly different subset of cases.

In New England there were 21 suburbs divided among Boston (16) and Providence (5). In the Mid-Atlantic region there were 368 suburbs distributed across eight SMSAs: Allentown (12); Buffalo (19); Newark (34); New York (74); Paterson (66); Philadelphia (48); Pittsburgh (100); and Rochester (15).

In the East North Central region, 451 municipalities were located in eleven SMSAs: Chicago (163); Cincinnati (55); Cleveland (56); Columbus (11); Davenport (9); Detroit (69); Gary (14); Grand Rapids (12); Indianapolis (17); Milwaukee (36); and Peoria (9). In the West North Central, 160 municipalities were found in: Kansas City (23); Minneapolis (61); St. Louis (76).

In the South Atlantic region, there were 112 suburbs: Atlanta (23); Baltimore (5); Ft. Lauderdale (17); Greenville (8); Miami (17); Tampa (14); Washington, D.C. (24); Wilmington (4).

In the East South Central, 29 suburbs were in two SMSAs: Birmingham (21); and Louisville (8). In the West South Central, there were 141 suburban municipalities in the following SMSAs: Dallas (45); Houston (47); New Orleans (7); Oklahoma City (16); San Antonio (15); and Tulsa (11).

There were 34 surburbs in Mountain SMSAs: Denver (8); Phoenix (11); and Salt Lake City (15) and 176 suburban municipalities in the Pacific region: Anaheim (21); Los Angeles (66); Portland (14); San Francisco (8); Seattle (12); and Tacoma (5).

NOTES

CHAPTER 1. The Local Market for Public Goods

1. Stein 1987 shows that the relationship between contracting and spending is quite complex. Also see DeHoog 1984, for a careful analysis of contracting for services.

2. A key assumption of Tiebout's model is thus the mobility of citizen/consumers—the market is powered by their willingness to move when exposed to a preferred service/tax bundle. This key assumption has been addressed by numerous scholars because the transaction costs of moving are so high that the assumption may be unrealistic. See, for example, Cebula and Avery 1983, or Mills and Oates, 1975.

3. This has been most widely discussed in the analysis of local school district finances, but the issue also affects the analysis of other municipal services (see, for example, Lineberry 1977 on central cities; and Schneider and Logan 1981 on suburbs).

CHAPTER 3. Suburban Expenditure Patterns

1. There are limits in my empirical analysis which make it less than an ideal test of the Niskanen model applied to the behavior of local bureaucrats. I have no measure of what local bureaucrats actually produce with the money they receive. Nor do I have information on the average or marginal costs of bureaucratic production. As a result, many of the insights into the bureaucratic production process flowing from the Niskanen model are beyond the scope of the empirical analysis that follows.

2. Overproduction does not automatically mean that the bureaucratic production process is inefficient: a Niskanen-like bureaucratic agency may have highly rational and orderly production which are simply more resource-consuming than society prefers. Thus, a Niskanen-like bureaucracy can be efficient technically, while at the same time costing society more than it wants to spend. However, Miller and Moe (1983) and Moe (1984) link overproduction and inefficiency more closely than does Niskanen.

3. The belief that competition will limit the size and growth of local government is evident in other lines of research besides Niskanen's—most notably in arguments for the structural design of systems of local government which maximize competition between alternate service providers (see Bennett and Johnson 1980; Wagner and Weber 1975) and in the related literature advocating the creation and maintenance of polycentric metropolitan markets (Bish 1971; Ostrom et al. 1961; Ostrom 1972).

4. Miller and Moe argue that Niskanen's original model is really a model of

agency output at one point in time, not a model of governmental growth (1983: 297). Yet as Conybeare (1984) points out, the Niskanen model can contribute to the analysis of growth and has informed growth models rooted in dynamic general equilibrium analysis. Furthermore, the model suggests that bureaucratic power increases government output relative to what would occur in competitive situations. In the analysis which follows, I undertake cross-sectional analysis that reflects the resolution of competing demands at a point in time. I also report an analysis of change in local expenditures as a function of the competition in the polycentric market, thus pushing the Niskanen model beyond its original formulation.

5. There are two major approaches to this question of functional responsibility. Liebert used a simple count of functions, while Clark, Ferguson, and Shapiro (1982) developed a much more complex weighted index, called the "index of functional performance." Following Liebert, I use an unweighted count variable.

6. The percent poor is defined as the percentage of the population in a community which earns less than 50 percent of the median income computed for the entire SMSA. To estimate the 1972, 1977, and 1982 value of this and the other demographic variables based on 1970 and 1980 values, I followed the procedure used by the Census Bureau. Using population as an example, compute $"r" = \log(\text{pop}1980/\text{pop}1970)/(10 \log e)$. Population 1972 = Population $1970(e^{**}2r)$. The 1977 estimate substitutes 7 in the last term of the equation, while the 1982 estimate substitutes the 1980 value for the 1970 term.

7. Note that Hill et al.'s data come from a single point in time in the mid 1970s, while my data are from three points in time between 1972 and 1982. By attaching Hill's data to cases in each of the three years, I am assuming that the patterns found by Hill are relatively stable.

8. If we assume the owner of the median priced home is also the median voter, the importance of this measure is clear.

9. While the data on taxes and true value are as close as possible to equalized values, there may still be measurement problems caused by differences in the equalization practices used by different county and/or state assessors. However, the only other source of equalized fiscal data is the census, which periodically reports corrected tax rates and tax base data. One possible way of verifying the data used here would be to correlate them with the data reported by the census. The problem with computing such a correlation is that in 1972, the year for which the census data are most complete, the equalization studies were only for large suburbs (population greater than 25,000). The 1972 data used in this paper are drawn from all suburban municipalities greater than *2,500* population, and the vast majority of suburbs in this sample are not surveyed by the census. In 1977, census data is scattered and incomplete. Thus for most of the corrections needed, state and county reports are the only source of information for most communities in the sample.

10. There is a known simultaneity bias in cross-sectional models of the effects of intergovernmental aid on expenditures, but the problem may not be

severe. In particular, cross-sectional analysis including intergovernmental aid *and* local expenditures in the same year can upwardly bias the estimated effect of such aid—by standard reporting procedures, grants are counted as received simultaneously with the subsidized expenditure. This simultaneity effect is a measurement problem more particular to models of grants-in-aid and not for models of revenue sharing programs, where monies are delivered independently of specific project expenditures. Indeed, Horowitz (1968) and O'Brien (1971) have shown that even when estimating the effects of "mixed" grant programs combining both revenue sharing and grants-in-aid, the upward bias of cross-sectional analysis is small.

11. Compared to using expenditures as the dependent variable, which reflects budgetary inputs into the bureaucratic production process, the use of expenditures on this side of the equation as an indicator of service availability and quality is a larger problem. Ideally, what is required is an indicator of the actual service levels enjoyed in different communities. However, the problems of gathering such data are as well known as the problems of using expenditures as a surrogate measure of service quality.

12. High collinearity between the contextual variables and the other variables in the equation, especially the SMSA dummy variables, is to be expected. I tested for multicollinearity by regressing the contextual variables on the remaining independent variables in the equation. While the regression of the total number of suburbs on the other variables produced an R square of over .90 (explaining why it falls out of the estimation process), a similar equation using the standard deviation of expenditures was only .38. The R square of the standard deviation of the tax bill equation was somewhat more troublesome at .68, most of which was accounted for by the regional variables.

13. Better measurement of the actual service levels found in communities might change this result and indicate an effect of competition along this dimension. Again, however, gathering such data for a large sample of communities is difficult, if not impossible.

14. See Schrodt and Ward (1981) for a discussion of some of the problems associated with this approach.

CHAPTER 4. Competition in the Three Worlds of Municipal Expenditures

1. Paralleling chapter 3, I ran the demand models without the competition measures and then with them. Coefficients across these two models for every type of expenditure are highly stable (as was evident in chapter 3). Given the extensive data analysis presented here, only the results which included competition indicators are reported.

2. While the definition of developmental expenditures leads to a relatively straightforward operationalization, the other two categories are less neat. Indeed, Peterson himself seems to have backed away from the allocational category (see Peterson et al. 1984). I define allocational services as those most

closely tied to the actual day-to-day operation and administration of general government—the basic concept underlying Peterson's original typology (see note 3 below). In my categorization there are three specific service areas which caused the greatest problems. I did not know how to classify police and fire expenditures. A reasonable case could be made to place them in either the developmental or allocational category. I chose not to use these expenditures at all. I also had a problem in classifying housing/community development money. Peterson classifies urban renewal as a developmental program. However, urban renewal was phased out as a separate program by the mid 1970s, and it was never a program in which many suburbs participated. The community development program was a much broader program than urban renewal and supported a range of programs, including a large low-to-moderate-income housing component. Given this subsidized housing component, I classified suburban outlays in this policy area as redistributive, although these monies can also be spent on development of the urban infrastructure.

3. The specific census defined areas included in this category are financial administration, general government, general control and general buildings.

4. These patterns of redistributive expenditures and service responsibility indicate only the role of suburban *municipalities* as service providers. Low scores may mean only that services are provided by other levels of government, such as the county. Indeed, the high level of redistributive service responsibility and expenditures of New England suburbs can be traced almost directly to the absence of viable county governments in that region.

5. This argument is supported by the literature on cut back management in which many of these functions are the last to be cut when local governments face reductions in aid (see, for example, Fitzgerald 1979; Kim 1982; McInturff 1980; Schneider 1986c). This argument is further reinforced by the fact that state mandates do not much affect the level of local expenditures on infrastructure—states do not need to force local policy action in this policy domain.

CHAPTER 5. Suburban Public Employment

1. As in previous chapters, some of the data come from the 1970 and 1980 Census of Population, while the fiscal and governmental data come from 1972, 1977, and 1982. The Census data were converted to estimates for the appropriate years. See note 6 in chapter 3.

2. The pay ratio is constructed on the basis of actual wages paid. Since a significant part of public-sector compensation may be in the form of fringe benefits and other forms of deferred compensation not reflected in actual wages, the *total* compensation package of public-sector workers may match more closely the private-sector package. However, data constraints make the comparison of total compensation packages impossible.

3. The way in which the factor supplier hypothesis is usualy developed is actually confusing. Government workers can live either inside or outside the

community in which they work. If a local government worker also lives in the community for which he works, it is clear he should support higher wages: the benefits of higher wages are concentrated, while the costs are diffused across the general population. However, the literature has not developed a clear expectation regarding public workers who do *not* live in the community for which they work. Such workers may support higher wages in the community in which they live on the expectation of reciprocity from the public-sector workers who live in the community in which they work. This case is obviously more difficult to evaluate.

4. I am using the term "categorical" broadly. What I have actually measured is the non-GRS component of federal aid and the non-general aid component of state aid. This actually includes specific project grants, formula grants, and block grants. These types of grants will all vary in the degree to which they stimulate the local public sector, but they are all more stimulative than revenue sharing grants.

5. There is a measurement problem in this procedure. Hill et al. measure financial mandates at one point in time, midway in the decade during which the suburbs in this sample are studied. I hope that these cross-sectional data reflect relatively consistent patterns of state involvement over time. I do not include federal mandates, assuming their effects are spread relatively evenly across local governments.

6. Clearly if the simultaneous effects are as large as theoretically postulated, two stage least squares estimation would be necessary. However, as will be seen later, the effects are in fact not statistically significant.

7. Reform is usually indicated by: the structural form of government (most commonly mayor versus city manager); and two dimensions of the local electoral system (at-large versus ward elections; partisan versus nonpartisan elections). Some studies investigate these dimensions separately, while others have scaled these reforms in various manners. Given the limitations in the data I was able to collect, I use only two indicators of reform and do not combine them.

8. The political variables are not measured at the exact same time as the other indicators. The city clerks who provided the electoral data were asked to indicate any changes in the form of election or in local government structure, but virtually none indicated such change. Second, the turnover data represent *cumulative* change between 1972 and 1982. I assigned that number to each community in each year, hoping these data reflect relatively consistent patterns of turnover in the local community. See note 4 above.

9. Among central cities, Stein (1984) shows that, by 1977, the increased reliance on intergovernmental aid changed the relationship between wage rates and the size of the local work force. For these suburbs, however, there were no differences in structural relationships over time. This stability may indicate differences in the decision processes and conditions facing central cities compared to suburbs during the decade under analysis: while the decade 1972–1982 was difficult for all local governments, central cities were more exposed to the turbulence of those years, and their responses were more dramatically different over time than were the responses of suburbs.

CHAPTER 6: The Flypaper Effect: Bureaucrats and Residents in Conflict

1. Gramlich (1977) provides an extensive discussion of the types of inter-governmental grants in which he actually identifies a third type: open-ended grants such as Medicare. However, these grants are generally not available to local governments.

2. There are known methodological problems in testing the effects on expenditures of intergovernmental aid in cross-sectional analysis. See note 10 in chapter 3.

3. I use beta coefficients here instead of elasticities because for many localities several indicators, particularly percent black, have zero values. The estimation of elasticities requires taking logs. Since the log of zero is undefined, many cases would have been dropped from the analysis.

4. There is a methodological problem in the computation of these interaction terms. General revenue sharing is positively associated with total expenditures, while some of the market indicators, including the two with statistically significant coefficients, are negatively related to the dependent variable. When the original terms in an equation have opposite signs, the interpretation of their interaction terms is difficult. To solve this problem, the two market indicators with negative coefficients (the border variable and the standard deviation in taxes) were multiplied by negative one (-1). The interaction terms of the other market variables were computed with no transformations, since table 24 shows they have the same sign as the GRS variable.

CHAPTER 7. Local Wealth and Personal Income

1. The attempt by municipalities to control the income of *new* residents underlies these various studies. The wealth of a community will also rise if existing local residents increase their incomes. We can think of this as "incumbent up-grading." It is difficult empirically to disentangle these two processes, but the analysis of the concentration of affluent and poor families in a community is logically centered on the question of in-migration while the analysis of median income more clearly mixes the two routes to higher personal income in a community.

2. While the interests of these three sectors is relatively easy to identify, *a priori*, it is hardest to predict the interests of wholesale firms. To the extent that they provide goods and services to manufacturing firms and to the extent their business activities produce heavy traffic or noise, they may also be adversely affected by growing income levels in the community, sharing the qualms of manufacturers. However, empirically, wholesale firms have increased in number more rapidly in wealthier communities (Schneider 1985). Apparently they derive benefits from increased local wealth.

3. There are known problems with this type of regression model, again see Schrodt and Ward (1981).

4. Grants from higher level to lower level governments have significantly different implications for local budgets depending on whether they are categorical or less restricted general revenue sharing type grants (Gramlich 1977; Inman 1979). Limitations in the 1972 Census of Governments prevent the computation of separate indicators.

5. The estimation procedure here is the same used in earlier chapters. See chapter 3.

6. As noted in earlier chapters, both the tax rate and the true value measure are gathered from local sources, such as state or county boards of assessors, and adjusted (equalized) for differences in assessment practices.

7. Note that these budgetary indicators appeared on the left hand side of equations in chapter 4 and income appeared on the right. Here the order of variables is reversed, producing a possible simultaneity bias which could require estimation techniques other than Ordinary Least Squares. The problem with implementing this more rigorous estimation procedure is that the reversal of variables in parts 2 and 3 requires a system of approximately a dozen simultaneous equations to take into account all the instances where the order of variables has been changed. I used two stage least squares to check "pair-wise" many equations (such as the income equation of this chapter and each of the expenditure equations of chapter 4) and found only minor changes in the size of the coefficients compared to the OLS coefficients I report (also see Peterson and Rom 1987).

Moreover, I have inspected the strength of the relationships and the most likely order of bias in each of the equations in this section and believe that in most instances bias is small because the strength of the feedback between variables is minimal or that the direction of the bias is *against* the conclusions I draw. Consider the possible bias using OLS in the relationship between developmental expenditures and income. Following existing theory and the argument presented so far, we know that, on the margin, higher income individuals demand more expenditures on developmental services. But, according to Peterson, developmental expenditures will also attract higher income individuals. Thus theoretically there is a positive feedback loop which, using OLS, should inflate the estimates of the positive effects of developmental expenditures on community wealth. Yet when we look at the empirical results (see table 27) using OLS, we find that the effects are not statistically significant. Thus even though there is most likely a bias toward a positive result, we find no relationship. The same pattern holds true for allocational expenditures. With regard to redistributive expenditures the absence of a relationship between these expenditures and income reduces the problem of nonrecursivity.

8. The coefficients reported in the tables for the lagged variable differ somewhat from those reported in the text. The text reports the "simple" regression coefficients before any other variables are added, while the tables report the partial regression coefficients controlling for region and other community conditions.

9. As described in note 1, there is a measurement problem here. If the

residents of a community increase their own incomes faster than the rate of increase found in the entire SMSA, the concentration of wealthy in the community could also increase (that is, incumbent up-grading can also affect the dependent variable). However, both ecological theory and the persistence model emphasize the importance of migration decisions. I assume here that changes in the concentration of the affluent in any given community is determined more by the ability of the community to lure new affluent residents than by the changing income of its individual members.

CHAPTER 8. *Economic Development of Local Communities*

1. The pattern for suburbs in the sample directly parallels the figures for all suburbs nationwide: in 1972, manufacturing jobs represented about 46 percent of all employment in the major sectors of the suburban economy (manufacturing, wholesale, retail, selected services, and government). By 1977, however, jobs in the manufacturing sector accounted for only 42 percent of jobs and continued to decline through 1982, to about 35 percent. The similarity in the national and sample level patterns increases confidence in the generalizability of the following analysis. Note that I have accepted the definitions used by the Census Bureau in their enumerations of jobs.

2. The average community ratio is higher than the ratio of manufacturing and service jobs based on aggregate numbers would suggest. This results because the distribution of manufacturing jobs is highly skewed, and some communities have very high ratios. Between 1972 and 1982 the ratio dropped sharply because many manufacturing suburbs lost jobs (decreasing the numerator) and new service jobs were much more evenly distributed across communities than were manufacturing jobs. Both these factors contribute to the lower ratios (see Schneider and Fernandez 1989).

3. The fact that the data are for *net* change poses a measurement problem. There is high turnover in the economy, and change in the number of jobs is the product of the birth of firms, the death of firms, and the expansion or contraction of jobs in existing firms. However, the detailed data needed to decompose net change is not available at the level of community which I am investigating. For the largest central cities in the United States, Dun & Bradstreet collect appropriate data. Similarly, data are sometimes available for counties or for scattered communities. But for the suburban municipalities in this sample, the Census of Manufacturing and the Census of Services report only totals, allowing solely for the study of net change.

4. As in chapter 7, the problem of nonrecursivity between expenditures and the location of jobs may exist. But again the weakness of the feedback loop and the direction of the bias reduces the problem (see note 7 in chapter 7). There is also a potential feed back loop between true value and job creation. But in chapter 9, we will see that the location of jobs in neither the manufacturing nor the service sectors is associated with growth in the tax base.

5. Analysts often make a distinction between "consumer-oriented" services and "production-oriented" ones (which aid in the production of goods). See, for example, Shelp (1981). This empirical pattern implies that suburban service firms specialize in consumer services.

6. Note that I am not dealing with specific programs of local government such as tax abatements or industrial development bonds, which are often used as parts of packages designed to lure a specific firm. Instead, the focus is on the general policy tools available to all local governments.

7. A similar problem was noted by Humberger (1983) in his analysis of manufacturing firms—what government officials thought were important inducements to firm location were *not* the same items emphasized by business leaders.

CHAPTER 9. Maximizing the Local Tax Base

1. These figures, from the Advisory Commission on Intergovernmental Relations (ACIR), are for the nation as a whole. Across the three major sources of local revenues (taxes, intergovernmental transfers, and user charges), the distribution for the suburbs in this sample is close to that reported by the ACIR. Between 1972 and 1982, for the suburbs in this sample, taxes provided almost two-thirds of all revenues, of which property taxes accounted for an average of about 65 percent. User charges accounted for less than 14 percent of total revenues, while intergovernmental aid accounted for about 25 percent.

2. There are multiple sources of wealth defining the suburban property tax base—most notably business firms, families, and utilities. Communities may vary in the precise strategies they use to maximize the tax base. In this analysis, I focus on the *outcome* of such attempts (as reflected in the size of the tax base) rather than on the movement of specific components of the tax base.

3. This was first widely discussed in the analysis of local school district finances, where disparities between the level of local property tax base across different school districts allowed rich districts to support high expenditures on education at lower tax rates than poorer districts. A major impetus was a series of court cases, such as *Serrano* v. *Priest* in California, challenging the use of local property taxes for education. These court cases often resulted in state policies designed to equalize the educational disparities derived from unequal property tax bases. The issue also affected the more general analysis of municipal service (see, for example, Lineberry 1977, or Schneider and Logan 1981).

4. Recall that this equation is of the type Schrodt and Ward (1981) call "incremental equations," distinct from "difference equations," where the dependent variable is the rate of change.

5. As noted in earlier chapters, these data are from reports of state or county assessors (or the equivalent offices) and represent the value of property in each municipality equalized for differences in local assessment practices.

6. Because of limitations in the Census of Manufacturing, many suburbs

have no data reported for either the number of manufacturing firms or manufacturing workers. I reran the analysis dropping those two variables. This increased the sample size to over 1000. The results of the analysis using the larger sample, however, were virtually identical to those reported. Since manufacturing firms are potentially major contributors to local property wealth, the equations with the smaller number of cases and including the two manufacturing variables are reported.

7. As in previous chapters, the tax bill is computed by multiplying the effective tax rate by the median home value in the community. Again note that while the data on taxes and true value are as close as possible to equalized values, there may still be some measurement problems caused by differences in the equalization practices used by different county and/or state assessors. See note 9, chapter 3.

8. There was an overall difference in the rate at which true value increased in this sample of communities between 1972–1977 and 1977–1982. True value increased by 93 percent in the first period, but by only 50 percent in the second period. This difference persists even after other variables are entered into the first equation—note the coefficient for the time variable in table 36.

9. There are major regional differences in changes in the local property tax base, most of which follow a predictable "Sunbelt" versus "Snowbelt" dichotomy. For the suburbs in this sample, the fastest growth in true value per capita between 1972 and 1977 occurred in suburbs located in Dallas, Fort Lauderdale, Houston, Seattle, and Tampa, while the slowest growth occurred among suburbs located in Chicago, Peoria, Grand Rapids, and St. Louis. This pattern was largely repeated between 1977 and 1982, with the fastest growth evident among suburbs in Seattle, Anaheim, Ft. Lauderdale, and Phoenix, and slow growth in Allentown, Chicago, and St. Louis. I do not report the individual SMSA coefficients, but these differences are significant at the .05 level.

10. The failure of both indicators to have an effect may result from the high correlation of debt and construction expenditures.

11. It is possible that if all communities relied on the same expenditures to maximize the property tax base, in the long run an equilibrium could result in which any potential benefits to individual communities from manipulating service/tax bundles would disappear. It is also possible that alternate institutional arrangements could increase the total welfare of the system. However, I am analyzing the benefits to individual communities successfully playing the "game" in the present system and within a time frame of ten years.

CHAPTER 10. *Intergovernmental Aid as a Local Resource*

1. See note 1, chapter 6.

2. It is not as easy to measure unrestricted grants from the states to their local governments as it is to measure unrestricted federal aid. Federal general revenue sharing grants are separately measured, and the characteristics of that

program are well known. The state programs most similar to GRS are what the Census of Governments reports as "General State Aid." But there is wide varia-tion between states in the degree to which this aid is actually unrestricted.

3. I developed similar models for the study of categorical aid. However, the results of this analysis were virtually identical to those of total aid and are not reported.

4. I measure this term as the percentage of families with median incomes less than 50 percent of the SMSA median income. I include it because an important question in the analysis of intergovernmental aid is the extent to which such aid is targeted on the most needy populations (see, for example, the Dommel and Rich 1987).

5. There are known methodological problems in testing the relationship between intergovernmental aid and expenditures. See chapter 3, note 10.

REFERENCES

Advisory Commission on Intergovernmental Relations (ACIR). 1972. *Profiles of County Government.* Washington, D.C.: Government Printing Office.

———. 1981. *Significant Features of Fiscal Federalism, 1981.* Washington, D.C.: Government Printing Office.

———. 1985. *Regulatory Federalism.* Washington, D.C.: Government Printing Office.

———. 1985. *Significant Features of Fiscal Federalism, 1984.* Washington, D.C.: Government Printing Office.

Allison, G. 1971. *The Essence of Decision.* Boston: Little Brown.

Aronson, J. R. 1974. "Financing Public Goods and the Distribution of Population in Metropolitan Areas: An Analysis of Fiscal Migration in the United States and England." In *Economic Policies and Social Goals.* A. J. Culyer, ed., 313–41. London: Martin Robertson.

Bahl, R. 1984. *Financing State and Local Government.* New York: Oxford University Press.

Banfield, E., and J. Q. Wilson. 1963. *City Politics.* New York: Vintage.

Baumol, W. J. 1982. "Contestable Markets: An Uprising in the Theory of Industry Structure." *American Economic Review* 72: 1–15.

Beaumont, E. F., and H. A. Hovey. 1985. "State, Local and Federal Development Policies: New Federal Patterns, Chaos, or What?" *Public Administration Review* 45: 327–32.

Bendor, J. 1987. "Formal Models of Bureaucracy. A Review Essay." Paper presented at the 1987 Annual Meeting of the American Political Science Association, Chicago, Ill.

Bendor, J., S. Taylor, and R. Van Galen. 1987. "Politicians, Bureaucrats, and Asymmetric Information." *American Journal of Political Science* 31: 796–828.

Bennett, J. T., and M. H. Johnson. 1980. *The Political Economy of Federal Government Growth: 1959–1978.* College Station, Texas: Center for Education and Research in Free Enterprise.

Bennett, J. T., and W. P. Orzechowski. 1983. "The Voting Behavior of Bureaucrats: Some Empirical Evidence." *Public Choice* 40: 271–83.

Bergstrom, T., and R. Goodman. 1973. "Private Demand for Public Goods." *American Economic Review* 63: 286–96.

Bish, R. 1971. *The Political Economy of Metropolitan Areas.* Chicago: Markham.

Blair, J. P., R. H. Fichtenbaum, and J. A. Swaney. 1984. "The Market for Jobs: Locational Decisions and the Competition for Economic Development." *Urban Affairs Quarterly* 20: 64–77.

Bowman, J. 1981. "Urban Revenue Structures: An Overview of Patterns, Trends, and Issues." *Public Administration Review* 41: 131–45.

Bradford, D., and H. Kelejian. 1973. "An Econometric Model of Flight to the Suburbs." *Journal of Political Economy* 81: 566–89.

Branfman, E. J., B. I. Cohen, and D. M. Trubek. 1973. "Measuring the Invisible Wall: Land Use Controls and Residential Patterns of the Poor." *Yale Law Review* 82: 483–508.

Breton, A., and Wintrobe, R. 1982. *The Logic of Bureaucratic Action.* Cambridge: Cambridge University Press.

———. 1984. "The Equilibrium Size of Budget-Maximizing Bureaus." *Journal of Political Economy* 92: 195–207.

Brudney, J. L., and R. E. England. 1983. "Toward a Definition of the Coproduction Concept." *Public Administration Review* 43: 59–65.

Buchanan, J. 1981. "Principles of Urban Fiscal Strategy." *Public Choice* 36: 1–14.

Burgess, E. W. 1927. "The Determinants of Gradients in the Growth of Cities." *American Sociological Review* 21: 178–84.

Burkhead, J., and S. Grosskopf. 1980. "Trends in Public Employment and Compensation." In *Public Employment and State and Local Government,* ed. R. Bahl, J. Burkhead, and B. Jump, Jr., 197–216. Cambridge, Mass.: Ballinger.

Buss, Terry F., and F. Stevens Redburn. 1983. *Shutdown at Youngstown.* Albany: State University of New York Press.

Cebula, R., and C. Avery. 1983. "The Tiebout Hypothesis in the United States: An Analysis of Black Consumer-Voters, 1970–1975." *Public Choice* 41: 307–11.

Charney, A. H. 1983. "Intraurban Manufacturing Location Decisions and Local Tax Differentials." *Journal of Urban Economics* 22: 184–205.

Chubb, J. E. 1985. "The Political Economy of Federalism." *American Political Science Review* 79: 994–1015.

Clark, T. N., and L. Ferguson. 1983. *City Money.* New York: Columbia University Press.

Clark, T. N., L. Ferguson, and R. Shapiro. 1982. "Functional Performance Analysis: A New Approach to the Study of Municipal Expenditures and Debt." *Political Methodology* 9: 87–123.

Collver, A., and M. Semyonov. 1979. "Suburban Change and Persistence." *American Sociological Review* 44: 480–86.

Committee for Economic Development. 1967. *Modernizing Local Government.* New York: Committee for Economic Development.

Conlon, T. J. 1981. "Back in Vogue: The Politics of Block Grant Legislation." *Intergovernmental Perspective* 7: 8–17.

Conybeare, J.A.C. 1984. "Bureaucracy, Monopoly, and Competition: A Critical Analysis of the Budget-Maximizing Model of Bureaucracy." *American Journal of Political Science* 28: 479–502.

Courant, P. N., E. M. Gramlich, and D. L. Rubinfeld. 1979a. "The Stimulative Effects of Intergovernmental Aid: or Why Money Sticks Where It Hits." In *Fiscal Federalism and Grants-in-Aid,* ed. Peter Mieszkowski and William H. Oakland, 5–22. Washington, D.C.: The Urban Institute.

———. 1979b. "Public Employee Marketing Power and the Level of Government Spending." *American Economic Review* 69: 806–817.

Cummings, J., and W. E. Ruther. 1980. "Some Tests of the Factor Supplier Pressure Group Hypothesis." *Public Choice* 35: 257–66.

Cyert, R. M., and J. G. March. 1963. *A Behavioral Theory of the Firm.* Englewood Cliffs, N.J.: Prentice Hall.

Czamanski, D. Z., and S. Czamanski. 1977. "Industrial Complexes." *Papers of the Regional Science Association* 38: 93–111.

Danielson, M. 1976. *The Politics of Exclusion.* New York: Columbia University Press.

Deacon, R. T. 1979. "The Expenditure Effects of Alternative Public Sector Supply Institutions." *Public Choice* 33: 381–98.

DeAllesi, L. 1969. "Implications of Property Rights for Government Investment Choices." *American Economic Review* 58: 13–24.

DeHoog, R. H. 1984. *Contracting Out for Human Services: Economic, Political and Organizational Perspectives.* Albany: State University of New York Press.

DiLorenzo, T. J. 1981a. "The Expenditure Effects of Restricting Competition in Local Public Service Industries: The Case of Special Districts." *Public Choice* 37: 569–78.

_____. 1981b. "An Empirical Assessment of the Factor-Supplier Pressure Group Hypotheis." *Public Choice* 37: 559–68.

_____. 1983. "Economic Competition and Political Competition: An Empirical Note." *Public Choice* 40: 203–09.

Dommel, P., and M. J. Rich. 1987. "The Attenuation of Targeting Effects of the Community Development Block Grant Program." *Urban Affairs Quarterly* 22: 552–79.

Downs, A. 1967. *Inside Bureaucracy.* Boston: Little Brown.

Dunleavey, P. 1985. "Bureaucrats, Budgets and the Growth of the State." *British Journal of Politics* 15: 299–328.

Eavey, C., and G. Miller. 1984. "Bureaucratic Agenda Control: Imposition or Bargaining?" *American Political Science Review* 78: 719–33.

Ehrenberg, R. 1973a. "The Demand for State and Local Government Employees." *American Economic Review* 63: 366–79.

_____. 1973b. "Municipal Government Structures, Unionization and the Wages of Fire Fighters." *Industrial and Labor Relations Review* 27:36–48.

Ellwood, John W., ed., 1982. *Reductions in U.S. Domestic Spending: How They Affect State and Local Governments.* New York: Transaction Books

Epple, D., and A. Zelenitz. 1981. "The Implications of Competition Among Jurisdictions." *Journal of Political Economy* 89: 1197–217.

Fainstein, S. S., N. I. Fainstein, R. C. Hill, D. Judd, and M. P. Smith, 1984. *Restructuring the City.* New York: Longman.

Farley, R. 1964. "Suburban Persistence." *American Sociological Review* 29: 38–47.

Filimon, R., T. Romer, and H. Rosenthal. 1982. "Asymmetric Information and Agenda Control: The Bases of Monopoly Power in Public Spending." *Journal of Public Economics* 17: 51–70.

Fischel, W. 1975. "Fiscal and Environmental Considerations in the Location of

Firms in Suburban Communities." In *Fiscal Zoning and Land Use Controls,* ed. E. S. Mills and W. E. Oates, 119–74. Lexington, Mass.: Lexington Books.

Fitzgerald, M. 1979. "Proposition 13: An Overview," *Tax Revolt Digest* 1: 1–14.

Flanigan, W. H., and N. H. Zingale. 1980. "Ticket Splitting and the Vote for Governor." *State Government* 53: 157–60.

Fox, W. 1981. "Fiscal Differentials and Industrial Locations." *Urban Studies* 18: 105–11.

Frey, B. S., and W. W. Pommerehne. 1982. "How Powerful are Public Bureaucrats as Voters." *Public Choice* 38: 253–62.

Friedland, R. 1983. "Profits of Poverty. The Geography and Politics of Economic Growth." *Urban Affairs Quarterly* 18: 41–54.

Gramlich, E. M. 1977. "Intergovernmental Grants: A Review of the Empirical Literature." In *The Political Economy of Fiscal Federalism,* ed. Wallace E. Oates, 219–40. Lexington, Mass.: Lexington Books.

Gramlich, E. M., and D. Rubinfeld. 1982. "Micro Estimates of Public Spending Demand." *Journal of Political Economy* 90: 536–60.

Gray, J., and D. Spina. 1980. "State and Local Industrial Location Incentives: A Well-Stocked Candy Store." *Journal of Corporation Law* 14: 517–687.

Guest, A. 1978. "Suburban Social Status: Persistence or Evolution?" *American Sociological Review* 43: 251–64.

Hansen, N. 1965. "Municipal Investment Requirements in a Growing Agglomeration." *Land Economics* 41: 49–56.

———. 1977. *Capital and Region.* New York: St. Martin's.

Hartman, C. 1984. *The Transformation of San Francisco.* Totowa, N.J.: Rowman and Allanheid.

Hatry, H. 1977. *How Effective are Your Community Services? Procedures for Monitoring the Effectivess of Municipal Services.* Washington, D.C.: The Urban Institute.

Hawley, A., and V. P. Rock, eds. 1975. *Metropolitan American in Contemporary Perspective.* New York: John Wiley & Sons.

Hill, M. B., et al. 1978. *State Laws Governing Local Government Structure and Aministration.* Athens: Institute of Government, University of Georgia.

Hill, R. C. 1974. "Separate and Unequal: Government Inequality in the Metropolis." *American Political Science Review* 68: 1557–68.

Hirsch, W. Z. 1967. *About the Supply of Urban Public Services.* Los Angeles: Institute for Government and Public Affairs.

Hirschman, A. O. 1970. *Exit, Voice, Loyalty.* Cambridge: Harvard University Press.

Hofstadter, R. 1955. *The Age of Reform.* New York: Knopf.

Holland, S. 1975. *Capital Versus Region.* New York: St. Martin's.

Horowitz, A. R. 1968. "A Simultaneous Equation Approach to the Problems of Explaining Interstate Differences in State and Local Government Expenditures." *Southern Economic Journal* 34: 459–76.

Humberger, E. 1983. *Business Location Decisons and Cities.* Washington, D.C.: Public Technology, Inc.

Inman, R. P. 1978. "Testing Political Economy's 'As If' Proposition: Is the Median Income Voter Really Decisive?" *Public Choice* 33: 45–65.

_____. 1979. "The Fiscal Performance of Local Governments: An Interpretative Review." In *Current Issues in Urban Economics,* ed. Peter Mieszkowski and Mahlon Straszheim, 270–321. Baltimore: The Johns Hopkins University Press.

Jackson, J. E. 1975. "Public Needs, Private Behavior, and Metropolitan Governance." In *Public Needs and Private Behavior in Metropolitan Areas,* ed. John Jackson, 1–29. Lexington, Mass.: Lexington Books.

Jennings, E. T. 1977. "The Policy Consequences of the Long Revolution and Bifactional Rivalry in Louisiana." *American Journal of Political Science* 21: 225–46.

Jones, B. 1981. "Party and Bureaucracy: The Influence of Intermediary Groups on Urban Public Service Delivery." *American Political Science Review* 75: 688–703.

Jones, B., with S. Greenberg and J. Drew. 1980. *Service Delivery in the City.* New York: Longman.

Jones, B., S. Greenberg, C. Kaufman, and J. Drew. 1977. "Bureaucratic Response to Citizen-Initiated Contacts." *American Political Science Review* 71: 148–65.

Jones, B., and L. W. Bachelor with C. Wilson. 1986. *The Sustaining Hand: Community Leadership and Corporate Power.* Lawrence: University of Kansas Press.

Jones, T. E. 1974. "Political Change and Spending Shifts in the American States." *American Politics Quarterly* 2: 159–78.

Kasarda, J. 1980. "The Implications of Contemporary Redistribution Trends for National Urban Policy." *Social Science Quarterly* 61: 373–400.

Kau, J. B., and P. H. Rubin. 1981. "The Size of Government." *Public Choice* 37: 261–274.

Kettl, D. F. 1980. *Managing Community Development in the New Federalism.* New York: Praeger.

Key, V.O. 1949. *Southern Politics.* New York: Random House.

Kim, K. E. 1982. "Post 2½ Changes: Municipal Appropriations Levels." *Impact 2½* 37 (November 1): 1–8.

Langbein, L. I. 1980. "Production or Perquisites in the Public Bureaus." Paper presented at the 1980 meeting of the Public Choice Society, San Francisco, Calif.

Larkey, P. D., C. Stolp, and M. Winer. 1981. "Theorizing About the Size of Government: A Research Assessment." *Journal of Public Policy* 1: 157–220.

Leinberger, C. B., and C. Lockwood. 1986. "How Business Is Reshaping America." *The Atlantic* (October): 43–63.

Liebert, R. 1976. *Disintegration and Political Action.* New York: Academic Press.

Lineberry, R. 1977. *Equality and Urban Services*. Beverly Hills, Calif.: Sage.

Lineberry, R., and E. Fowler. 1967. "Reformism and Public Policies in American Cities." *American Political Science Review* 71: 701–16.

Logan, J. R. 1978. "Growth, Politics and the Stratification of Places." *American Journal of Sociology* 84: 404–16.

Logan, J. R., and H. Molotch. 1987. *Urban Fortunes*. Berkeley and Los Angeles: University of California Press.

Logan, J. R., and M. Schneider. 1981. "Stratification of Metropolitan Suburbs, 1960–1970." *American Sociological Review* 46: 175–86.

Lovell, C., et al. 1979. *Federal and State Mandating on Local Governments: An Exploration of Issues and Impacts*. Washington, D.C.: National Science Foundation.

Lowery, D., and W. D. Berry. 1983. "The Growth of Government in the United States: An Empirical Assessment of Competing Explanations." *American Journal of Political Science* 27: 665–94.

McGuire, T. G., M. Coiner, and L. Spancake. 1979. "Budget Maximizing Agencies and Efficiency in Government." *Public Choice* 34: 333–59.

McGuire, T. G. 1981. "Budget Maximizing Government Agencies: An Empirical Test." *Public Choice* 36: 313–22.

McInturff, P. 1980. "Proposition 13: The Impact on the Inland Empire." San Bernadino: Department of Public Administration, California State University.

Mackay, R. J., and C. L. Weaver. 1978. "Monopoly Bureaucrats and Fiscal Outcomes: Deductive Models and Implications for Reform." In *Policy Analysis and Deductive Reasoning*, ed. G. Tullock and R. Wagner, 141–65. Lexington Mass.: Lexington Books.

MacKenzie, R. B. 1979. *Restrictions on Business Mobility*. Washington, D.C.: American Enterprise Institute.

Markus, G. 1980. *Models for the Analysis of Panel Data*. Beverly Hills, Calif.: Sage.

Meier, Kenneth J. 1986. *Politics and the Bureaucracy*. Monterey, Calif.: Brooks-Cole.

Miller, G. 1981. *Cities by Contrast*. Cambridge, Mass.: MIT Press.

Miller, G., and T. M. Moe. 1983. "Bureaucrats, Legislators, and the Size of Government." *American Political Science Review* 77: 297–322.

Mills, E., and W. Oates. 1975. *Fiscal Zoning and Land Use Controls*. Lexington: Lexington Books.

Mique, J. L., and G. Belanger. 1974. "Toward a General Theory of Managerial Discretion." *Public Choice* 27: 24–43.

Mitnick, B. M. 1986. "The Theory of Agency and Organizational Analysis." Paper presented at the 1986 Annual Meeting of the American Political Science Association, Washington, D.C.

Mladenka, K. 1978. "Organizational Rules, Service Equality and Distributional Decisions in Urban Politics." *Social Science Quarterly* 59: 192–201.

Moe, T. M. 1984. "The New Economics of Organization." *American Journal of Political Science* 28: 739–77.

Molotch, H. 1976. "The City as Growth Machine." *American Journal of Sociology* 82: 309–32.

Molotch, H., and J. R. Logan. 1984. "Tensions in the Growth Machine." *Social Problems* 31: 483–99.

Morgan, D. R., and J. L. Brudney. 1985. "Urban Policy and City Government Structure: Testing the Mediating Effects of Reform." Paper presented at the 1985 Annual Meeting of the American Political Science Association, New Orleans.

Morgan, D. R., and J. P. Pelissero. 1981. "Urban Policy: Does Political Structure Matter?" *American Political Science Review* 75: 999–1006.

Moriarity, B. M. 1980. *Industrial Locational and Community Development.* Chapel Hill: University of North Carolina Press.

Moses, L., and H. Williamson. 1967. "The Location of Economic Activity in Cities." *American Economic Review* 52: 211–22.

Muller, P.O. 1982. *Contemporary Suburban America.* Englewood Cliffs, N.J.: Prentice Hall, Inc.

Nathan, R. P., P. M. Dearborn, C. A. Goldman, and Associates. 1982. "Initial Effects of the Fiscal Year 1982 Reductions in Federal Domestic Spending on State and Local Governments." In *Reductions in U.S. Domestic Spending: How They Affect State and Local Governments,* ed. J. W. Ellwood, 315–50. New York: Transaction Books.

Nathan, R. P., A. D. Manvel, and S. E. Calkins. 1975. *Monitoring Revenue Sharing.* Washington, D.C.: Brookings Institution.

Niskanen, W. A. 1971. *Bureaucracy and Representative Government.* Chicago: Aldine.

_____. 1974. "Comment on Mique and Belanger." *Public Choice* 17: 43–45.

_____. 1975. "Bureaucrats and Politicians." *Journal of Law and Economics* 18: 617–43.

Noll, R. G., and M. P. Fiorina. 1978. "Voter, Bureaucrats, and Legislators: A Rational Perspective on the Growth of Bureaucracy." *Journal of Public Economics* 9: 239–54.

Norton, R. D., and J. Rees. 1979. "The Product Cycle and the Spatial Decentralization of American Manufacturing." *Regional Studies* 13: 141–51.

Noyelle, T., and T. Stanback. 1983. *Economic Transformation of American Cities.* Totowa, N.J.: Allanheld and Rowman.

Oakland, W. H. 1978. "Local Taxes and Intraurban Industrial Location." In *Metropolitan Financing and Growth Management Policies,* ed. G. Break, 13–30. Madison: University of Wisconsin Press.

Oates, W. E. 1969. "The Effects of Property Taxes and Local Spending on Property Values: An Empirical Study of Tax Capitalization and the Tiebout Hypothesis." *Journal of Political Economy* 77: 957–71.

_____. 1979. "Lump-Sum Intergovernmental Grants Have Price Effects." In *Fiscal Federalism and Grants-in-Aid,* ed. P. Mieszkowski and W. H. Oakland, 23–30. Washington, D.C.: The Urban Institute.

O'Brien, T. 1971. "Grants-in-aid: Some Further Answers." *National Tax Journal* 24: 65–77.

O'Connor, J..1973. *The Fiscal Crises of the State.* New York: St. Martin's.

Olson, M. 1982. *The Rise and Decline of Nations.* New Haven, Conn.: Yale University Press.

Ostrom, E. 1972. "Metropolitan Reform: Propositions Derived From Two Traditions." *Social Science Quarterly* 53: 474–93.

———. 1981. "Modeling Bureaucratic Incentives in a Local Public Economy." The Edmund Janes James Lecture. Urbana: Department of Political Science, University of Illinois.

Ostrom, V., C. Tiebout, and R. Warren. 1961. "The Organization of Government in Metropolitan Areas." *American Political Science Review* 55: 835–42.

Pack, H., and J. R. Pack. 1978. "Metropolitan Fragmentation and Local Public Expenditures." *National Tax Journal* 31: 349–61.

Parks, R., and E. Ostrom. 1981. "Complex Models of Urban Service Delivery Systems," In *Urban Policy Analysis,* ed. T. N. Clark, 171–200. Vol. 21, Urban Affairs Annual Review. Beverly Hills, Calif.: Sage.

Pascal, A. H., et al. 1979. *Fiscal Containment of Local and State Government.* Santa Monica, Calif.: Rand Corporation.

Peltzman, S. 1980. "The Growth of Government." *Journal of Law and Economics* 23: 209–87.

Percy, S. L. 1984. "Citizen Participation in the Coproduction of Urban Services." *Urban Affairs Quarterly* 19: 431–66.

Peterson, P. 1981. *City Limits.* Chicago: University of Chicago Press.

Peterson, P., B. Rabe, and K. Wong. 1984. *When Federalism Works.* Washington, D.C.: Brookings Institution.

Peterson, P., and M. C. Rom. 1987. "Federalism and Welfare Reform: The Determinants of Interstate Differeneces in Poverty Rates and Benefit Levels." Paper presented at the 1987 Annual Meeting of the American Political Science Association, Chicago.

Pindyck, R. S., and D. L. Rubinfeld. 1976. *Econometric Models and Econometric Forecasts.* New York: McGraw Hill.

Pressman, J. L., and A. Wildavsky. 1973. *Implementation.* Berkeley and Los Angeles: University of California Press.

Rees, J. 1979. "Technological Change and Regional Shifts in American Manufacturing." *Professional Geographer* 32: 45–55.

Rich, R. 1981. "Interaction of the Voluntary and Governmental Sectors: Toward an Understanding of the Co-production of Municipal Services." *Administration and Society* 13: 59–70.

Rodriguez, N. P., and J. R. Feagin. 1986. "Urban Specialization in the World System: An Investigation of Historical Cases." *Urban Affairs Quarterly* 22: 187–220.

Romer, T., and H. Rosenthal. 1982. "Median Voters or Budget Maximizers: Evidence from School Expenditure Referenda." *Economic Inquiry* 20: 556–78.

Rubin, I. S., and H. J. Rubin. 1987. "Economic Development Incentives: The Poor (Cities) Pay More." *Urban Affairs Quarterly* 22: 37–62.

Sanders, H. T., and C. N. Stone. 1987. "Developmental Politics Reconsidered." *Urban Affairs Quarterly* 22: 521–39.

Savas, E. S. 1982. *Privatizing the Public Sector*. Chatham, N.J.: Chatham House.

———. 1987. *Privatizing: The Key to Better Government*. Chatham, N.J.: Chatham House.

Saunders, P. 1981. *Social Theory and the Urban Question*. New York: Holmes and Meir.

Schmenner, R. W. 1982. *Making Business Decisions*. Englewood Cliffs, N.J.: Prentice-Hall.

Schneider, M. 1980a. *Suburban Growth*. New Brunswick, Ohio: Kings Court.

———. 1980b. "Resource Reallocation and the Fiscal Condition of Metropolitan Communities." *Social Science Quarterly* 61: 545–566.

———. 1985. "Suburban Fiscal Disparities and the Location Decisions of Firms." *American Journal of Political Science* 29: 587–605.

———. 1986a. "The Market for Local Economic Development: The Growth of Suburban Retail Trade, 1972–1982." *Urban Affairs Quarterly* 21: 24–41.

———. 1986b. "Fragmentation and the Growth of Local Government." *Public Choice* 48: 255–64.

———. 1986c. "Intergovernmental Aid and Local Government Expenditure Patterns," *Polity* 19: 254–69.

———. 1987. "Income Homogeneity and the Size of Suburban Government." *Journal of Politics* 49: 36–53.

Schneider, M., and F. Fernandez. 1989. "The Emerging Suburban Service Economy." *Urban Affairs Quarterly*. Forthcoming.

Schneider, M., and J. R. Logan. 1981. "The Fiscal Implications of Class Segregation: Inequalities in the Distribution of Public Goods and Services in Suburban Municipalities." *Urban Affairs Quarterly* 17: 23–36.

———. 1982a. "The Effects of Local Government Finances on Community Growth Rates: A Test of the Tiebout Model." *Urban Affairs Quarterly* 18: 91–106.

———. 1982b. "Suburban Racial Segregation and Black Access to Local Resources." *Social Science Quarterly* 63: 762–70.

Schneider, M., and B. M. Ji. 1987. "The Flypaper Effect and the Size of Local Government." *Public Choice* 54: 27–39.

Schnore, L. 1961. "The Sociological and Economic Characteristics of American Suburbs." *Sociological Quarterly* 21: 107–18.

Schrodt, P., and M. D. Ward, 1981. "Statistical Inference in Incremental and Difference Equation Formulations." *American Journal of Political Science* 25: 815–32.

Scott, A. S. 1982. "Locational Patterns and the Dynamics of Industrial Activity in the Modern Metropolis." *Urban Studies* 19: 111–42.

Sears, D. O., and J. Citrin. 1983. *The Tax Revolt*. Cambridge, Mass.: Harvard University Press.

Sharp, E. B. 1984. "Exit, Voice and Loyalty in the Context of Local Government." *Western Politics Quarterly* 37: 67–83.

Sharpe, L. J., and K. Newton. 1984. *Does Politics Matter? The Determinants of Public Policy.* New York: Oxford University Press.

Shelp, R. K. 1981. *Beyond Industrialization: Ascendancy of the Global Service Economy.* New York: Praeger.

Sjoquist, D. L. 1982. "The Effect of the Number of Local Governments on Central City Expenditures." *National Tax Journal* 35: 79–88.

Smith, M. 1984. *Cities in Transformation.* Vol. 26, Urban Affairs Annual Reviews. Beverly Hills, Calif.: Sage.

Spizman, L. M. 1980. "Unions, Government Services and Public Employees." *Public Finance Quarterly* 8: 427–42.

Staaf, R. J. 1977. "The Growth of the Educational Bureaucracy." In *Budgets and Bureaucrats,* ed. T. E. Borcherding, 148–68. Durham, N.C.: Duke University Press.

Stein, R. M. 1984. "Municipal Public Employment: An Examination of Intergovernmental Influence." *American Journal of Political Science* 28: 636–53.

————. 1986. "Tiebout's Sorting Hypothesis: An Intergovernmental Perspective." Paper presented at the 1986 Annual Meeting of the Midwest Political Science Association, Chicago.

————. 1987. "The Budgetary Effects of Municipal Service Contracts: 1977–1982." Paper presented at the 1987 Annual Meeting of the Midwest Political Science Association, Chicago.

Stigler, G. J. 1970. "Directors Law of Public Income Distribution." *Journal of Law and Economics* 13: 1–10.

Stimson, J. A. 1985. "Regression in Space and Time: A Statistical Essay." *American Journal of Political Science* 29: 914–47.

Stockfish, J. A. 1976. *Analysis of Bureaucratic Behavior: The Ill-Defined Production Process.* RAND P–5591. Santa Monica, Calif.: The Rand Corporation.

Stone, C. N. 1980. "Systemic Power in Community Decision-Making: a Restatement of Stratification Theory." *American Political Science Review* 74: 978–90.

Stone, C. N., and H. T. Sanders, eds. 1987. *The Politics of Urban Development.* Lawrence: University of Kansas Press.

Swanstrom, T. 1985. *The Crisis of Growth Politics: Cleveland, Kucinich, and the Challenge of Urban Populism.* Philadelphia: Temple University Press.

Tiebout, C. 1956. "A Pure Theory of Local Expenditures." *Journal of Political Economy* 64: 416–24.

Tullock, G. 1974. "Dynamic Hypotheses on Bureaucracy." *Public Choice* 19: 127–31.

Wagner, R., and W. Weber. 1975. "Competition, Monopoly and the Organization of Government in Metropolitan Regions." *Journal of Law and Economics* 18: 670–84.

Walker, D. 1980. *Toward a Functioning Federalism.* Cambridge, Mass.: Winthrop.

Wasylenko, M. 1980. "Evidence on Fiscal Differentials and Intrametropolitan Firm Location." *Land Economics* 56: 339–48.

————. 1981. "The Location of Firms: The Role of Taxes and Fiscal Incentives." In *Urban Government Finance,* ed. R. Bahl, 216–34. Beverly Hills, Calif.: Sage.

Wilson, J. Q. 1980. "The Politics of Regulation." In *The Politics of Regulation,* ed. J. Q. Wilson, 357–94. New York: Basic Books.

Winters, R. 1976. "Party Control and Policy Change." *American Journal of Political Science* 20: 597–36.

Wright, D. S. 1982. *Understanding Intergovernmental Relations.* Monterey, Calif.: Brooks/Cole.

Wu, S. Y. 1986. *Manufacturing Decline and Fiscal Stress of Local Governments.* Ph.D. diss., State University of New York, Stony Brook.

Yago, G., H. Korman, S. Y. Wu, and M. Schwartz. 1984. "Investment and Disinvestment in New York, 1960–1980." *The Annals* 475: 28–38.

INDEX

Allocational expenditures, 18, 19, 160, 190; effect of competition on, 71, 72, 81, 82, 83, 88; patterns in, 73–74, 80–83; and tax base, 169, 170–71, 172–73. *See also* Developmental expenditures; Expenditures; Redistributive expenditures

Antigrowth policies, 28, 148–50, 207

Baumol, W. J., 203
Beame, Abe, 84
Benefit/cost ratio, 20, 35, 123, 163, 164, 200, 201, 209–10; and expenditure levels, 60; and intergovernmental aid, 134; and no-growth politics, 149; and types of governmental services, 17–19, 21, 71–72, 84, 87, 210. *See also* Allocational expenditures; Developmental expenditures; Redistributive expenditures; Tax base
Boston, 149, 150
Buchanan, J., 28
Budgets. *See* Expenditures
Building codes, 136, 145
"Bureaucratic decision rules," 37
Bureaucrats, 15, 19, 23, 210; budget maximizing by, 32–35, 47–48, 72, 88, 112, 203–04; and economic development, 31–32, 148; and intergovernmental aid, 26, 110–20, 177, 178, 179–80; and personal income level, 127–28; and politicians, 34, 37; and privatization, 27; and total expenditures, 47–48, 63, 68, 69; and types of governmental expenditures, 72, 82, 84, 86. *See also* Flypaper effect; Public work force
Business firms, 30–32, 201–02; and allocational expenditures, 80, 82; decentralization of, 30–31, 40, 147–48; and developmental expenditures, 76, 78, 160, 173, 202; effect of fiscal policies on location of, 31–32, 154–55, 158–60, 162–63, 165; and intergovern-

mental aid, 112–13, 179–80, 192; and personal income level, 129–30, 131, 140, 162, 201, 202; and privatization, 27; and public work force, 92, 100, 104; and tax base, 21, 35, 160, 168, 201, 210; and total expenditure levels, 56, 61, 66, 68. *See also* Developmental expenditures; Economic development; Service industry

Capital investments. *See* Construction projects; Developmental expenditures; Economic development; Infrastructure
Carter administration, 26, 60
Categorical aid, 179–80, 181, 194–95; and flypaper effect, 111, 116, 177; and size of public work force, 96, 100. *See also* Intergovernmental aid; Revenue sharing
Census of Government Employment, 63, 94
Census of Government Finance, 49
Census of Governments, 16, 114, 184, 215
Census of Manufacturing, 215–16
Census of Population, 57, 96, 134, 215
Central Park, 149
Chicago, 37
Cities by Contract (Miller), 126, 206
Citizens. *See* Residents
City Limits (Peterson), 17, 201, 206, 209. *See also* Peterson's Model of Strategic Budgeting
City managers, 38, 97, 104, 186–87, 193
Clark, Terry, 27, 208
Collver, A., 40, 132
Commission governments, 97
Community development. *See* Redistributive expenditures
Community Development Act of 1974, 181
Community Development Block Grant program, 181
Competition: and allocational expendi-

Pitt Series in Policy and Institutional Studies
Bert A. Rockman, Editor

Tage Erlander: Serving the Welfare State, 1946–1969
Olof Ruin

Urban Alternatives: Public and Private Markets in the Provision of Local Services
Robert M. Stein

The U.S. Experiment in Social Medicine: The Community Health Center Program, 1965–1986
Alice Sardell